TRAVELS

INTO

BOKHARA,

&c. &c.

VOL. II.

LONDON:
Printed by A. SPOTTISWOODE,
New-Street-Square.

Costume of Bokhara

TRAVELS

INTO

BOKHARA;

CONTAINING

THE NARRATIVE OF A VOYAGE ON THE INDUS

FROM THE SEA TO LAHORE,

WITH PRESENTS FROM THE KING OF GREAT BRITAIN:

AND AN ACCOUNT OF

A JOURNEY FROM INDIA TO CABOOL,

TARTARY, AND PERSIA.

PERFORMED BY ORDER OF THE SUPREME GOVERNMENT OF
INDIA, IN THE YEARS 1831, 32, AND 33.

BY LIEUT. ALEXʀ BURNES, F.R.S.

OF THE INDIA COMPANY'S SERVICE.

——— " Per syrtes iter æstuosas,
              per inhospitalem
Caucasum, vel quæ loca fabulosus
Lambit Hydaspes."   Hor.

Second Edition.

IN THREE VOLUMES.

VOL. II.

LONDON:

JOHN MURRAY, ALBEMARLE STREET.

MDCCCXXXV.

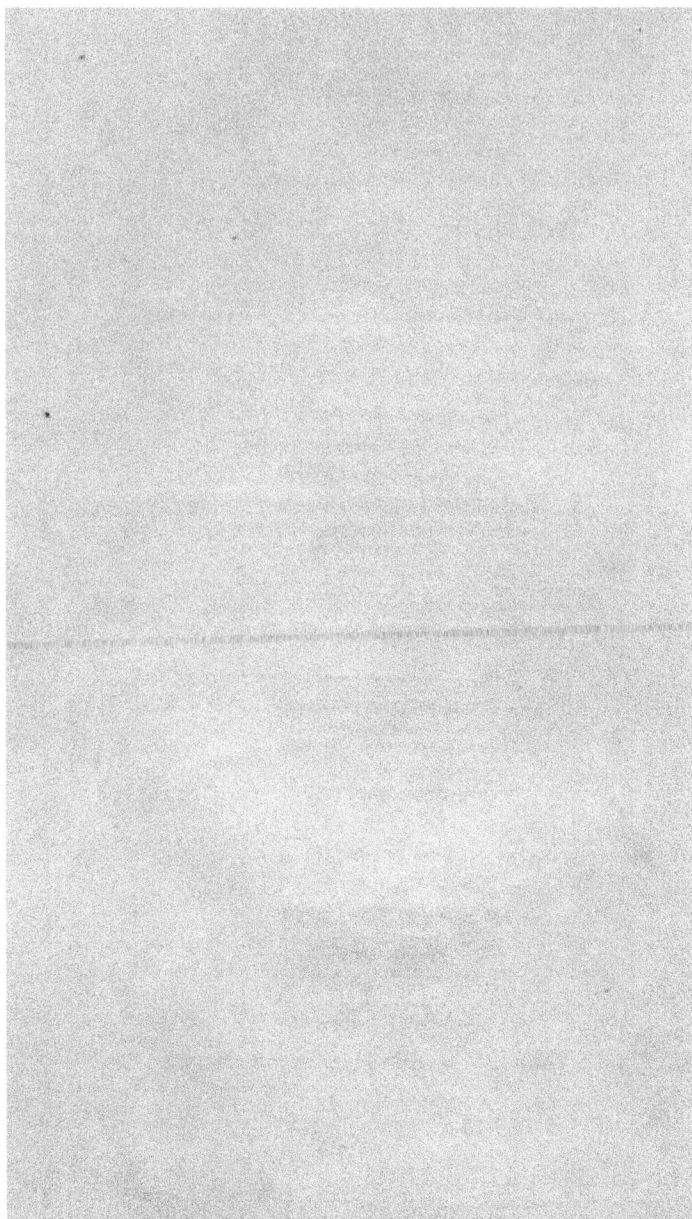

NARRATIVE

OF

TRAVELS INTO BOKHARA,

&c. &c.

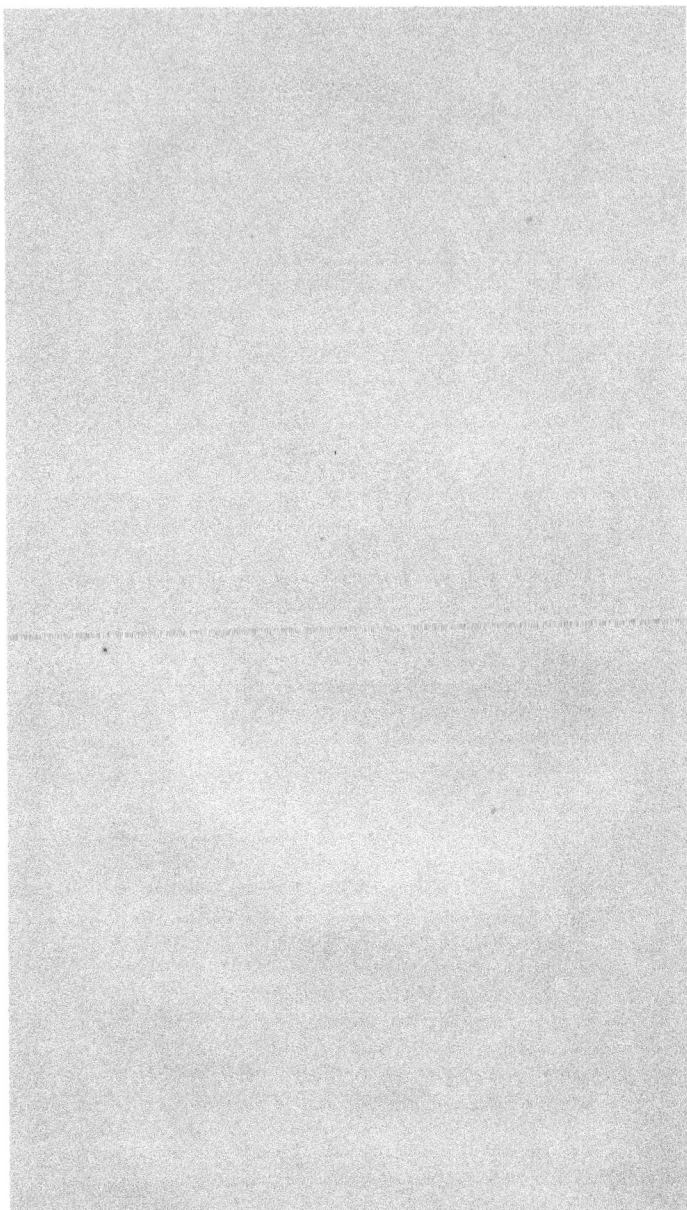

CONTENTS

OF

THE SECOND VOLUME.

CHAPTER I.

LAHORE.

CHAP. II.

ACROSS THE PUNJAB TO THE INDUS.

CHAP. III.

PESHAWUR.

CHAP. IV.

JOURNEY TO CABOOL.

CHAP. V.

CABOOL.

CHAP. VI.

JOURNEY OVER THE HINDOO KOOSH, OR SNOWY MOUNTAINS.

CHAP. VII.

SERIOUS DIFFICULTIES. — JOURNEY TO KOONDOOZ.

CHAP. VIII.

BALKH, AND JOURNEY TO BOKHARA.

CHAP. IX.

BOKHARA.

NARRATIVE.

CHAPTER I.

LAHORE.

In the end of December, 1831, I had the honour to obtain the final sanction of the Governor-general of India to proceed to Central Asia. I received my passports from his lordship at Delhi on the 23d of that month, and proceeded by express to Lodiana on the frontiers, where I had the pleasure of meeting my fellow-traveller Mr. James Gerard, of the Bengal army. We here experienced many acts of kindness and assistance from Capt. C. M. Wade, the political agent, whose good offices I have to acknowledge with gratitude. The society of this, the most remote station of British India, also evinced an interest in our welfare which was truly gratifying. We took leave of it at a convivial party given for the occasion on the 2d of January, and on the following day bade a long farewell to such scenes, and plunged into the solitude of an Indian desert. We took the route that leads along the left bank of the Sutlege, till that river is joined by the Beas, or Hyphasis.

Before crossing the boundaries of India it was both prudent and necessary to receive the permission of Maharaja Runjeet Sing, the ruler of the Punjab. It was suggested to me that a private application was in every respect preferable to an official letter from government, since the most favourable reception which I had already experienced from his highness left no doubt of his ready compliance. I consequently addressed his highness, and solicited the indulgence of again entering his territories. I gave him a brief outline of the objects which I had in view, and congratulated myself on having to traverse, at the outset, the territories of so friendly an ally. In the true style of Oriental hyperbole, I assured his highness, that " when I had again the pleasure of seeing him it would add to my happiness, because it would afford me an opportunity of renewing my terms of friendship with a prince whose exalted virtues filled me with recollections of perpetual delight ! " In the course of three days we were joined by a small escort of cavalry sent to welcome us, and their commandant brought a most friendly reply from the Maharaja, expressive of his pleasure at our approach. It was also intimated to us that we should receive presents of money and gifts as we advanced; but, as it would better suit our character to pass without these attentions, I civilly declined them. Reports would precede us, and doubtless in an exaggerated enough shape, which made it desirable to shun all pomp and show, and the more so since we had really no right to them.

As we descended the banks of the Sutlege, we gradually lost sight of the Himilaya mountains. For the first twenty miles they could be seen in great grandeur, clothed in snow from base to summit, without an inferior ridge to hide their majesty. They were about 150 miles distant, and not so peaked in their outline as the same range of mountains to the eastward. The hoary aspect of this stupendous chain formed a striking contrast with the pleasing verdure of the plains of the Punjab. In the morning these, indeed, were covered with hoar-frost, but it disappeared under the first rays of the sun, and left, in this alternation of heat and cold, a hard green sward, which is not often seen in tropical countries.

On the banks of the river we passed innumerable villages, the houses of which were terrace-roofed, and formed of sun-dried brick on a wooden framework. They had a clean and comfortable look, and the peasantry appeared well clad and happy. They consist of Juts, both Hindoo and Mahommedan, and a few Seiks. All the Mahommedans have been converted from Hindooism; and it is a curious fact, that the Moslems predominate on the southern bank, where, from the vicinity to the Hindoo world, one would have expected to find those of that persuasion. In the upper parts of the Sutlege, near Lodiana, the inhabitants are exclusively agricultural; but, after that river has been joined by the Beas, or Hyphasis, the habits of the people are pre-

datory. There they are known under the various
denominations of Dogur, Julmairee, Salairee, &c.
and by the general designation of Raat, and live in
a perpetual state of opposition to one another. In
the cultivated parts this country has the appearance
of an extensive meadow. It is entirely free from
underwood, and some of the wheat fields extend
for miles without a hedge. The grain is raised
without irrigation, though the water is but twenty-
six feet from the surface. There are no trees except in the vicinity of the villages; and such is the
scarcity of fuel, that cow dung is universally used
in its stead. This is dried and stacked. The fire
formed of it throws out a most powerful heat, which
leaves the people no cause to regret the want of
other fuel. The country below that stripe which
fringes the river is known by the name of Malwa.
It has a dry climate and soil, and produces gram
and barley, with bajree* and mut, which are exported to the Punjab.

After a journey of fifty miles from Lodiana, we
encamped at Huree, on the banks of the Hyphasis,
below the confluence of that river and the Sutlege.
In all our maps this junction takes place some fifty
miles lower down, which appears to have been only
correct at a remote period. These united rivers
form a beautiful stream, which is never fordable;
and, at this season, was 275 yards wide. The actual channel exceeded a mile and a half, and the
high bank lay on the northern shore; the water was

* Holcus spicatus.

running at the rate of two miles and a quarter an hour, and was at this season perfectly clear, and free from the foul, muddy appearance of a river that is swollen by the water of the mountains.   The depth did not exceed twelve feet since the river had retired to its summer bed, and the melting snow had ceased to feed it.   Both rivers stood at a temperature of 57°, which was 6° below that of the atmosphere.   The people informed us, that about fifty years ago the Sutlege had been hemmed in among the mountains, by a hill falling in upon its bed.   After an obstruction for some weeks, it vomited forth its imprisoned stream with great destruction.   A similar case occurred about eight years ago, in the Ravee, or river of Lahore.   It did little injury, and the terror of the inhabitants was excited only by the black earthy colour of the water which forced itself over the obstructing mound.   The Sutlege has altered its course at no distant period, and swept away some of the villages on its banks.   These are of a clayey, crumbling nature, easily undermined by the current.   Near the existing point of union between the rivers, we passed the dry bed of the old Sutlege, which is said to have once joined the Hyphasis at Feerozpoor. The space between this and the present channel, from twelve to fifteen miles across, is entirely destitute of trees, and covered by a rich mould, the deposit of the river.

In a country subject to such changes, how are we to look for an identity between the topography of modern and ancient days?   Yet we were now in the vicinity of the altars of Alexander; and if we sought for these ancient relics of the " Macedonian madman" without success, we sought not without industry and enthusiasm. When the army of Alexander mutinied on the banks of the Hyphasis, he crossed that river, and raised twelve colossal altars, to indicate the limit and glory of his expedition. Major Rennell has placed the site of these monuments between the Beas and Sutlege; but that eminent geographer is not here supported by the text of Alexander's historians. They do not even mention the Sutlege; and their allusions to a desert that lay beyond the Hyphasis can only be identified with the country beyond that river, and below its junction with the Sutlege, where that desert is still to be found. Nor is it probable that Alexander would erect the trophies of his conquest, where a small and fordable river yet separated him from India. We wandered about for a few days, and extended our researches on every side. We crossed the Sutlege, and found, at the point of its junction with the Beas, a brick ruin, of small dimensions, called Andreesa, which sounded like Greek, but the building was of a Mahommedan age. We then embarked on the Hyphasis, and passed the confluence of the two streams, where the waters meet each other gently, and glide smoothly along. Both rivers have an equal breadth of 200 yards, but the Sutlege discharges a greater volume of water. It was with faint hopes of success that we prosecuted our enquiries after these remnants of antiquity, since the inhabitants did not remember to have even seen an European. It is an approximation, nevertheless, to discovery, to ascertain where these altars are not; and if any traces of them be hereafter found, they probably lie lower down, and on the left bank of the united stream of the Beas and Sutlege, there called the Garra. I should here mention that, on our way from Lodiana, and about twenty miles from that cantonment, we heard of the ruins of Tiharu, on the southern bank of the Sutlege, which had been washed into the river within the last thirty years. Kilnburnt bricks of large dimensions and peculiar shape are yet found on this site, which may have been an ancient ruin. If the altars stood here, my surmises are erroneous.

On the 11th we crossed by the ferry boats at Huree ka Puttun, and landed in the Punjab at the village of that name. There are twenty-three boats at this ferry; and it is protected by a party of 400 horse, whom the ruler of the Punjab has stationed here to prevent the fanatics of the Seik creed from passing into the British territories. As we entered the village, we were met by a crowd of females and children, who approached to chant our welcome. They are the poorer peasantry, and, of course, actuated by the hope of reward; but the custom has something pleasing in it. The boys of the village had also assembled to gratify their curiosity; while we approached, they were silent, and looked with attention: when we had passed, all was bustle and uproar, running and falling, jumping and laughing, till the head man and his troopers called the urchins

to order. I remember well when no one more delighted in such scenes than myself. Human nature
is the same everywhere.

We had no sooner set foot on the Punjab than
a sirdar, or chief, of the name of Sham Sing, appeared by order of his master. He presented me
with a bow, according to the custom of the Seiks,
and two bags of money; which latter I declined,
being amply satisfied at the readiness with which
we had received permission to enter the country.
I wished also to dispense with this personage and
his cavalcade; but it was impossible, since he had
been deputed from Lahore to escort us, and the
road was described as not altogether safe for a small
party. It was well we did not separate ourselves
from the chief, as we afterwards passed a village on
fire, and in possession of the Seik fanatics, to whom
I have before alluded. We met a body of 500
horse, with two field-pieces, proceeding to chastise
these " wrong-headed and short-sighted" men, as
they are styled in the language of the Punjab
cabinet.

On the following morning we commenced our
march across the " Doab*," between the Beas and
Ravee (Hydraotes), which has the name of Manja.
It is the highest portion of the Punjab east of the
Hydaspes; a fact which is established by the eastern
bank of the one river as well as the western one of
the other being both elevated. The left bank of
the Ravee is about forty feet high, and so is the

* A country between two rivers is so called.

right bank of the Beas.   The wells are also much
deeper than south of the Sutlege; here they exceed sixty feet, there they are not twenty-six.
The soil is a hard, indurated clay, sometimes
gravelly, producing thorny shrubs and brambles,
called by the natives jund, khureel*, and babool.†
Cultivation depends upon the rain, and irrigation
is by no means general.   Herds of neelgaee roam
over it.   In former years the Mogul emperors,
seeing the comparative sterility of this tract, fertilised it by canals from the Ravee, which connected
that river with the Beas.   The remains of one of
them may be yet traced at the town of Puttee,
running down at right angles upon the Beas, though
it has been choked up for the last 150 years.   The
district of Manja is celebrated for the bravery of
its soldiers, and the breed of its horses, which would
always entitle it to the patronage of a sovereign.

The first town we entered was Puttee, which
contains about 5000 people, and, with the adjoining
town of Sooltanpoor, was built in the reign of
Akbar.   The houses are constructed of bricks, and
the streets are even laid with them.   Some work-
men, digging a well in this neighbourhood, lately
hit upon a former well, on which was a Hindoo inscription.   It set forth that it had been built by one
Agurtuta, of whom tradition gives no account.   The
district of Puttee held, at one time, a supremacy,
over 1360 villages, and yielded a revenue of nine
lacs of rupees, when fertilised by its canal.

* Capparis.   † Mimosa Arabica.

At Puttee we visited one of the royal studs of
Runjeet Sing. We found about sixty brood mares,
chiefly of the Dunnee breed, from beyond the Hydaspes, where the country is of the same description as Manja, dry and elevated. May not this
aridity, as resembling the soil of Arabia, where the
horse attains such perfection, have something to do
with its excellence? These animals are exclusively
fed on barley, and a kind of creeping grass called
" *doob*," which is considered most nutritive. The
horses at this stud were lately attacked by an epi-
demic disease, of which a Mahommedan, who resides in a neighbouring sanctuary, is believed to
have cured them. Though a Mahommedan, the
Seiks have in gratitude repaired and beautified his
temple, which is now a conspicuous white building,
that glitters in the sun. The Seik people are tolerant in their religion; and I have remarked in
India generally much more of this virtue than the
people receive credit for. It may be superstition
which induces this general respect of all religions;
but, however originating, it is a sound and wholesome feeling. The Mahommedans have, no doubt,
been overbearing in their conquests; (and what
conquerors have not been overbearing?) but, as they
settled among the people, their prejudices disappeared, to the mutual benefit of themselves and
their subjects.

On the 13th we received a message from the
Acali who had set fire to the village a few days
previous, and whose acts of fanaticism had called
for the interference of the court. This outlaw, by

name Nehna Sing, wished to visit us, and I felt
equal anxiety to hear from so notorious a character
some history of himself and his adventures.   These
fanatics of the Seik creed acknowledge no superior,
and the ruler of the country can only moderate their
frenzy by intrigues and bribery.   They go about
every where with naked swords, and lavish their
abuse without ceremony on the nobles, as well as
the peaceable subjects ; nor are they always so
harmless, since they have, on several occasions, even
attempted the life of Runjeet Sing.   An interview
with such a person excited considerable anxiety on
the part of our conductors, who strongly dissuaded
me from it, and, at length, completely frustrated our
wishes by informing the Acali that he must come
unattended.   This he declined, and we were obliged
to forego the pleasure of seeing a man who had
dared Runjeet Sing himself, within a few miles of
his capital.   We were obliged to rest satisfied with
a hearsay account of this Seik bigot ; nor could I
discover any difference in the shades of fanaticism
here and in other countries.   These Acalis or Ni-
hungs are not numerous, but commit the grossest
outrages, and shield themselves under their religious
character.   They evince no greater hostility to those
of another creed than to a Seik, and would appear
to be at war with mankind.   Their fanaticism borders
on insanity.   The creed of the Seiks is well known :
it has been ably described by Sir John Malcolm.
Like their neighbours, the Mahommedans, they have
forgotten much of its primitive form, and found their
distinction from other sects on a few ritual ob-

servances. A Seik will tell you that tobacco is the most debasing of stimulants, since the founder of their sect, Gooroo Govind Sing, proved it by exhibiting the contamination in the interior of a tobacco pipe, as a type of its corruption in the human body! A Seik once told me that tobacco and flies were the greatest of ills in this degenerate age (*kul yoog:* literally, dark age).

About half way across the " Doab" we reached Pidana, the seat of one of the principal chiefs of the Punjab, Sirdar Juwala Sing, who had been sent from Lahore to entertain us at his family mansion. He met us about a mile out, and delivered a letter with a bow and a bag of money. The chief had robed himself in a rich dress of brocade, and his retainers were arrayed in tunics of yellow, which is the favourite colour of the Seiks. Juwala Sing has the reputation of a brave soldier, and possesses a suavity of manner and address which appear to great advantage in a fine soldier-looking person about six feet high. It was twilight as he led us through his fort and under his baronial castle to our camp, which gave a favourable idea of the residence of a Seik chief. The castle stood in the centre, surrounded by a village, peopled by his retainers, the whole being enclosed by a mud wall and outer ditch. Within this space is to be found a bazar, extensive stables, and, in the present instance, these were built on a plan of great regularity. In the tranquillity which has followed the conquest of this country, most of the chiefs have turned their minds to improving their places of residence; and their habitations have at a distance a most imposing and respectable appearance, though inferior to the fortified dwellings of the Rajpoot chiefs in Marwar. They are always built in a military style, of a quadrangular shape, with lofty walls and turrets. Our worthy host made us such welcome guests, that we remained with him for two days. From the top of his castle we had a commanding view of the surrounding country, which, from its vicinity to the two capitals of the country, Lahore and Umritsir, is industriously cultivated, though the soil is unproductive.

In our progress to Lahore, we entered the great road of Juhangeer, which was once shaded with trees, and studded with minarets and caravanserais. It conducted the traveller

"From Agra to Lahore of Great Mogul,"

and has been celebrated in Lalla Rookh, in the royal procession to Cashmeer. In the lapse of time the trees have disappeared; but many minarets and superb caravanserais still mark the munificence of the Mogul emperors. The road itself is yet a broad and beaten way; nor was it possible to tread upon it without participating in the excitement which the author of Lalla Rookh has raised, and I may almost say gratified.

On the morning of the 17th we entered the imperial city of Lahore, which once rivalled Delhi. We wound among its ruins; and, when yet three miles distant, were met by Monsieur Allard, and two natives of rank sent to welcome us. The Chevalier came in his carriage drawn by four mules,

into which the Doctor and myself stepped, and drove
to his hospitable mansion, where we alighted and took
up our quarters. After the ceremony of receiving
various friendly and formal messages from Runjeet,
the native part of the deputation withdrew, leaving
a profusion of the fruits of Cashmere and Cabool as
an earnest of the condescension of their master.
In the evening, a purse of 1100 rupees was sent
to us; nor was it possible to refuse the money
without giving offence.

We next morning paid our respects to the Maharaja, and were received with marked affability in a
garden about two miles from the city. We found
him in great spirits, and continued with him for
about two hours. His conversation ranged from
points of the utmost importance to mere trifles: he
expressed much satisfaction at the interview which
he had lately had, for the first time, with the Governor-general; and said, that he might now reduce
the pay of his troops, after having seen so efficient
an army as the Indian with so little pay. His
highness was much interested in shell practice;
and conducted us to the front of his garden, to show
the success which had attended his exertions. They
are unacquainted with the mode of fusing iron in this
country, and the shells are constructed of brass.
Monsieur Court, one of his French officers, exhibited
these to him on the day of our arrival, and was presented with a purse of 5000 rupees, jewels, and other
gifts. Runjeet made the most particular enquiries
regarding our intended journey; and, since it was
no part of my object to develope the entire plans

in view, we informed his highness that we were proceeding *towards* our native country.   He requested
me to take a complimentary letter to the King of
England; which I declined, on the excuse of its
endangering my safety in the intermediate territories.   I then presented a handsome brace of pistols,
that drew forth his highness's commendation, and
which he said he would keep for my sake. The Doctor
produced a spy-glass as the token of his homage.
Runjeet received us, surrounded by troops: four
regiments of infantry could be seen at parade from
his audience tent.   We passed through a street
formed by his infantry and cavalry, and were honoured by a salute.   On taking leave, he requested
that we would continue as long as possible at his
court, since he wished to show us some tiger-hunt-
ing, and give an entertainment in his palace, —
honours which we duly appreciated.   We meanwhile returned to enjoy the friendly society of M.
Allard and his brother officers.   I shall make no
further mention of Lahore, since it is described in
my first visit to the court, and was now no longer
a scene of curious novelty.

Near midnight on the 22d, we were much alarmed
by an earthquake, which continued for about ten
seconds with great violence.   The house in which
we were lodged, though a substantial dwelling of
brick and mortar, shook with great violence. The atmosphere had indicated nothing unusual; the baro-
meter underwent no variation either before or after
it; and the thermometer stood so low as 37°, and fell
four degrees under the freezing point before sunrise.
In July last it had risen to 102°. I was informed that

earthquakes were of frequent occurrence at Lahore,
particularly during winter. In Cashmeer they are still
more common; and appear to be more usual on approaching the mountains. The lofty minarets of
Lahore afford, however, the most convincing proof,
that there can have been no very violent commotion
of nature since they were built,—nearly two hundred
years ago. The shock on the present occasion appeared to run from south-east to north-west; and it
was singular to discover, after crossing Hindoo
Koosh, that this was the exact direction of its course.
In the valley of Badukhshan, and the whole upper
course of the Oxus, the greater portion of the villages had been overthrown, which had buried some
thousands of people in their ruins. The shock
had occurred there at the same time, and, as far as
I could judge, at the same hour, since they mentioned the midnight horrors of the sad event.

A week after our arrival we received the promised
invitation to join his highness in the sports of the
field. He himself had quitted the capital, and sent
a friendly letter, along with four elephants to convey
us and our baggage. We immediately mounted,
and took the route by the banks of the Ravee, in
which direction the court had proceeded. On our
way, we passed an hour in the celebrated garden of
" Shalimar," which was now more beautiful than
ever. Though it was winter, the trees were loaded
with oranges. We halted for the night, near the
village of Lakodur, famous in history as the spot
at which Nadir Shah crossed the river and captured
Lahore. The stream has forsaken its former channel, which is now dry and cultivated. The hordes

of the destroying Nadir have been in like manner long withdrawn, and given place to the industrious and reformed inhabitants of this country. On the following morning we entered the royal camp, which was about twenty miles from the city. On the road we passed crowds of soldiers, porters and messengers bearing fruits and rarities. Since leaving Lahore, it was evident that we were approaching a hive of men. About a mile distant we were welcomed by a Rajah and his train, who came on elephants, and conducted us to the camp, pitched close to the banks of the river. The scene, as we approached, was magnificent. A large pavilion of red cloth, surrounded by extensive walls of the same materials, marked the encampment of Runjeet, while his troops and chiefs were cantoned in picturesque groups around. The suite of tents which had been pitched for our accommodation was most elegant. They were made of scarlet and yellow cloth, and the ground was covered with Cashmeer carpets and pieces of French satin. It was with some reluctance that I set foot upon such valuable materials. In each tent was a camp bed, with curtains of yellow silk, and coverlets of the same description. Such costly splendour was ill suited to men who had so little prospect even of comfort; but I must say that it was exhilarating at the moment. One of the officers of the court welcomed us in the name of his highness; and in the evening we were joined by Captain Wade and Dr. Murray, who had been sent on a political mission to the court of Lahore.

On the morning of the 27th, we marched with the Maharaja : and, fording the Ravee, proceeded inland. The order of the march was very picturesque, and the retinue in every respect that of a *soldier* king. His horses were led in front of him, but the journey was performed on elephants. Two of these stupendous animals bore *houdas* of gold, in one of which his highness sat. Six or seven others followed with his courtiers and favourites. A small body of cavalry, and a field-piece, formed his escort; and the carriage, which he had received from the Governor-general, drawn by four horses, completed the procession.

Runjeet was very talkative during the march, and detained us in conversation for about an hour after it had terminated. He spoke of the good fortune of Ameer Khan, in receiving so large a grant of land from the Indian Government without military service ; and commented on his rise from so low an origin to such an elevation. He need not have gone farther than himself for a remarkable instance of the caprice of fortune. Runjeet said that a disciplined army did not suit the manners of an Eastern prince, for it could not be regularly paid, and complained, consequently, of its duties : he wished to know if our troops ever clamoured for pay, and expressed surprise to learn that such behaviour was viewed as mutinous. A conversation could not, of course, conclude without his favourite topic of wine ; and, as he first sat down, he remarked that the site of his tent was an agreeable one for a drinking-party, since it commanded a fine view of the surrounding country. He enquired of the doctors, whether wine was best before or after food; and laughed heartily at an answer from myself, when I recommended both. During this conversation, a peasant rushed in upon our party, calling loudly for justice: he was stopped by the guards, and gagged; but Runjeet called out in a stern voice, — " Strike him not !"   An officer of high rank was sent to hear his complaint; but I fear that, if reports be true, justice is here an equally expensive article as in other Asiatic governments.

On taking leave of his Highness, we proceeded to our tents, which were a distinct suite from that which we had yesterday occupied. They were made of Cashmeer shawls, and about fourteen feet square. Two of these were connected by tent walls of the same superb materials; while the intervening space was shaded by a lofty screen, supported on four massy poles, adorned with silver. The shawls of one tent were red; of the other, white. In each of them stood a camp bed, with curtains of Cashmeer shawls, which gave one an impression of a fairy abode more than an encampment in the jungles of the Punjab.

Among our visiters in the camp, I must not omit to mention the sage Uzeezodeen, the physician and secretary of Runjeet Sing, who, according to Eastern notions, is a very learned person, deeply versed in theology, metaphysics, and physics, which he professes to have acquired from the Greek authors. He displayed his acquirements in many

long discourses, from which I have extracted the
following, as a specimen of what sometimes passes
for wisdom in the East. "The world possesses
three different atoms, all excellent, and all of which
enter into the 'noblest work of God,' man.—Neither
the gem nor the precious metals can multiply or
increase their size or number; in their beauty we
find their excellence. In the vegetable kingdom,
we see the trees and plants, sucking moisture from
the earth and moulding it to their nature, increase
in size and glory. In the animal kingdom, we see
the beasts of the field cropping those plants which
afford them nourishment, and avoiding such as are
noxious. We see them propagating the species
without the institutions of society. In man alone
have we every excellence; he possesses the beauty
and ornament of the gem: understands and wields
the properties of the vegetable kingdom; and to
the instinct of the animal creation he adds reason,
and looks to futurity. As the learned physician
said, 'he chooses his wife considerately, nor herds
in flocks like the other animals of the creation.'"

But we had come to hunt, not to philosophise;
and next day accompanied the Maharaja on a
sporting expedition at noon. He rode a favourite
bay horse, covered with an elegant saddle-cloth of
the richest embroidery, ornamented, in its border,
by almost every beast and bird which the sportsman calls his own. Runjeet was dressed in a tunic
of green shawls, lined with fur; his dagger was
studded with the richest brilliants; and a light
metal shield, the gift of the ex-King of Cabool,

completed his equipment. A train of elephants followed him; and a pack of dogs, of motley breed, natives of Sinde, Bokhara, Iran, and his own dominions, led the van. His falconers supported their noble birds on their fists. They fluttered at his side, and shook the bells suspended from their feet. A company of infantry in extended order, with two or three hundred horsemen, swept the ground; and we followed the foresters with their rude halberds, who soon disturbed the game. We were to encounter hogs instead of tigers. The swords of the Seiks glittered in the sun: and in the course of half an hour eight monsters had bitten the dust, and many more were entrapped by snares. Most of the animals had been slain by the horsemen with their swords; a few had been first wounded by the matchlock. The sport might not be duly appreciated by a European sportsman, since the hogs had but a small chance of escape; yet I am sure the excitement of the field was great. The scene took place in a plain covered with high grass, in the open patches of which we could see from our elephants the brilliant display with great advantage. The bright coloured dresses of the courtiers had a striking effect. Runjeet himself viewed each hog as it fell, and keenly turned to the scenes of passing slaughter. In the course of an hour and a half we returned to our tents, and saw each of the successful sportsmen rewarded. The live hogs were then brought, tied by one leg to a stake, and baited with dogs. It is a cruel sport, and does not afford any great amusement: the courage and fire of the

animals are renewed by dashing water over them.
After witnessing it for a short time, an order was
given to set all the live hogs at liberty, as Runjeet
said that they might praise his humanity; and the
infuriated animals scampered through the crowded
encampment, to the great delight of the assembled
multitude.

After the bustle had passed, we continued for
some time with the Maharaja, who gave us an
animated account of his exploits beyond the Indus.
He described the bravery of a Nihung, or Seik
fanatic, who had perished on that occasion. He
had fought on foot and received a wound, which he
dressed, and returned to the field on horseback.
He received a second wound; but, not discomfited,
seated himself on an elephant; and was at last shot
through the lungs. " He was a brave man," continued he, " but a great villain; and had he not
fallen on that day, I must have imprisoned him for
life: he wished to cross the frontier and set fire to
some of the British cantonments." The particular
battle to which his highness now alluded was fought
at Noushero, near Peshawur, and was the most
glorious victory which he gained after passing the
Indus in a heroic manner, without a ford. It was
quite delightful to hear Runjeet speak of his charges,
his squares, his battles, and his success; and his
only eye brightened with the description. " You
will pass the field of battle," added he, " and you
must reconnoitre it well. I shall give you letters
to the neighbouring chiefs and the marauding Khyberees, who will describe the ground, and ensure

you protection and honourable treatment." The favour was well meant; and I felt it the more, as it was unsolicited, though the letters proved useless.

We continued in these enjoyments till the end of the month, when we returned to Lahore, with the same pomp and pageantry that we had witnessed in the field. On the way we had some sport with the hawks, which is an amusement that can be enjoyed even by those who are no sportsmen. A hundred cannon announced the arrival of Runjeet Sing in his capital; and we again took up our abode with our worthy friend Monsieur Allard.

On the 6th of February, the festival of the " Busunt," which simply means the Spring, was celebrated with great splendour. Runjeet invited us on the occasion; and we accompanied him on elephants to witness the demonstration of joy with which returning spring is here hailed, as in other countries. The troops of the Punjab were drawn out, forming a street of about two miles long, which it took upwards of thirty-five minutes to traverse. The army consisted entirely of regular troops — cavalry, infantry, and artillery; and the whole corps was uniformly dressed in yellow, which is the gala costume of this carnival. The Maharaja passed down the line, and received the salute of his forces. Our road lay entirely through the ruins of old Lahore, over irregular ground, which gave the line a waving appearance, that greatly heightened the beauty of the scene. At the end of this magnificent array stood the royal tents, lined with yellow silk. Among them was a canopy, valued at a lac

of rupees, covered with pearls, and having a border
of precious stones. Nothing can be imagined more
grand. At one end Runjeet took his seat, and
heard the Grinth, or sacred volume of the Seiks,
for about ten minutes. He made a present to the
priest ; and the holy book was borne away wrapped
in ten different covers, the outside one of which,
in honour of the day, was of yellow velvet. Flowers
and fruits were then placed before his highness ;
and every kind of shrub or tree that produced a
yellow flower must have been shorn of its beauties
on this day. I could discover no reason for the
selection of so plain a colour, but the arbitrary will
of a ruler. After this came the nobles and com-
mandants of his troops, dressed in yellow, to make
their offerings in money. Two sons of the fallen
Kings of Cabool, Shah Zuman and Shah Eyoob,
then entered, and conversed for some time. The
Nawab of Mooltan, clad also in yellow, and accompanied by five of his sons, followed to pay his homage, and was most kindly received. This is the
same individual who was so much frightened at the
Cabool mission, now a subservient vassal of Runjeet Sing. His name is Surufraz Khan. The agents
from Bhawulpoor and Sinde approached in their
turn, and were closely questioned about a subject
of great political importance at the present time,—
the opening of the Indus. One could ill discover,
from the sycophancy of these persons, that they
were the representatives of those who so cordially
hated the Maharaja. With these ceremonies the
dancing girls were introduced ; and as they largely

share the favour of his highness, they partook
bounteously of the pile of money now lying before
him.   He appeared almost to divide it among them.
They were desired to chant the amorous songs of
the festival; also an ode on wine.   Runjeet then
introduced the bottle, and insisted on our drinking
a stirrup-cup, with which we parted.

Our departure from Lahore was stayed by the
entertainment which his highness had resolved on
giving us in his palace of the Sumun Boorj.   We
met in a garden, and proceeded with him to the
appointed place, which was superbly illuminated
with waxen tapers on the occasion.   Bottles filled
with different-coloured water were placed near the
lights and increased the splendour.   We were first
conducted to the great hall, the ancient seat of the
Mogul Emperors, which is about seventy feet long,
and opened to the front by an arched colonnade of
marble.   The ceiling and walls are entirely inlaid
with mirrors, or gilded; and on this occasion presented a scene of great magnificence.   There are
many parts of this place, which, like that of Delhi,
evidently owe much of their architectural beauty
to the genius of an European artist.   We withdrew
from the great hall to a small apartment, the bed-
room of the Maharaja, where it was intended that
the festivities of the evening should take place.
Captain Wade and Dr. Murray were likewise present; and we sat round his Highness on silver
chairs.   In one end of the room stood a camp bed-
stead, which merits a description.   Its framework,
posts, and legs were entirely covered with gold, and

the canopy was one massy sheet of the same precious metal. It stood on footstools, raised about ten inches from the ground, also of gold. The curtains were of Cashmeer shawls. Near it stood a round chair of gold ; and in one of the upper rooms of the palace we saw the counterpart of these costly ornaments. The candles that lighted up the apartment were held in branch sticks of gold. The little room in which we sat was superbly gilded ; and the side which was next the court was closed by a screen of yellow silk. Here we enjoyed the society of our royal entertainer, and duly celebrated the rites of Bacchus. Runjeet circulated the wine most freely, filled our glasses himself, and gave every encouragement by his own example. He drinks by the weight, and his usual dose does not exceed that of eight *pice** ; but on this occasion he quaffed the measure of eighteen. His favourite beverage is a spirit distilled from the grapes of Cabool, which is very fiery, and stronger than brandy. In his cups he became very amusing, and mentioned many incidents of his private life. He had quelled two mutinies among his troops ; three of his chiefs had, at different times, fallen by his side ; and he had once challenged his adversary to settle the dispute by single combat. The battles of his highness infected the dancing ladies whom he had introduced, at a late period of the evening, according to his custom. He gave them spirits ; and they tore and fought with each other, much to his amusement, and to the

---

* A small copper coin.

pain of the poor creatures, who lost some ponderous ornaments from their ears and noses in the scuffle. Supper was introduced, and consisted of different kinds of meats, richly cooked, and which, in contrast to the surrounding magnificence, were handed up in leaves sewed into the shape of cups. They contained hare, partridge, pork, and all sorts of game, &c., of which Runjeet partook freely, and handed to us. There were also a variety of confections and ices: but it is easier to describe these matters of fact than the scene in which they took place. We broke up long past midnight.

During these gay and festive scenes, we were not forgetful of the difficulties which awaited us; and availed ourselves of the experience of Messrs. Allard and Court, who had travelled overland from Persia through a part of the countries we were now about to traverse. These gentlemen seemed to vie with each other in every act of kindness. They furnished us with various letters to their acquaintances in Afghanistan, and gave us many hints to guide our conduct. Monsieur Court, indeed, drew up a précis of them, the result of his own experience, which I annex*, since it conveys, at the same time, most valuable information to a traveller, and gives me an opportunity of expressing my gratitude both to him and M. Allard, and the reasons on which I found it. These gentlemen did not disguise from me the many apprehensions which they entertained for our safety; but our visit to Lahore had not been made to discuss

* See the end of the chapter.

the chances of our success, but only in prosecution
of the journey.

On the evening of the 10th of February, we took
our leave of Maharaja Runjeet Sing on the parade-
ground, where he again exhibited to us, with apparent pride, the progress which his troops had made
in throwing shells.   On this occasion he asked for
my opinions on opening the Indus; and remarked,
that, as that river and its five great tributaries passed
through his territories, he ought to derive greater
advantages than the British government.   He spoke
of the scheme as might have been expected from a
man of his enlightened views; but said that he did
not relish the idea of vessels navigating all parts of
his territories.   He fears collision with the British
government.   His Highness then proceeded to dictate letters in our behalf to the chiefs of Peshawur
and Cabool, as well as several other personages
beyond the Indus.   He also issued orders to all the
chiefs and agents between his capital and the frontier; and stretching his hand from the elephant,
gave each of us a hearty shake, and said farewell.
He particularly requested me to write to him frequently, and give an account of the countries I traversed, with their politics and customs, and never
forget him in whatever region I might be placed.
We received letters from Runjeet Sing himself in
the deserts of Tartary and in Bokhara; nor did we
fail to comply with his request when far from his
territories.   I never quitted the presence of a native
of Asia with such impressions as I left this man:
without education, and without a guide, he conducts

all the affairs of his kingdom with surpassing energy and vigour, and yet he wields his power with a moderation quite unprecedented in an Eastern prince.

MONSIEUR COURT'S INSTRUCTIONS.

" A Monsieur Burnes, par son Ami, M. Court.

" Le proverbe Français dit, ' Si tu veux vivre en paix en voyageant, fais en sorte de hurler comme les loups avec qui tu te trouves :' c'est-à-dire, Conforme-toi en tout aux mœurs et coutumes des habitans des contrées que tu parcours.   C'est là la base de vos instructions.

" Commencez d'abord par vous dépouiller de tout ce qui pourrait faire connaître que vous êtes Européen ; car si l'on vient à savoir que vous êtes tel, on va se figurer que vous emportez avec vous toutes les mines de Pérou.   Par là vous vous attirez sur les bras une nuée d'ennemis, vu que les peuplades barbares que vous allez traverser n'en veulent qu'à l'argent, et non à la personne.   Evitez donc de produire le moindre objet qui puisse tenter leur cupidité. Songez que souvent je les ai entendu se glorifier, comme d'un acte héroïque, d'avoir fait assassiner telle et telle personne, pour lui enlever un objet qu'ils avaient convoité.

Evitez autant que possible les occasions qui pourraient donner atteinte à votre honneur.   Si des cas imprévus surviennent, n'y répondez jamais avec em-

portement; car répondre à l'insolence Asiatique
c'est ajouter de la matière combustible à un feu qui
brûle déjà. Si vous vous voyez forcé d'y répondre,
il faut alors leur présenter des raisons solides accom-
pagnées d'expressions obligeantes et courageuses.

" Ayez pour maxime qu'il ne faut pas faire d'amitié
particulière avec les Orientaux, vu qu'ils sont inca-
pables d'attachement sincère. Vivez bien avec tous,
mais ne vous attachez à aucun. Par ce moyen il
vous en coûtera moins. Sachez qu'ils n'ont ni la
bonne foi, ni la franchise, ni la loyauté qui nous
caractérisent. Ils sont doux, flatteurs, caressans,
il est vrai ; mais sous ces formes séduisantes ils
cachent presque toujours de sinistres desseins. La
perfidie, la trahison, le parjure n'ont rien qui leur
paraisse répréhensible. A leurs yeux le droit n'est
rien, la force fait tout. N'allez pas vous imaginer
que ce que vous appelez bonté, douceur, complai-
sance, puisse vous être utile. Ils ne savent nullement apprécier de telles qualités. Comme Européen,
ne craignez pas de faire usage de la flatterie. Etant
d'usage parmi eux, vous ne sauriez trop l'employer ;
elle peut même vous être avantageuse.

" En quittant Lahore, dites adieu à Bacchus,
pour ne le revoir que dans la belle Europe. C'est
là un sacrifice essentiel à faire. Il vous évitera bien
des querelles que pourraient vous susciter les Mahométans. Soyez modeste dans vos dépenses :
moins vous en ferez, moins vous tenterez la cupidité
des Orientaux. Evitez surtout de donner le moindre
cadeau : car si vous faites tant que de régaler quel-
qu'un, vous vous trouverez bientôt assiégé par une

infinité d'autres, qui ne désempareront que quand
vous les aurez satisfaits.   Paraissez en public le
moins qu'il vous sera possible.   Evitez toute sorte de
conversation, surtout celles qui traitent de théologie,
point sur lequel les Mahométans aiment à tomber
avec un Européen.   Donnez leur toujours raison
lorsque vous vous verrez forcé de donner votre avis.
Que vos mémoires soient écrits en secret, autrement
vous donneriez lieu à des soupçons qui pourraient
vous être préjudiciables.

"En prenant des renseignemens, faites le avec
adresse et prudence ; n'ayez jamais l'air d'insister à
les avoir.   Si le pays offre des curiosités, visitez les
comme pour passer le tems : si elles sont écartées,
n'y allez jamais qu'en bonne compagnie.

"Ne vous mettez en route qu'avec des caravanes
sûres, et ayez surtout l'attention de ne jamais vous
en écarter.   Ayez de petites attentions pour le
caravanseraskier, car c'est toujours de lui que dépend
l'heureux succès des voyageurs.   En vous attirant
son amitié, il pourra vous donner des renseignemens que vous pourrez désirer, et par là vous évi-
terez de vous adresser à des personnes étrangères.
Que votre campement soit toujours à ses côtés ;
mais, nonobstant cela, que l'un de vous ait sans cesse
l'œil au guet.

"Soyez toujours armé jusqu'aux dents pour en
imposer.   Evitez les gens qui font les empressés
pour vous servir, car ce sont là ordinairement des
marauds qui en veulent à votre bourse.   Avant
votre départ, tâchez de faire connaître que vous
partez sans argent, et que ce qu'il vous en faut vous

l'avez pris en lettres de change. Faites en sorte
d'avoir toujours la moitié de votre argent sur vous,
et bien caché. Dans les endroits où vous craindrez
d'être visité, cachez le d'avance pour qu'il ne soit
pas vu. Songez que j'ai été plus d'une fois visité,
et que cela pourrait fort bien vous arriver ; trouvez
donc de bonnes cachettes pour l'argent.

" Lorsqu'il s'agira de payer la traite foraine,
soldez la sans difficulté, à moins que les exigeances
du douanier ne soient trop fortes. Sachez que ce
sont là des coquins qui peuvent vous susciter plus
d'une querelle.

" Quoique voyageant dans des contrées livrées au
plus affreux despotisme, vous ne pourrez vous em-
pêcher d'admirer la grande familiarité qui existe du
petit au grand, ainsi ne soyez nullement étonné si
vous vous voyez par fois accosté par des vauriens
qui vous arracheront des mains le kalion pour en
tirer de la fumée. N'ayez donc aucun air hautain
avec qui que ce soit ; l'air de fakhir est celui qui
vous convient le plus.

" Le Nevab Dgiabar Khan peut vous aplanir
toutes les difficultés que vous pourrez rencontrer
de Caboul à Bokhara ; tâchez donc de lui plaire :
c'est d'ailleurs le plus parfait honnête homme que
j'ai rencontré en Asie. Quant à votre projet de
traverser la Khiva pour vous rendre sur les bords de
la mer Caspienne, je le trouve impraticable : je désire,
cependant, que vous puissiez le surmonter. Dans
le cas contraire, repliez-vous sur Hérat ou Méched,
mais alors ne vous mettez en route qu'avec une
nombreuse caravane bien armée, car le pays que

vous devez traverser est infesté de Turcomans, qui ravagent impunément toutes ces contrées. D'ailleurs, l'expérience que vous acquerrez en traversant ces contrées vous fournira des lumières propres à vous guider mieux que ne le feroient mes instructions.

" Que Dieu vous fasse arriver à bon port !"

CHAP. II.

ACROSS THE PUNJAB TO THE INDUS.

AFTER taking an affectionate farewell of Messrs.
Allard and Court, we quitted Lahore in the forenoon of the 11th of February, and alighted at the
tomb of Juhangeer, a splendid mausoleum across
the Ravee. Without any depression of spirits, or
diminution of zeal, I felt no small degree of solitude
at being separated from our hospitable friends ; and
I now look back on the few weeks which I passed
at Lahore as some of the happiest of my life. Nor
was there much in our first night's lodging to cheer
us — the wreck of a royal cemetery, which the
manes of a king had once rendered sacred, but
lately converted into a barrack for a brigade of infantry, who had further contributed to its desolate
appearance. We put up for the night in one of the
garden-houses which surround it, and listened to
the puerile stories of the people, who assured us
that the body of the emperor, like the fabled tale
of that of Mahommed, was suspended by loadstones.
One has only to enter a chamber underneath to see
it resting on the ground.

It now became necessary to divest ourselves
almost of every thing which belonged to us, and
discontinue many habits and practices which had

become a second nature; for the success of our
enterprise depended upon these sacrifices. We
threw away all our European clothes, and adopted,
without reserve, the costume of the Asiatic. We
exchanged our tight dress for the flowing robe of
the Afghans, girt on swords and *" kummur-bunds "*
(sashes) ; and with our heads shaved, and groaning
under ponderous turbans, we strutted about slip-
shod; and had now to uncover the feet instead of
the head. We gave away our tents, beds, boxes,
and broke our tables and chairs. A hut, or the
ground, we knew, must be our shelter, and a coarse
carpet or mat our bed. A blanket, or *" kummul,"*
served to cover the native saddle, and to sleep under
during night; and the greater portion of my now
limited wardrobe found a place in the *" khoorjeen,"*
or saddle-bags, which were thrown across the horse's
quarter. A single mule for each of us carried the
whole of our baggage, with my books and instruments ; and a servant likewise found a seat upon the
animal. A pony carried the surveyor, Mohammed
Ali ; and the Hindoo lad had the same allowance.
These arrangements took some time and consideration ; and we burned, gave away, and destroyed
whole mule-loads of baggage — a propitiatory offering, as I called it, to those immortal demons the
Khyberees, who have plundered the traveller, from
time immemorial, across the Indus. Every one
seemed sensible of the imperious necessity of the
sacrifice, since we valued our lives more than our
property. Of what use would it have been to have
adopted the costume and customs of the country,

and to be yet burdened with the useless paraphernalia of civilisation? It is, nevertheless, a curious feeling to be sitting cross-legged, and to pen a journal on one's knees. Custom soon habituated us to these changes; and we did not do the less justice to our meals because we discarded wine and spirits in every shape, and ate with our fingers from copper dishes without knives and forks.

Half-way across to the Chenab, we halted in a garden at Kote, the residence of one of Runjeet Sing's colonels, and an agreeable place. It was not 100 yards square, but well stored with fruit-trees and flowers: most of the former were now in blossom, and an enumeration of them would give a favourable idea of this climate. They consisted of the peach, apricot, greengage, fig, pomegranate, quince, orange sweet and bitter, lime, lemon, guava, grape, mango, jamboo, bair, date, cardamom, almond, and the apple; with seven or eight other kinds, of which I can only give the native names — the *gooler*, *sohanjna*, *goolcheen*, *umltass*, *bell*, *bussoora*. The walks of the garden were lined with beautiful cypresses and weeping willows; and in the flower-beds were the narcissus, and rose-bushes of the " *sidburg*," or an hundred leaves. Most of the trees and flowers are indigenous; but many had been introduced from Cashmeer, and a native of that valley was the gardener. The proprietor of this pleasant spot was absent: his villa was in disorder, and neglected, since he is suffering from the avarice of his ruler. His son, a sharp boy of nine years old, paid us a visit, and repeated some lines of a Persian poet which he was reading at school. Little fellow! he is growing up to witness scenes of blood, at all events of alteration, in this land.

At a distance of about twenty miles from the river, we again sighted the towering Himilaya, which burst forth in all their glory. They were the mountains over Bimbur, on the road to Cashmeer, where Bernier had deplored his sufferings from the heat, now over-topped with snow. It is impossible to look on these mountains without feelings of delight; for they afford a relief to the eye after the monotony of the vast plains of the Punjab. Judging from the heights which have been determined more to the eastward, they cannot be lower than 16,000 feet. It is difficult to estimate their distance, since the map gives no correct notion of the range. Making every allowance, the loftiest of them could not be nearer than 160 miles, and subtended an angle of 51 minutes. There was scarcely a single peak, or feature, in any way remarkable throughout the range. May not this regular lineation indicate a trap or limestone formation?

We reached the banks of the Chenab, or Acesines, at Ramnuggur, a small town, the favourite resort of Runjeet Sing, and where he has often mustered his troops when proceeding on his campaigns beyond the Indus. It stands on a spacious plain where he can exercise his troops. The name of the place has been altered from Russool to Ramnuggur since the Mahommedan supremacy has been overthrown. The one name signifies the city

of the prophet ; the other, the city of God ; nor is
it remarkable that the name of the Deity should
prevail.

The " Doab," between the Ravee and Chenab, is
a little better cultivated, and more fertile, than that
which we had passed. Its soil is sandy, and in its
centre the wells are but twenty-five feet deep.
Their temperature averaged about 70° of Fahren-
heit. In the morning, vapour or clouds of smoke
ascended from them, till the atmosphere was sufficiently heated to hide it. At this season the climate is cold and bleak, frequently rainy, and always
cloudy. The wind generally blows from the north.
The sugar-cane thrives here ; and they were now
expressing its juice, which is extracted by placing
two wooden rollers horizontally on the top of each
other, and setting them in motion by a pair of oxen.
They turn a wheel which acts on two lesser ones,
placed vertically at right angles to it, and these
communicate with the wooden rollers. While I
examined one of these machines, the head man of
the village explained it ; and then made me a present of some " goor," or coarse sugar, the first-fruits
of the season. He was an ignorant Jut: his son
accompanied him. When I enquired into the
knowledge of the boy, and advised his being sent to
school, he replied, that education was useless to a
cultivator of the soil. The same opinion, I am sorry
to say, prevails in higher quarters ; for Runjeet and
his son are equally unlettered, and he objects to the
education of his grandson, who is otherwise a pro-
mising boy.

At Ramnuggur we had a visit from a venerable Seik chief, of eighty-two, who had fought in the wars under the grandfather of Runjeet Sing. His beard was silvered by age; but he was a hale old man, and appeared in an entire suit of white clothes, which in this country mark the old school as distinctly as the queue and spencer of England. The garrulity of years had overtaken him; yet he gave us a lively account of his early career, and the increasing power of the Seik nation. " It had been predicted," he said, " in their Grinth, or Bible, that wherever there was a horse or a spear, there would be chiefs and soldiers in the land. Every day serves to verify the prediction," continued he; " since the number of converts to the Seik creed increases, and now averages about 5000 yearly." When political aggrandisement follows the religious supremacy of a sect, it requires little prediction or foresight to know that that sect will increase. With the Patan invasion the Hindoo became a Mahommedan; and with the Seik power both he and the Hindoo have become Seiks, or Sings. The genuine Sing, or Khalsa, knows no occupation but war and agriculture; and he more affects the one than the other. The follower of Baba Nanuk is a merchant. The Seiks are doubtless the most rising people in modern India. Our venerable acquaintance spoke of the degeneracy of the land; but the vigorous government and tone of the people do not countenance his opinions.

There is a curious subject for speculation in the appearance of the Seik people, and their general resemblance to each other. As a tribe they were unknown 400 years ago; and the features of the whole nation are now as distinct from those of their neighbours as the Indian and the Chinese. With an extreme regularity of physiognomy, and an elongation of the countenance, they may be readily distinguished from the other tribes. That any nation possessing peculiar customs should have a common manner and character, is easily understood; but that, in such a short period of time, some hundred thousand people should exhibit as strong a national likeness as is to be seen among the children of Israel, is, to say the least of it, remarkable.

We crossed the Chenab, or Acesines, by the usual ferry, which is about three miles from the village. It was three hundred yards wide, and had a depth of nine feet for two thirds of the channel. Its banks are low on either side, and speedily inundated in the hot and rainy seasons. We are informed that Alexander the Great had to move his camp precipitately from the Acesines, which Arrian describes to be a rapid river. During the rains it is so; but the current did not now exceed one mile and a half an hour, and it is passable by a ford. The temperature of this river was 53°, and lower than the three other rivers of the Punjab which we had already crossed — the Sutlege, Beas, and Ravee.

We halted at a mosque on the right bank of the river, but our quarters must not be mistaken for a St. Sophia. These buildings consist of mud walls, over which a terrace roof is formed by wooden

rafters, also covered with mud.   The "faithful" are
luxurious enough to have a fireplace inside, to heat
the water used in their ablutions.   Our violation of
a place so holy was, in some degree, compensated
by the liberal distribution of our medicines.   Some
noxious wind, as the people had it, had lately blown
over this country, which, with the arrival of such a
personage as a Firingee (European) physician,
made every person sick.   As in other countries,
the ladies had the most numerous catalogue of complaints; and if the doctor did not actually cure, I
believe he worked on their imaginations, which is of
some consequence.   The people are much afflicted
with a disease called " *Noozlu* " (literally defluxion),
which I thought meant cold.   They describe it as
a running at the nostrils, which wastes the brain
and stamina of the body, and ends fatally.   It is
attributed to the salt used in the country, which is
procured from the salt range.   There is much eye
disease in the Punjab, which may be caused by the
nitrous particles on the banks of its different rivers.
Ask a native for an explanation of it or any other
complaint, and he will tell you that it, and all other
inflictions, are the punishment of offences committed
by ourselves, or in the former state of our being.
In the doctrine of metempsychosis, they have, at all
events, found a future state of punishments, and,
I also trust, rewards.

A journey of forty-five miles brought us to the
banks of the Jelum, or the famous Hydaspes of the
Greeks.   It winds its way through an alluvial plain,
at the base of a low rocky range of hills.   We em-

barked upon this fine river, and sailed down with
the stream for a distance of five miles. On the
voyage we disturbed several crocodiles from the
different islands, which are more numerous than in
the other Punjab rivers. The same fact is mentioned by Arrian, who speaks of the Hydaspes as a
" muddy and rapid" river, with a current of three
or four miles an hour, which is correct. It had
rained on the day preceding our arrival; the stream
was discoloured, and the water bubbled in eddies
at various places. The Jelum is a smaller river than
the Chenab, but at this season their breadth is
similar. On disembarking, we crossed a rich and
beautiful sheet of verdure that stretches to the
town of Pind Dadun Khan, where we halted. Historical association and natural beauties united to
please as we trod the routes of Hyphestion and Cra-
terus, and sailed on the stream which had wafted
the fleet of Alexander. In our progress from the
Chenab, we had been travelling in the domain which
that conqueror had added to the kingdom of Porus
after the battte of the Hydaspes. In Arrian's description I see the existing population : — " The
inhabitants are strong-built and large-limbed, and
taller in stature than all the rest of the Asiatics."
Nothing, however, can be more miserable than the
country between the Acesines and Hydaspes, — a
sterile waste of underwood, the abode of shepherds,
scantily supplied with water, which is sixty-five
feet below the surface. At one of the few villages
in this tract, we halted at the well of a vestal virgin,
who had dug it, and founded a mosque from feelings

of charity. Such people are called "*pak damun*," which literally means pure garment. They marry themselves to the Koran. The Mahommedans of our party visited the lady, and we repaired her well by fixing new pots for drawing the water.

At Pind Dadun Khan we were met and welcomed by the authorities on the banks of the river. They presented us with a purse of 500 rupees, and some jars of sweetmeats. Pind Dadun Khan is the capital of a small district, and has a population of about 6000 souls. It consists of three small towns situated close to each other, and about four miles from the river. Its houses are like others in the Punjab; but their frameworks are made of cedar (deodar), which is floated down with the inundations of the river from the Himilaya. The durability and fragrance of this wood recommend it for building of every description. We saw a cedar-tree lying on the banks of the Hydaspes, with a circumference of thirteen feet. On this river the Macedonians constructed the fleet by which they navigated the Indus; and it is a remarkable fact, that in none of the other Punjab rivers are such trees floated down, nor do there exist any where else such facilities for the construction of vessels.

Pind Dadun Khan lies within five miles of the salt range, which stretches from the Indus to the Hydaspes, and in which numerous mines are dug for the extraction of that mineral. We halted a day to examine these curious excavations, which I shall now describe. We found about 100 persons at work in one of the mines, who were as much surprised to see us, as we were to behold the bright and beautiful crystals of red salt which formed the walls of the cave. We converted our visit into a day of rejoicing, by a liberal distribution of some of the money which was every where heaped upon us; nor could it be better bestowed, for the poor creatures presented to us a spectacle of misery. Mothers with their infants, children, and old men, were alike employed in bringing the salt to the surface, and their cadaverous looks and stifled breathing excited the utmost compassion. We gave them a rupee each, the value of which could be justly appreciated, since they could only earn it after extracting 2000 pounds of salt.

In the high lands of Cabool, between the city of that name and Peshawur, a range of hills springing from the roots of the White Mountain (Sufeed Koh) crosses the Indus at Karabagh, and terminates on the right bank of the Jelum, or Hydaspes of the ancients. This range formerly figured in our maps under the name of Jood, after it had passed the river; but it has been more appropriately denominated the " Salt Range," from the extensive deposits of rock-salt which it contains. An account of that part of it near Karabagh, where the Indus, in its course southwards, cuts this range, and lays open its mineral treasures, will be found in Mr. Elphinstone's work.* In the neighbourhood of Pind Dadun Khan, a town about 100 miles N. W. of Lahore, the salt mines which supply the northern provinces of

* Vide Introduction, vol. i. p. 58.

India with that necessary of life are excavated in the same range. The following particulars pretend not to rank as a scientific account of these mines, my only object being to convey that information which a journey to so unfrequented a part of the Punjab has enabled me to collect.

The salt range forms the southern boundary of a table land, between the Indus and Hydaspes, which rises about 800 feet from the plains of the Punjab. The hills attain an actual height of 1200 feet from the valley of the Jelum, which gives them an elevation of about 2000 feet from the sea. They exceed five miles in breadth. The formation is sandstone, occurring in vertical strata with pebbles or round stones imbedded in various parts of it. Vegetation is scanty; and the bold and bare precipices, some of which rise at once from the plain, present a frightful aspect of desolation. Hot springs are found in various places. Alum, antimony, and sulphur also occur; but a red clay, which is chiefly seen in the valleys, is a sure indication of a salt deposit, and is to be found at intervals throughout this range. The supply of the mineral is now drawn from Pind Dadun Khan, whence it can be conveyed with facility both up and down a navigable river.

At the village of Keora, five miles from Pind Dadun Khan, we examined one of the principal mines. It was situated near the outside of the range, in a valley, which was cut by a rivulet of salt water. It opened into the hill through the red clayey formation above mentioned, at a distance of about 200 feet from the base. We were con-

ducted by a narrow gallery, sufficient to admit of
one person passing another, for about 350 yards, of
which fifty may be taken as actual descent. Here
we entered a cavern of irregular dimensions, and
about 100 feet high, excavated entirely in salt. The
mineral is deposited in strata of the utmost regularity, occurring, like the external rock, in vertical
layers. Some of them, however, subtend an angle
of from twenty to thirty degrees, and have the same
appearance as bricks that have been placed upon
one another. None of the layers exceed a foot
and a half in thickness, and each is distinctly separated from its neighbour by a deposit of argilla-
ceous earth about an eighth of an inch thick, which
lies like mortar between the strata. Some of the
salt occurs in hexagonal crystals, but oftener in
masses: the whole of it is tinged with red, varying
from the slightest shade to the deepest hue; when
pounded, the salt is white. The temperature of the
cavern exceeded that of the open air by twenty
degrees, where the thermometer stood at sixty-four
(in February). The natives state that these mines
are much colder in the hot season; but this only
shows that they undergo little or no alteration,
while the heat outside alters with the season.
There was no moist feeling, which one might have
expected in a salt mine.

There were upwards of 100 persons, men, women,
and children, at work in the mine; and their little
dim burning lamps on the sides of the cavern and its
recesses shone with reflected lustre from the ruby
crystals of the rock. The cavity has been ex-

cavated from the roof downwards. The salt is hard and brittle, so that it splinters when struck with the sledge-hammer and pickaxe. The rock is never blasted with gunpowder, from fear of the roof falling in; and accidents of this kind sometimes happen in the present simple mode of excavation. The mines are not worked for two months during the rains, for the same reason. The miners live in villages among the hills. They have a most unhealthy complexion, but do not appear to be subject to any particular disease. They receive a rupee for every twenty maunds of salt brought to the surface; a task which may be performed by a man, his wife and child, in two days. In those mines where the mineral is near the surface, it is hewn into blocks of four maunds, two of which load a camel; but it is usually broken in small pieces. This salt holds a high reputation throughout India, with native practitioners, from its medical virtues. It is not pure, having a considerable mixture of some substance (probably magnesia), which renders it unfit for curing meat. The natives of the Punjab ascribe the prevalence of "noozlu" to its effects.

As the salt range contains a supply which is inexhaustible, the mines yield any quantity that may be desired. Two thousand five hundred maunds of Lahore (one of which is equal to 100 lbs. English) are extracted daily, which gives about 800,000 maunds annually. A few years since, the salt was sold at the mine for a half, and even a quarter, of a rupee per maund; but its price has been now raised to two rupees per maund, exclusive

of duties. It is closely monopolised by the Punjab
government; and Runjeet Sing hopes to derive an
annual revenue of sixteen lacs of rupees, with two
and a half more for the duties. A lac and a half
of rupees, however, is expended in working the mineral. The profits amount to about 1100 per cent.,
though the salt is sold for one third the price of
that of Bengal, which averages five rupees per
maund of 80 lbs.* The Punjab salt is exported by
the Jelum to Mooltan and Bhawulpoor, where it
meets that of the Sambre lake. It finds its way to
the banks of the Jumna and Cashmeer, but it is not
exported westward of the Indus. Runjeet Sing has
prohibited the manufacture of salt in all parts of his
dominions; yet it is very questionable if he will
permanently derive so large a revenue from it as he
now receives. The farmer of the monopoly, a cruel
and tyrannical man, is now mercilessly oppressing
the people to extract it. The natives do not know
the period at which these mines were first worked;
but it must have been at an early date, since the
mineral is laid open by the Indus. They were used
by the emperors of Hindostan; but the enquiring
Baber does not mention them in his Commentaries.

We marched up the right bank of the Jelum to
Jelalpoor for about thirty miles by a tract of rich
land and great fertility. The husbandmen were
mowing down the green wheat for the use of their
cattle. The salt range runs parallel with the river,

---

* Vide Mr. Ramsay's evidence before the Committee of the
Lords.

and presents a perfect contrast of desolation to its
fertile valley; for it has no vegetation. Many villages, however, are perched upon the outer hills,
which rise over one another in a picturesque manner. Nor are they more remarkable for their romantic situation than their comfort. We halted at
one of them, which was neat and well kept, and
lodged in a room which was about sixteen feet long,
and half that breadth. It had cupboards and shelves,
while the magazines for grain, which are formed
of earth, answered the purposes of tables. The
whole buildings, both inside and out, are plastered
with a grey-coloured earth, which gives them a
cleanly appearance; and since these villages stand
on the declivity of the hills, the rain washes down all
that is disagreeable with it. In return for the hospitality which gave us this house, Dr. Gerard had
the good fortune to save the life of a poor woman
who was dying of inflammation, and whom he bled
copiously.

It has been conjectured that Julalpoor is the scene
of Alexander's battle with Porus, when he crossed
the stream by a stratagem, and defeated that prince.
There is much to favour the opinion; for, in the
words of Quintus Curtius, we have " islands in the
stream, projecting banks, and waters dilated." Yet
the mention of "sunken rocks" seems to point
higher up the river, near the village of Jelum. The
high roads from the Indus pass this river at two
places, at Julalpoor and Jelum; but the latter is the
great road from Tartary, and appears to have been
the one followed by Alexander. The rocky nature

of its banks and bed here assists us in identifying
the localities of the route, since the course of the
river is not liable to fluctuation. At Jelum the
river is also divided into five or six channels, and
is fordable at all times, except in the monsoon.

About fifteen miles below Jelum, and about a
thousand yards from the Hydaspes, near the modern
village of Darapoor, we hit upon some extensive
ruins called Oodeenuggur, which seem to have been
a city that extended for three or four miles. The
traditions of the people are vague and unsatisfactory,
for they referred us to the deluge, and the time of
the prophet Noah. Many copper coins are found,
but those which were brought to me bore Arabic
inscriptions. A slab, with an inscription in that
language, which had been lately dug up, was also
shown to us; and I learn from M. Court that he
found a fluted pillar near this site with a capital
very like the Corinthian order. It, however, had a
Hindoo figure on it. At present there are no buildings standing; but the ground is strewed with broken pieces of kiln-burnt bricks and pottery, the
latter of a superior description. On the opposite
side of the Hydaspes to Darapoor stands a mound
said to be coeval with Oodeenuggur, where the
village of Moong is built, at which I procured two
Sanscrit coins. There are likewise some extensive
ruins beyond Moong, near Huria Badshapoor. I
do not conceive it improbable that Oodeenuggur
may represent the site of Nicæ, and that the mounds
and ruins on the western bank mark the position of
Bucephalia. We are told that these cities were

built so close to the river, that Alexander had to
repair them on his return from the Punjab campaign, since they stood within the influence of the
inundation. It is to be observed that towns which
have an advantageous locality are seldom deserted;
and if so, that others rise near them, which will account for the Arabic coins found in the neighbourhood. Alexander is said to have pitched his camp
at a distance of 150 stadia from the river, on a plain;
and there is an extensive champaign tract behind
this very site.

In our search for the remnants of Alexander's
cities, we are led into reflections on the state of the
country in those days; and it is curious to compare
them with our own times. We are informed that
Porus, with whom Alexander fought on the banks
of this river, maintained a force of 30,000 infantry
and 4000 cavalry, with 200 elephants and 300 war
chariots; and that he had subdued all his neighbours.
Now, if we change the war chariots into guns, we
have precisely the regular force of Runjeet Sing,
the modern Porus, who has likewise overwhelmed
all his neighbours. The same country will generally produce the same number of troops, if its
population be not reduced by adventitious circumstances.

We quitted the banks of the Jelum, and entered
the country of Potewar, inhabited by a tribe of
people called Gukers, famed for their beauty, and
claiming a Rajpoot origin. The credulity of these
people is as great as in other parts of India. A
grave and respectable man assured me that he had

seen a lake, called Ruwaesir, in the hill district of
Mundee, on the Sutlege, which had three small
islets floating upon it.   These are a place of Hindoo
pilgrimage; and my informant assured me that
they approach to receive the votaries who embark
upon them, and are floated out with their offerings!
It is obvious that there must be some delusion or
deception, which is practised with no small dex-
terity, as the place retains its character.   A native
told me that he had heard it was an artificial heap
of soil placed over reeds; but he had not visited the
spot, and seemed to proffer his information from
hearing my doubts as strongly expressed as I felt
them.   In the valley of Cashmeer there are mov-
able beds of melons, which in some degree may be
considered in the light of islands.   The ingenious
people of that valley spread a thick mat on the surface of their lake, and sprinkle it over with soil: it
soon acquires a consistency, from the grass growing
upon it.   On the following year they sow melons
and cucumbers, and reap the harvest from a boat;
and thus turn to account the very surface of the
lake in their rich country.   The melon islands of
Cashmeer may have supplied a hint to the Hindoo
priests of Mundee.

Our approach to the Mahommedan countries became evident daily, and showed itself in nothing
more than the costume of the women, many of
whom we now met veiled.   One girl whom we saw
on the road had a canopy of red cloth erected over
her on horseback, which had a ludicrous appearance.
It seemed to be a framework of wood; but as the

cloth concealed every thing as well as the countenance of the fair lady, I did not discover the contrivance. The costume of the unveiled portion of the sex had likewise undergone a change; they wore wide blue trousers, tightly tied at the ankle, which taper down, and have a graceful appearance. A narrow web of cloth sixty yards long is sometimes used in a single pair, for one fold falls upon the other.

On the 1st of March we reached the celebrated fort of Rotas, considered to be one of the great bulwarks between Tartary and India. As we wound through the dismal defiles, and might be ruminating on the various expeditions which had traversed this very road, the fort burst upon our view like the scene of a magic lantern. It had been hidden from us by towering precipices. We approached its ponderous walls by a straggling path which time had chiselled in the rock, and soon reached its lofty gateway. The black hoary aspect of the fort, and the arid sterility of the surrounding rocks, inspired us with no favourable idea of the neighbourhood, which has been the resort of many a desperate band. We had omitted to provide ourselves with Runjeet Sing's order for admission into this fortress; but we proceeded to the gateway, as a matter of course, and after a parley the doors were thrown open. The official permission arrived from Lahore on the following day.

We soon found ourselves among friends, and listened to the tales of the veterans without any fear of witnessing the scenes of their ancestors.

The Afghan officers of the Mogul empire under the
Emperor Humaioon dethroned that monarch, and
fortified themselves in Rotas, in the year 1531.
Shere Shah was its founder. Twelve years, and
some millions of rupees, are said to have been
wasted in its construction ; yet it was betrayed and
fell. Humaioon returned from his wanderings with
the auxiliaries of Iran, and recovered the kingdom
of his forefathers. He commanded that the fort of
Rotas should be levelled ; but so massy are its walls,
and so strong is the whole edifice, that his Ameers
and Oomrahs ventured to ask his majesty, whether
he came to recover his throne, or destroy a single
fort, since the one undertaking would require as
much energy as the other. Humaioon contented
himself with levelling a palace and a gateway as the
monument of his conquest, and prudently marched
to Delhi. We examined its walls and outworks, its
gateways and bastions ; and the people pointed out
to us the orifices for pouring oil on the besiegers.
We viewed with admiration the elaborate loopholes
for the matchlock, the deep wells cut in the live
rock, and the bomb-proof magazines of the fortification. From one of the towers we had a commanding view of the plain, in which we could distinguish a spacious caravansary, the work of the
generous and tolerant Akbar. He here eclipsed his
father Humaioon as much as he did in all the acts
of his protracted reign. The son raised an edifice
to shelter the weary traveller in his pilgrimage ; the
parent, full of wrath, wasted a greater sum in the
demolition of a palace. These caravansaries have

been erected at every stage as far west as the Indus; and the traveller cannot pass them without a
pleasurable feeling at the enlightened design of
their founder. The Emperor Akbar was a phil-
anthropist.

From Rotas we entered into a mountainous and
rugged country of great strength, and our road lay
in ravines. The chaos of rocks, their vertical strata,
terminating in needles from decomposition, the
round pebbles that lay imbedded in the sandstone,
and the wild scenery, made this an interesting
neighbourhood. Humboldt mentions somewhere,
that deposits of rock-salt and mineral springs mani-
fest some connection with volcanoes; and among
these hills we had both. One may almost convince
himself of the upheavings of nature, from a glance
at the rock. Though generally vertical, it may be
observed in some places to descend upon the ravines, as if the one half of the hill had been suddenly raised, or the other as suddenly depressed.
Water is abundant in the ravines, and is also found
in wells at a depth of thirty-five feet. To our right
we could see the spot at which the Jelum or Hydaspes issues from the mountains. It is called
Damgully. There is no route into the valley of
Cashmeer by this river; and the most frequented
one lies by Meerpoor and Poonch, about twelve
miles to the eastward. Near the point where the
Jelum enters the plain, there is an isolated rock
about sixty feet high, called Raoka, which may be
ascended by steps. A Mahommedan saint resides
on it. In searching for an obelisk called Rawjee,

mentioned by Mr. Elphinstone, we heard of Raoka; but since it only appeared to be a detached portion of rock, we did not visit it.

On the 6th of March we reached the village of Manikyala, at which there is a singular " *tope*" or mound of masonry. It has been described by Mr. Elphinstone, who gives a correct drawing of it, and tells us, that " it was, indeed, as like Grecian architecture as any building which Europeans, in remote parts of the country, could now construct by the hands of unpractised native builders." * It has been lately opened by M. Ventura, a general in Runjeet Sing's service. We are much indebted to that gentleman, since his labours were conducted at considerable expense and trouble. Through the kindness of my friend M. Allard, I had an opportunity of looking at the reliques which that officer found. A brief description of them has been published in the Researches of the Asiatic Society of Bengal; but I may here observe that they consist of three cylindrical boxes of gold, pewter (or some mixed metal), and iron, which were found cased within one another, and placed in a chamber cut in a large block of stone at the foundation of the pile. The gold box is about three inches long and an inch and a half in diameter, filled with a black dirty substance like mud, half liquid, and mixed up with small pieces of glass or amber; which would suggest an opinion of its once being cased in a glass that had been fractured and shivered. Among this substance, two

* Introduction to Elphinstone's Caubul, page 131.

coins or medals were found: the smaller one is of gold, and about the size of a sixpence, having a human figure, and the four-pronged instrument which marks all the Manikyala coins; the other has two lines of rude character, probably Hindee, on one side, and no writing or symbol on the reverse. Many other coins and reliques were found during the opening of the tope; and the people informed me that some human bones had been disinterred. On my arrival at Manikyala, I had an opportunity of appreciating the valuable services of M. Ventura, by a personal inspection of the "tope," which his persevering labour has now laid open. That gentleman had first endeavoured to enter the building from below, but failed on account of the great solidity of the structure. Further observation had discovered to him that there was a shaft or well (if I can use the expression) descending into the building from the top; and here M. Ventura dug with success. He first cleared the well, which reaches half way down, and is flagged at the bottom with large blocks of stone. He then completed his work by tearing up these enormous blocks till he reached the foundation, where he was rewarded by finding the cylinders which I have described, as well as a variety of coins, which have been forwarded to Paris, but are yet undeciphered.

In a place of such celebrity I did not expect to find my search for coins and antiques rewarded beyond the most sanguine expectations, since none are mentioned to have been seen by the gentlemen of the Cabool mission. I procured two antiques

and seventy copper coins. The value of the latter
is much heightened by their corresponding with
those found in the interior of the tope by M. Ventura. One of the antiques is a ruby or red crystal
cut in the shape of a head, with a frightful countenance and very long ears: while the other is an
oval cornelian, with the figure of a female holding
out a flower, and gracefully dressed in a mantle.
The execution is superior.* I shall notice these
coins hereafter, having presented some of them to
the Asiatic Society of Bengal, and received the
most ample return from Mr. James Prinsep, its able
secretary, in various notes regarding them.

I was much struck with the position of Manikyala,
for it stands on a spacious plain, and the " tope" is
to be distinguished at a distance of sixteen miles.
Various surmises have been thrown out regarding
this site, but I do not hesitate to fix upon it as
Taxilla, since Arrian expressly tells us that " that
was the most populous city *between* the Indus and
Hydaspes;" which is the exact position of Manikyala. M. Ventura decides on it as Bucephalia,
from a derivation that interprets Manikyala to mean
the city of the horse; but this is not founded on
history, as Bucephalia stood on the banks of the
Hydaspes, and, I believe, I have already described
its true position.

I shall describe the " tope" of Belur, which we
afterwards visited, before I give any conclusion regarding these buildings.

* It is with regret that I record the loss of these antiques,
though impressions of them have been preserved.

We reached Rawil Pindee on the 7th, and alighted
at the house which the ex-King of Cabool built in
his exile. It was a miserable hovel. The town of
Rawil Pindee is agreeable ; and we were pleased to
find the mountains covered with snow, and but
twelve miles distant. Some specimens of crystallised
sulphur, in its native state, were brought to me
from these hills ; and there is a town among them
called Porewala, which led me to think that it might
have some relation to the renowned Porus of the
Hydaspes.

We were now fast leaving Hindoostan and its
customs behind us. The dandelion had become a
common weed. At Manikyala, we halted next door
to a bakery, where the whole bread of the village is
baked. How much more sensible is this custom,
than that every family should prepare it separately,
as in India, and live in perpetual terror of defile-
ment from one another ! We were glad to be considered customers of the village oven. On our
road we met a numerous body of Afghans, and also
Hindoo pilgrims, crowding from beyond the Indus
to the great religious fair of Hurdwar : they looked
more like Mahommedans than the followers of
Brahma. The festival occurs every twelve years,
and distance serves to increase the devotion of the
pilgrim. The sight of these people from beyond
the Indus gave rise to many curious sensations.
We wore their dress, and they knew us not ; we
received their salutations as countrymen, and could
not participate in their feelings. Some of them
would ask, as we passed, whether we were going to

Cabool or Candahar; and from their looks and questions, I found many a secret and doubtful thrill pass across me. This I found to arise from the novelty of our situation, for it soon wore off after we mingled familiarly with the people; and, in course of time, I gave and returned the usual salutations with all the indifference of a practised traveller.

At Rawil Pindee we had a visit from the government officers, among whom was a Seik priest, or Bedee, who had taken the singular vow, never to repeat three or four words without the name of "Vishnu," one of the gods of the Hindoo trinity. His conversation was, therefore, most remarkable; for, on all subjects, and in all answers, he so interlarded the words "Vishnu, Vishnu," that I could not suppress a smile. This personage presented us with a purse of 200 rupees; but it appeared to come from Vishnu, and not from the Maharaja Runjeet Sing.

About fifteen miles from Rawil Pindee, we passed the defile of Margulla, and descried with joy the mountains beyond the Indus. This is a narrow pass over the low hills, and paved with blocks of stone for 150 yards. A Persian inscription, let into the rock, commemorates the fame of the civilised Emperor who cut the road. The defiles continue for about a mile; when a bridge across a rivulet conducts the traveller to the next caravansary. A bridge, a caravansary, and a road cut through a hill, within a distance of two miles, bespeak a different rule from that of the Punjab in modern times. We

continued our march to Osman, about twenty miles
from Rawil Pindee. It stands on a plain, at the
mouth of a valley, close to the base of the outlying
hills. Its meadows are watered by the most beautiful and crystal rivulets, that flow from the mountains. Some of them are conducted by artificial
means through the village, and turn little water-
mills that grind flour. Up the valley stands the fort
of Khanpoor, with some beautiful gardens; and over
it snow-clad mountains rear their peaks. The fields
of this fruitful valley lie neglected, from the exorbi-
tant assessment of the person who farms it. The
peasants have no hope of redress but by such an
expedient; and this entire suspension of the labours
of the husbandmen may open the understanding of
the misguided governor.

We visited Osman, which is about four miles
from the King's road, at the base of the lower Himilaya, to examine a mound or " tope," like that of
Manikyala, which stands on the nook of a range of
hills near the ruined village of Belur, about a mile
beyond Osman. The construction of the building,
as depicted in the annexed sketch, gives it to the
same era as that of Manikyala. Neither of the
buildings are perfect; and the one now delineated
differs from the other in the greater length of the
shaft. It is fifty feet high, or about two thirds of
the height of Manikyala. It has also been opened,
and the square aperture formed of cut stone has
descended into the building. The small pilasters
are likewise to be recognised, but the mouldings are
more numerous, and the general outline of the build-

ing is somewhat different. The " tope " of Belur is a
conspicuous object, from its elevated situation, but

TOPE OF BELUR.

I could not gather a tradition regarding it from the
numerous population. Like one in search of the
philosopher's stone, I was led from place to place,
and now learned that there were two buildings
similar to these " topes," beyond the Indus, between Peshawur and Cabool. We also discovered
the ruins of another tope, three miles eastward of
Rawil Pindee. The few coins which I found at the
tope of Belur were of the same type as those already
described. Seeing that both the structures of
Manikyala and Belur are pierced by a shaft that

descends into the building, I incline to a belief that in these " topes " we have the tombs of a race of princes who once reigned in Upper India, and that they are either the sepulchres of the Bactrian kings, or their Indo-Scythic successors, mentioned in the Periplus of the second Arrian. The rudeness of the coins would point to the latter age, or second century of the Christian era.

From the beautiful rivulets of Osman we passed down the valley, and, after a march of seven miles, found ourselves in the garden of Hoosn Abdall, — a spot which attracted the munificent Emperors of Hindoostan. It is situated between two bare and lofty hills, whose brown and naked tops do not contribute much to its beauty; still it must be an enchanting place in the hot months. The garden-houses are now mouldering to decay, and weeds hide the flowers and roses; yet the peach and apricot trees glowed with blossom, vines clung to them, and the limpid water gushed in torrents from the rock. Some hundred springs rise in the limit of this small garden, and, after washing its beds, pay their tribute to a brook which passes on to the Indus. They form pools, which are stored with fish, that may be seen darting about in the clear water. The spring had commenced when we visited this delightful place. As we passed it, our view opened upon the valley of Drumtour, that leads to Cashmeer; and the range of hills at Puklee, covered with snow, were to be traced in chain with more lofty mountains beyond them. The fertile plain of Chuch and Huzara also lay before us.

We came in sight of the Indus, at a distance of fifteen miles. It could be traced from its exit through the lower hills to the fort of Attok, by the vapour which hung over it like smoke. As the water of the Indus is much colder than the atmosphere, it may account for this phenomenon. We encamped at Huzroo, which is a mart between Peshawur and Lahore. The people were now quite changed; they were Afghans, and spoke Pooshtoo. I was struck with their manly mien, and sat down with delight on a felt, along with an Afghan, who civilly invited me to converse with him. I did not regret to exchange the cringing servility of the Indians for the more free and independent manners of Cabool. An itinerant goldsmith, who had heard of our intended journey to Bokhara, came and chatted with us. He had travelled there, and even in Russia; and showed us a copper copec which he had brought with him on his return. He spoke of the equity and justice of the people among whom we were to travel, which made this rambling jeweller a welcome visiter. He was a Hindoo.

On the morning of the 14th of March, we had the pleasure of encamping on the banks of the Indus, with the troops of Runjeet Sing, now on the frontier, under Sirdar Huree Sing. That chief came to meet us with all the forms of Eastern pomp, and conducted us to a comfortable suite of tents which he had prepared for us. On our march to the river, we passed the field of battle where the Afghans made their last stand, now some twenty years ago, on the eastern side of the Indus. They

were commanded by the Vizier Futteh Khan, who
fled, panic-struck, though not defeated. A horde as
numerous as that of Xerxes or Timour might en-
camp on this spacious plain, which is an entire sheet
of cultivation. It was covered with rounded stones
(many of which were granite) — an unerring proof
of the agency of water. We visited our host, the
commandant, who welcomed us with his troops and
officers in array, and gave us the cordial reception
of friends. Our conversation turned on the warlike deeds of Runjeet, and his passing the Indus
both with and without a ford. We grew interested
in the subject, and soon made up our minds to, at
least, make the attempt of fording this great river.

We mounted one of the chief's elephants; and,
accompanied by himself and 200 horsemen, passed
a few miles down the river to the village of Khy-
rakhuel, about five miles above Attok. The stream
was here divided into three branches, and in the
two first gushed with amazing violence. I did not
like the appearance of the torrent; and, though I
said nothing, would have willingly turned back:
but how could that be, when I had been the foremost to propose it? The chief rallied his escort
round him, threw a piece of silver money into the
river, according to custom, and dashed into it. We
followed, and the whole of our party reached in
safety. While on the island, and preparing to enter
the principal branch, a melancholy accident occurred
to some stragglers who attempted to follow us.
They were seven in number; and, instead of crossing at the exact point where we had effected the

passage, they passed a few yards lower down, with
the water but knee deep, yet very rapid.   The
whole seven were unhorsed in a moment, and
swept into the stream.   The ferrymen ran to their
assistance, and extricated them all but one poor
fellow and two horses, whom we could see struggle,
and at last sink.   The others were rescued with
great difficulty, and two of them were all but dead.
We were shocked at the catastrophe, and proposed
to return, but the chief would not listen to it.   He
gave a laugh, and said, " What know ye, that these
fellows (we thought they had all gone) may be
kings in another world; and what is the use of a
Seik if he cannot pass the Attok ?" (Indus).   The
principal branch, however, was still in our front;
and I only agreed to cross if the horsemen were
left behind.   " Leave my guard," cried the chief,
" impossible!" but we did leave it, and safely passed
the ford.   The footing was slippery, and the current shot with great rapidity: the colour of the
water was blue, and it was exceedingly cold, which
makes it trying to both man and beast.   The
elephants pressed up against the stream, and roared
as we advanced.   The excitement of such an undertaking is great, and would have been exhilarating, had not our joy been dimmed by such a cala-
mity.   This ford has often been used by the Seiks,
but the passage has involved many serious accidents.

A tale of a desperate soldier was here related to
me, as having occurred at Lahore.   He was a native
of Hindoostan, and had murdered the adjutant of

the regiment in which he was serving, in Runjeet's
army.   An example was called for in the support
of discipline; but Runjeet Sing has never shed
blood since he attained his throne, and refused to
put him to death, though urged to it by the French
officers.   The hands of the culprit were ordered to
be amputated on the parade ground, before the
troops, and were chopped off by an axe; the
hemorrhage was arrested by immersing the stump
in burning oil.   The hands were nailed on a board,
as a warning to the army, and the unfortunate man
was dismissed with ignominy.   A comrade conducted him to a ruined mosque, where he passed
the night; but his spirit forbade him to survive his
disgrace, and he resolved on committing suicide.
Next day he threw himself into the river (Ravee):
his resolution was shaken, and, instead of drowning
himself, he crossed the river, swimming with his
handless stumps!

We now proceeded to the fortress of Attok,
which stands on a black slaty ridge, at the verge of
the Indus, the "forbidden river" of the Hindoos.
It was, indeed a forbidden one to us, for the garrison had mutinied, ejected their officers, and seized
upon the ferry-boats.*   Their arrears of pay were

* A critical journal, in alluding to our fording the Indus
above Attok, finds a difficulty in reconciling that fact with
this passage.   The reply is simple: at Attok the Indus is
not fordable, and above it, though we crossed in safety, the
river of Cabool still separated us from Peshawur, not being
fordable, and it was our object to visit that city.   Had the
military information which I collected during my journey been
published, this obscurity would not have occurred.

not forthcoming, and they had taken this means of informing Runjeet of their grievances. It was in vain that we produced the most peremptory orders, to receive us inside the walls, and show us the curiosities of the place; they replied, that their complaints would now be heard, as the Maharaja would know of their ill treatment towards us. Since they evinced no further contumacy, we halted outside, in a dilapidated mosque, and were not molested. It was useless to parley with irritated men, and I thought we were fortunate in prevailing on them, after a detention of two days, to give us a boat, in which we were ferried across the grand boundary of India, on the afternoon of the 17th of March. The water was azure blue, and the current exceeded six miles an hour. We passed in four minutes. About 200 yards above Attok, and before the Indus is joined by the Cabool river, it gushes over a rapid with amazing fury. Its breadth does not here exceed 120 yards; the water is much ruffled, and dashes like the waves and spray of the ocean. It hisses and rolls with a loud noise, and exceeds the rate of ten miles in the hour. A boat cannot live in this tempestuous torrent; but after the Cabool river has joined it, the Indus passes in a tranquil stream, about 260 yards wide and 35 fathoms deep, under the walls of Attok. This fortress is a place of no strength: it has a population of about 2000 souls.

Before crossing the Indus, we observed a singular phenomenon at the fork of the Indus and Cabool river, where an ignis fatuus shows itself every

evening. Two, three, and even four bright lights
are visible at a time, and continue to shine throughout the night, ranging within a few yards of each
other. The natives could not account for them,
and their continuance during the rainy season is the
most inexplicable part of the phenomenon, in their
estimation. They tell you, that the valiant Man
Sing, a Rajpoot, who carried his war of revenge
against the Mahommedans across the Indus, fought
a battle in this spot; and that the lights now seen
are the spirits of the departed. I should not have
credited the constancy of this "will-o'-the-wisp," had
I not seen it. It may arise from the reflection of
the water on the rock, smoothed by the current;
but then it only shows itself on a particular spot,
and the whole bank is smoothed. It may also be
an exhalation of some gas from a fissure in the
rock; but its position prevented our examining it.

We found the fishermen on the Indus and Cabool
river washing the sand for gold. The operation is
performed with most profit after the swell has
subsided. The sand is passed through a sieve, and
the larger particles that remain are mixed with
quicksilver, to which the metal adheres. Some of
the minor rivers, such as the Swan and Hurroo,
yield more gold than the Indus; and as their sources
are not remote, it would show that the ores lie on
the southern side of the Himilaya.

CHAP. III.

PESHAWUR.

It required some arrangement to commence our advance into the country of the Afghans; for they and the Seiks entertain the most deep-rooted animosity towards each other. At Attok, a friendly letter was sent to us by the chief of Peshawur, expressive of his good wishes. I, therefore, addressed that personage, Sooltan Mahommed Khan, informing him of our intentions, and soliciting his protection. I likewise sent a letter of introduction from Runjeet to the chief of Acora; but so inconstant is power in these countries, that that person had been ejected during the few weeks we had been travelling from Lahore: but the usurper opened the communication, and kindly despatched a party to meet us. The subjects of Runjeet Sing escorted us to the frontier, which is three miles beyond the Indus; here we met the Afghans. Neither party would approach, and we drew up at a distance of about 300 yards from each other. The Seiks gave us their "*wagroojee futtih*," synonymous with our three cheers, and we advanced, and delivered ourselves to the Mahommedans; who said, *Wus-sulam alaikoom!* "Peace be unto you!" We trod our way to Acora, with our new people, the Khuttuks, a lawless race, and alighted at that village, which is nearly deserted, from the constant inroads of the Seiks. The chief immediately waited upon us, and expressed his dissatisfaction at our having purchased some articles from the bazar, since it was a reflection on his hospitality. I begged his pardon, and placed the mistake on my ignorance of Afghan customs, adding, that I would not forget, as I advanced, the hospitality of the Khuttuks of Acora. The chief took his leave, charging us, before his departure, to consider ourselves as secure as eggs under a hen; a homely enough simile, the truth of which we had no reason to doubt. Yet it was at this place that Mr. Moorcroft and his party encountered some serious difficulties, and were obliged to fight their way. We here received a second and most friendly letter from the chief of Peshawur, which was truly satisfactory, since it had been written before he had got any of the letters of introduction which we forwarded. It intimated that a person was approaching to conduct us.

We had now quitted the territories of Hindoostan, and entered on a land where covetousness of a neighbour's goods is the ruling passion: we therefore marched with our baggage. Our few servants were also divided into regular watches for the night. We had two Afghans, two Indians, and two natives of Cashmeer. A Cashmeerian paired with an Indian, and the trustworthy with the most lazy; while we ourselves superintended the posting of the sentries. Our people laughed heartily at this military disposition; but it was ever after enforced in all our travels. We ourselves were now living as natives, and had ceased to repine at the hardness of the ground and the miserable hovels in which we sometimes halted. I had also disposed of my valuables in what then appeared to me a masterly manner: a letter of credit for five thousand rupees was fastened to my left arm, in the way that the Asiatics wear amulets. My polyglot passport was fixed to my right arm, and a bag of ducats was tied round my waist. I also distributed a part of my ready money to each of the servants; and so perfect was the check that had been established over them, that we never lost a single ducat in all our journey, and found most faithful servants in men who might have ruined and betrayed us. We trusted them, and they rewarded our confidence. One man, Ghoolam Hoosn, a native of Surat, followed me throughout the whole journey, cooked our food, and never uttered a complaint at the performance of such duties, foreign as they were to his engagements. He is now with me in England.

Our conductor, on the part of Runjeet Sing left us at Acora. Choonee Lal, for that was his name, was a quiet inoffensive Brahmin, who did not seem at ease across the Indus. I gave him a farewell letter to his master; and, since his Highness had written for my sentiments regarding the salt-mines of the Punjab, and the best means of profiting by them, I gave him a long account of salt monopolies, telling him, that it was better to levy high duties upon salt than grain. I told him, also, in as many words, that the salt-range was as valuable a portion of his territory as the valley of Cashmeer; but I do not believe that his Highness stood in need of much counsel, as the measures which we had seen at the mines practically proved.

On our road to Acora, we passed a field of battle, at the small village of Sydoo, where, it is said, 8000 Seiks had defended themselves against an enraged population of 150,000 Mahommedans. Bood Sing, their commander, threw up a small breastwork of loose stones, and extricated himself from his dilemma, so as to secure the praise even of his enemies. We now saw the place, and the bleaching bones of the horses which had fallen on the occasion. On the next march we passed the more celebrated field of Noushero, to which our attention had been directed by Runjeet Sing himself. He here encountered the Afghans for the last time; but their chief, Azeem Khan, was separated from the greater part of his army by the river of Cabool. The Seiks defeated the divisions on the opposite side, mainly through the personal courage of Runjeet Sing, who carried a hillock with his guards, from which his other troops had three times retreated. Azeem Khan, of Cabool, fled without encountering the successful army, which had partly crossed the river to oppose him. It is believed, that he feared the capture of his treasure, which would have fallen into Runjeet's power if he had advanced; but it is also said, that he was terrified by the shouts of the Seiks on the night of their victory. He attributed their exclamations to the fresh arrival of troops : for they have a custom of shouting on such occasions. We have already compared this potentate with Porus ; and the similar stratagem by which Alexander defeated that prince will also be remembered. As the Greeks had terrified his predecessor on the Hydaspes, the Seiks now frightened the Afghans by their shouts and pæans.

As we traversed the plain to Peshawur, I felt elevated and happy. Thyme and violets perfumed the air, and the green sod and clover put us in mind of our native home. The violet has the name of "*gool i pueghumbur*," or the rose of the Prophet, *par excellence*, I suppose, from its fragrance. At Peerpaee, which is a march from Peshawur, we were joined by six horsemen, whom the chief sent to escort us. We saddled at sunrise, though it rained heavily, and accompanied the party to the city, trying sorely the patience of the horsemen, by declining to halt half way, that they might give timely information of our approach. We pushed on till near the city ; when their persuasion could be no longer resisted. " The chief sent us to welcome you, and has ordered his son to meet you outside the city," said their commander, " and we are now within a few hundred yards of his house." We halted, and in a few minutes the eldest son of the chief made his appearance, attended by an elephant and a body of horse. He was a handsome boy, about twelve years old, and dressed in a blue tunic, with a Cashmeer shawl as a turban. We dismounted on the high road, and embraced ; when the youth immediately conducted us to the presence of his father. Never were people received with more kindness: he met us in person at the doorway, and led us inside of an apartment, studded with mirror glass and daubed over with paint in exceedingly bad taste. His house, his country, his property, his all, were ours; he was the ally of the British government, and he had shown it by his kindness to Mr. Moorcroft, which he considered as a treaty of friendship. We were not the persons who wished to infringe its articles. Sooltan Mahommed Khan is about thirty-five years old, rather tall in stature, and of dark complexion. He was dressed in a pelisse, trimmed with fur and the down of the peacock, which had a richer look than the furniture that surrounded him. We were glad to withdraw and change our wet clothes, and were conducted to the seraglio of Sooltan Mahommed Khan, which he had prepared, *I need not add, emptied*, for our reception. This was, indeed, a kind of welcome we had not anticipated.

An hour had not passed before we were visited by Peer Mahommed Khan, the younger brother of the chief, a jolly and agreeable person. The chief himself followed in the course of the evening; and a sumptuous dinner succeeded, of which we all partook. The meat was delicious, and so was the cookery. We ate with our hands; and soon ceased to wonder at a nobleman tearing a lamb in pieces and selecting the choice bits, which he held out for our acceptance. A long roll of leavened bread was spread in front of each of us as a plate; and, since its size diminished as the meat disappeared, it did its part well. Pilaos and stews, sweets and sours, filled the trays; but the bonne bouche of the day was a lamb that had never tasted aught but milk. A bitter orange had been squeezed over it, and made it very savoury. Four trays of sweet-meats followed, with fruit; and the repast concluded with sherbet mixed with snow, the sight of which delighted us as much as our new friends. A watch of night was spent before we broke up; and after the chief had repeated in a whisper his devotion to our nation and anxiety for our welfare, he bade us good night. I had almost lost the use of my legs from the irksome position of constraint in which I had so long sat. If we had been prepared to like the manners of this people, there was much to confirm it on this evening.

On the following day we were introduced to the remainder of the family. There are two brothers besides the chief, and a host of sons and relations. The most remarkable person of the family was a son of Futtih Khan, the Vizier of Shah Mahmood, who had been so basely and cruelly murdered. The lad is about fourteen years of age, and the solitary descendant of his ill-fated father. The sons of the Meer Waeez and Mookhtar o-doula, who had dethroned Shah Shooja, were among the party, and the day passed most agreeably. The people were sociable and well-informed, free from prejudice on points of religion, and many of them were well versed in Asiatic history. They were always cheerful, and frequently noisy in their good-humour. During the conversation many of them rose up, and prayed in the room when the stated hours arrived. As we got better acquainted in Peshawur, our circle of acquaintance was widely extended, and visiters would drop in at all hours, and more particularly if they found us alone. The Afghans never sit by themselves, and always made some apology if they found any of us solitary, though it would have been sometimes agreeable to continue so. In the afternoon the chief invited us to accompany him and his brothers to see the environs of Peshawur. The doctor stayed away, but I rode with them. Of the town of Peshawur I shall say nothing, since the graphic and accurate descriptions of Mr. Elphinstone require no addition. Such, indeed, is the nature of the information contained in his valuable work, that I shall always avoid the ground on which he trod, and in Peshawur confine myself to incidents and adventures of a personal nature. I say this in my own defence. I had accompanied the chief on a day most favourable to a stranger, the "nouroz," or new year (the 21st of March), which is celebrated by the people. The greater part of the community were gathered in gardens, and paraded about with nosegays and bunches of peach-blossom. We entered the garden of Ali Murdan Khan, and seating ourselves on the top of the garden-house, looked down upon the assembled multitude. The trees were covered with blossom, and nothing could be more beautiful than the surrounding scene. The chief and his brothers took great pains to point out the neigh-

bouring hills to me, explaining by whom they were
inhabited, with every other particular which they
thought might interest. They also informed me,
that the nobleman who had prepared this garden
possessed the philosopher's stone (the " sung-i-
fars"), since there was no other way of accounting
for his great riches. They added, that he threw
it into the Indus; which at least eases them of the
dilemma as to his heir.

We soon got accustomed to our new mode of life,
and, as we made it a rule never on any occasion to
write during the day, or in public, had leisure to
receive every person who came to see us. In
a short time we became acquainted with the whole
society of Peshawur; and, during the thirty days
that we remained there, had an uninterrupted series
of visiting and feasting. Nothing, however, more
contributed to our comfort and happiness than the
kindness of our worthy host. Sooltan Mahommed
Khan was not the illiterate Afghan whom I expected to find, but an educated well-bred gentleman, whose open and affable manner made the
most lasting impression. As we were sitting down
to dinner, he would frequently slip in, quite unattended, and pass the evening with us. He would
sometimes be followed by various trays of dishes,
which he had had cooked in his harem, and believed
might be palatable to us. He is a person more
remarkable for his urbanity than his wisdom; but
he transacts all his own business: he is a brave
soldier; his seraglio has about thirty inmates, and
he has already had a family of sixty children. He

could not tell the exact number of survivors when
I asked him.

On the Friday after our arrival we accompanied
the chief and his family to some flower-gardens,
where we spent the greater part of the day in conversation. The chief himself sat under one tree,
and we ranged ourselves beneath another. Iced
sherbet and confections were brought to us, and
we heard much of the munificence of Mr. Elphinstone from Moollah Nujeeb, an elderly man, who
had accompanied him to Calcutta. In the afternoon we returned to the King's garden, which is a
most spacious one, and sat down on the ground with
Sooltan Mahommed Khan and his family, to partake of sugar-cane cut into small pieces. Four of
the chief's sons accompanied us; and it was delightful to see the affectionate notice which he took
of his children, none of whom were five years old.
Each of them sat on horseback in front of one of
his suite, and held the reins in a masterly manner:
for the Dooranees are taught to ride from infancy.
We then followed the chief to his family burying-
ground, where his two elder brothers, Atta and
Yar Mahommed Khan, who fell in battle, lie interred. The whole branches of the family were
present, and offered up their afternoon prayers in
a mosque, close to the cemetery. The sight was
very impressive, and the more so, since the sons of
the deceased brothers were among the party. The
day finished with a visit to a holy man named
Shekh Iwus: and such is the usual manner of
spending a Friday among the Dooranee nobles of

Peshawur. The chief's retinue consisted of his relations and servants: he had no guards; and, at first starting, was only accompanied by ourselves and two horsemen. There is a simplicity and freedom about these people greatly to be admired; and, whatever the rule may be, I can at least vouch for petitioners having an ear given to their complaints. Every one seems on an equality with the chief, and the meanest servant addresses him without ceremony. He himself seems quite free from every sort of pride or affectation, and is only to be distinguished in the crowd by his dress, in which he is fond of richness and ornament.

In one of our rides about Peshawur with the chief, we had a specimen of justice and Mahommedan retribution. As we passed the suburbs of the city we discovered a crowd of people, and, on a nearer approach, saw the mangled bodies of a man and woman, the former not quite dead, lying on a dunghill. The crowd instantly surrounded the chief and our party, and one person stepped forward, and represented, in a trembling attitude, to Sooltan Mahommed Khan, that he had discovered his wife in an act of infidelity, and had put both parties to death: he held the bloody sword in his hands, and described how he had committed the deed. His wife was pregnant, and already the mother of three children. The chief asked a few questions, which did not occupy him three minutes: he then said, in a loud voice, " You have acted the part of a good Mahommedan, and performed a justifiable act." He then moved on, and

the crowd cried out " Bravo !" (" Afreen !") The
man was immediately set at liberty. We stood by
the chief during the investigation ; and, when it
finished, he turned to me, and carefully explained
the law. " Guilt," added he, " committed on a
Friday, is sure to be discovered ;" for that happened to be the day on which it occurred. There
is nothing new in these facts ; but, as an European,
I felt my blood run chill when I looked on the
mangled bodies, and heard the husband justifying
the murder of her who had borne him three children : nor was the summary justice of the chief,
who happened to be passing, the least remarkable
part of the dismal scene. It seems that the exposure of the bodies on a dunghill is believed to
expiate in some degree the sins of the culprit, by
the example it holds out to the community ; they
are afterwards interred in the same spot.

We were invited, shortly after our arrival at
Peshawur, to pass a day with the chief's brother,
Peer Mahommed Khan. He received us in a
garden, under a bower of fruit-trees, loaded with
blossom. Carpets were spread, and before we sat
down the boughs were shaken, which covered them
with the variegated leaves of the apricot and peach.
The fragrance and beauty were equally delightful.
The party consisted of about fifty persons, all of
whom partook of the entertainment, which was on
a substantial and large scale. There were per-
formers in attendance, who chanted odes in Pooshtoo and Persian. The conversation was general,
and related chiefly to their own expeditions. The

children of the chief and his brothers were again
present: they rioted among the confectionery, and
four of them had a pitched battle with the blossom
of the trees, which they threw at each other like
snow. I do not remember to have seen any place
more delightful than Peshawur at this season: the
climate, garden, and landscape, delight the senses,
and to all we had been so fortunate as to add the
hospitality of the people. I had brought no presents to conciliate these men, and I therefore would
receive none at their hands; but, on the present
occasion, our host produced a small horse, of a hill
breed, and insisted on my receiving it. " Mr.
" Moorcroft," said he, " accepted one of these
" same horses, which availed him in his difficulties;
" and I cannot, therefore, take a refusal, since you
" are entering such dangerous countries." The
horse was forcibly sent to my house. The sequel
will show the strange Providence which is sometimes to be traced in the acts of man.

But our residence at the house of the chief was
not without inconvenience, and it required some
consideration to devise a plan for our extrication
with credit. The chief of Peshawur was at en-
mity with his brother of Cabool, and wished to
persuade us to pass through that city by stealth,
and without seeing him. He offered, indeed, to
send a Persian gentleman as our conductor beyond
Afghanistan; and, had I believed the arrangement
practicable, I would have rejoiced: but it was ob-
viously difficult to pass through the city of Cabool
and the country of its chief without his knowledge;

and a discovery of such an attempt might bring
down upon us the wrath of a man from whom we
had nothing to fear by openly avowing ourselves
as British officers. I was resolved, therefore, to
trust the chief of Cabool as I had trusted his brother
of Peshawur, so soon as I could persuade Sooltan
Mahommed Khan that our intercourse there should
never diminish the regard which we felt for him
personally. In a few days, he consented to our
writing to Cabool, and notifying our approach to
Nuwab, Jubbar Khan, the brother of the governor,
whom I addressed under a new seal, cut after the
manner of the country, and bearing the name of
" Sikunder Burnes." Sooltan Mahommed Khan
now confined himself to advice, and such good
offices as would conduct us in safety beyond his
dominions. He requested that we might still
further change our dress, which we did, and left
it as the best sign of our poverty. The outer garment which I wore cost me a rupee and a half,
ready made, in the bazaar. We also resolved to
conceal our character as Europeans from the common people, though we should frankly avow to
every chief, and indeed every individual with whom
we might come into contact, our true character.
But our compliance with this counsel subjected us
to the strongest importunities to avoid Toorkistan,
and pass by the route of Candahar, into Persia.
Nothing could save us from the *ferocious* and man-
selling Uzbeks; the country, the people, every-
thing was bad. They judged of the calamities of
Moorcroft and his associates, and I listened in si-

lence. The chief thought that he had so far worked upon us to abandon the design, that he prepared various letters for Candahar, and a particular introduction to his brother, who is chief of that place.

Shortly after our arrival in Peshawur, Sooltan Mahommed Khan illuminated his palace, and invited us to an entertainment, given, as he assured us, on our account. His mansion was only separated from ours by a single wall, and he came in person to conduct us in the afternoon. The ladies had been spending the day in these apartments, but the " krook" * was given before we entered; and a solitary eunuch, who looked more like an old woman, only now remained. In the evening the party assembled, which did not exceed fifteen persons, the most distinguished in Peshawur : we sat in the hall, which was brilliantly lighted; behind it there was a large fountain in the interior of the house, shaded by a cupola about fifty feet high, and on the sides of it were different rooms, that overlooked the water. The reflection from the dome, which was painted, had a pleasing effect. About eight o'clock we sat down to dinner, which commenced with sweetmeats and confections, that had been prepared in the harem. They were far superior to any thing seen in India; the dinner succeeded, and the time passed very agreeably. The chief and his courtiers talked of their wars and revolutions, and I answered their numerous questions regarding our

* A Tartar custom and word in clearing the outer apartments of the seraglio.

own country. The assembly were ever ready to draw comparisons between any thing stated, and the records of Asiatic history, referring familiarly to Timour, Baber, and Aurungzebe, and exhibiting at the same time much general knowledge. I gave them accounts of steam-engines, galvanic batteries, balloons, and electrifying machines, which appeared to give universal satisfaction. If they disbelieved, they did not express their scepticism. Many of the courtiers of course flattered the chief as they commented on his remarks; but their style of address was by no means cringing, and the mild affability of Sooltan Mahommed Khan himself quite delighted me. He spoke without reserve of Runjeet Sing, and sighed for some change that might release him from the disgrace of having his son a hostage at Lahore. The subject of the Russians was introduced, and a Persian in the party declared that his country was quite independent of Russia. The chief, with much good humour, remarked, that their independence was something like his own with the Seiks, unable to resist, and glad to compromise.

Among our visiters, none came more frequently than the sons of the chief and his brothers; and none were more welcome, for they displayed great intelligence and address. Nearly the whole of them were suffering from intermittent fever, that was soon cured by a few doses of quinine, of which we had a large supply. The knowledge exhibited by these little fellows induced me on one occasion to note their conversation. There were four of them

present, and none had attained his twelfth year.
I interrogated them, as they sat round me, on the
good qualities of Cabool, giving to each two answers; they replied as follows : — 1. The salubrity
of the climate ; 2. the flavour of the fruit ; 3. the
beauty of the people ; 4. the handsome bazar ;
5. the citadel of the Balar Hissar ; 6. the justice of
the ruler ; 7. the pomegranates without seed ; and,
8. its incomparable " *ruwash*," or rhubarb. Four
answers to its bad qualities gave the following information : — 1. Food is expensive ; 2. the houses
cannot be kept in repair without constantly re-
moving the snow from the roof ; 3. the floods
of the river dirty the streets ; and, 4. the immo-
rality of the fair sex, which last is a proverb, given
in a Persian couplet.* It does not appear to me
that boys in Europe show such precocity, and it is
no doubt attributable to their earlier introduction
into the society of grown up people. When a boy
has arrived at his twelfth year, a separate establishment is maintained here on his account ; and, long
before that time of life, he is prohibited from fre-
quenting his mother's apartments but on certain
occasions. Khoju Mahommed, the eldest son of
the chief of Peshawur, whom I have already mentioned, came one day to invite us to dinner, and I
expressed some surprise to hear that he had a house
of his own. " What !" replied the youth, " would
you have me imbibe the disposition of a woman,

* " Zun i Cabool be yar neest
  Arud i Peshawur be juwar neest."

when I am the son of a Dooranee ?" I occasionally accompanied these scions to the gardens of
Peshawur; and found them good associates, as no
person ever thought of disturbing us. I remember
of hearing from one of them, a tale of his father's
wars and untimely end in battle two years before,
and how he took the bloody head of his parent in
his arms, when brought from the field without its
trunk.

These rambles in Peshawur were not always
undertaken in such company; for I used latterly to
go unattended even by a capchee or door-keeper of
the chief, who used to accompany us on our first
arrival. I visited the Bala Hissar, in which Shah
Shooja had received so gorgeously the Cabool mission of 1809. It is now a heap of ruins, having
been burned by the Seiks in one of their expeditions
to this country. I also went to the large caravansary, where that amusing and talented traveller,
Mr. Forster, describes with such humour the co-
vetous Moollah, who wished to steal his clothes.
Circumstances were strangely changed since his
days, now some fifty years ago; he considered his
journey and dangers at an end on reaching Cabool,
where we looked for their commencement. Passing
a gate of the city, I observed it studded with horse
shoes, which are as superstitious emblems in this
country as in remote Scotland. A farrier had no
customers : a saint to whom he applied recommended his nailing a pair of horse shoes to a gate
of the city : he afterwards prospered, and the far-
riers of Peshawur have since propitiated the same

saint by a similar expedient, in which they place implicit reliance.

One of our most welcome visiters in Peshawur was a seal engraver, a native of the city, who had travelled over the greater part of Asia and Eastern Europe, though he had not yet attained his thirtieth year. In early life he had conceived the strongest passion to visit foreign countries; and with the avowed, but by no means the only, motive of making a pilgrimage to Mecca, quitted his house without the knowledge of his family, and proceeded by the Indus to Arabia. He had performed the *haj*, and then visited Egypt, Syria, Constantinople, Greece, and the islands of the Archipelago, supporting himself during the journey by engraving the names of the faithful, which appears to be a profitable sort of occupation. With his wealth he enjoyed the new scenes of the Levant, and united himself to other wanderers, from one of whom he had happily escaped a base attempt to poison. After an absence of five or six years, he returned to his family, who had long looked upon him as lost. His father took the earliest opportunity of settling him in life, to check his roaming propensities, so that he now lived quietly in Peshawur. He appeared quite delighted to visit us, and talk of the Nile and the pyramids, Istambool and its golden horn, the accounts of which he could get few of his countrymen to believe. He looked back upon his peregrinations with great delight, and sighed that his being the father of a family prevented his joining us. This disposition to wander is a curious trait in the character

of the Afghans, for they are great lovers of their
country. A Mahommedan, however, is at home
every where his creed is professed; for there is a
sort of fellowship in that religion, like free-masonry,
which binds its members together: among them
there are no distinctions of grade or rank, which so
strongly mark the society of other sects and countries.

We arrived at the season of the quails, when
every one who could escape from his other vocations
was engaged in hawking, netting, or fighting these
courageous little birds. Every Tuesday morning
the chief had a meeting in his court-yard, to en-
courage the sport. He used to send for us to
witness it: it is by no means destitute of amusement, whether we regard the men or the birds;
for chief, servant, and subject, were here on an
equality, the quails being the heroes, not the men.
They are carried about in bags, and enticed to
fight with each other for grain, which is sprinkled
between them. When the quail once runs he is
worthless, and immediately slain; but they seldom
make a precipitate retreat. Nothing can exceed
the passion of the Afghans for this kind of sport;
almost every boy in the street may be seen with a
quail in his hand, and crowds assemble in all parts
of the city to witness their game battles.

Seeing the interest which we took in these
scenes, the chief invited us to accompany him on
a hawking party, about five miles from Peshawur;
but we were unsuccessful, and killed nothing. We
went in search of water-fowl, and a party that pre-

ceded us had disturbed the ducks. We had, however, an Afghan pic-nic, and an insight into national
manners. We sat down under a slight awning, and
the servants produced eight or ten young lambs,
which had been slain on the occasion. The chief
called for a knife, cut up one of them, spitted the
pieces on a ramrod drawn from one of his attendant's matchlocks, and handed them to be roasted. He
remarked to me that meat so dressed had a better
flavour than if cooked by regular servants, and that
if we were really in the field he would hold one end
of the ramrod and give the other to some one else
till the meat was ready, which would make the
entertainment thoroughly Dooranee. I liked this
unaffected simplicity. There were about thirty in
the party to partake of the déjeûné, and not a morsel of it was left, so keen were our appetites, and so
good our fare ; but the Afghans are enormous eaters.

As the time of our departure drew near, we had
nothing but a continued succession of feasting. We
dined with all the chiefs and many of their sons,
with priests and Meerzas. Among the most pleasant of our parties was one given by Moollah Nujeeb, a worthy man, who had made an enterprising
journey into the Kaffir country at the suggestion of
Mr. Elphinstone, and for which he enjoys and
merits a pension. He gave us good counsel, and
showed much interest in our behalf, but strongly
dissuaded us from entertaining a holy person as our
guide, on which I had resolved.*   The Uzbeks are

---

* Among other pieces of advice, he suggested that we should
eat onions in all the countries we visited. It is a popular

described to be much under the influence of their
priests and Syuds, and I thought that the company of one might avail us on an occasion of
difficulty, since Moorcroft had entirely trusted to
one of them, who is now in Peshawur. Moollah
Nujeeb assured me, on the other hand, that such a
person could never extricate us from any difficulties, and would publish our approach every where;
and he further insinuated, that many of the disasters which had befallen the unfortunate Moorcroft were to be attributed to one of these worthies.
Such advice from one who was a priest himself
deserved notice, and I afterwards ascertained the
justness of the Moollah's views.

It was, however, necessary to conciliate the holy
man to whom I have alluded, and I visited him.
His name was Fuzil Huq, and he boasts a horde of
disciples towards Bokhara, nearly as numerous as
the inhabitants. My introduction to him was
curious; for Monsieur Court had desired his secretary to write to another holy man of Peshawur,
whose name he had forgotten. In his difficulties
he applied to me, and knowing the influence of
Fuzil Huq, I mentioned him at random: the letter
was written by the secretary; I delivered it, and
the saint was gratified at its receipt from a quarter
where he had no acquaintance. He received me
with kindness, and tendered his services most
freely, offering letters of introduction to all the

---

belief that a foreigner becomes sooner acclimated from the use
of that vegetable.

influential persons in Tartary. He had heard that I was of Armenian descent, though in the English employ; nor did I deem it necessary to open his eyes on the subject. I thanked him for his kindness with all the meekness and humility of a poor traveller, and he proceeded to give his advice with a considerable degree of kindness. Your safety, he said, will depend on your laying aside the name of European, at all events of Englishman; for the natives of those countries believe the English to be political intriguers, and to possess boundless wealth. Common sense and reflection suggested a similar line of conduct, but the performance was more difficult. The saint prepared his epistles, which he sent to us; they were addressed to the king of Bokhara and the chiefs on the Oxus, five in number, who owned him as their spiritual guide. We were described as "poor blind travellers," who are entitled to protection from all members of the faithful. They abounded in extracts from the Koran, with many moral aphorisms enlisted for the occasion on our behalf. The saint, however, made a request that we should not produce these letters unless an absolute necessity compelled us; but I looked upon them as very valuable documents. I did not quit this man's house without envying him of the influence over such tribes, which he owes to his descent from a respected parent, of whom he inherited a large patrimony. I had many misgivings about him, for he is not without suspicion of having increased Moorcroft's troubles; and it is certain that the family of one of his disciples was enriched by the wealth of

that ill-fated traveller.   He, however, possesses documents which lead me to acquit him of every
thing ; yet I would rather avoid than court the man,
and rather please than displease him.

Among other advice, we were strongly recommended to desist from giving medicines to the people; for it had already rallied round the doctor some
hundreds of patients, and would sound the tocsin of
our approach as we advanced.   I had thought that
the medical character would have been our passport,
and to adventurers I do not doubt its advantage;
but our only object being to pass through in safety,
it became a subject of great doubt if it should be
maintained at all ; besides the continued applications
of the people, which left us no time to ourselves,
many surmises were made as to the riches and treasures which we possessed, that enabled us gratui-
tously to distribute medicines.   It was therefore
resolved to withdraw from the field by the earliest
opportunity ; and a plan which I had thought from
the beginning as likely to aid us considerably in our
enterprise, was at once abandoned.   The bleeding
of the people would alone have furnished employment to a medical man, for the Afghans let blood
annually at the vernal equinox, till they reach their
fortieth pear.   The people were also labouring under
a tertian fever, which increased the number of patients.

The only antiquity which we discovered near
Peshawur was a " tope," or mound, about five miles
distant, on the road to Cabool, and evidently of the
same era as those of Manikyala and Belur.   It is in

a very decayed state, and the remains would not
suggest any idea of the design, had we not seen
those in the Punjab. It was nearly a hundred feet
high, but the stone with which it had been faced
had fallen down or been removed. We procured
no coins at it, and the natives could not give any
tradition farther than it was a " tope." We also
heard of another building similar to this in the
Khyber pass, about eighteen miles distant, which we
could not visit, from the unsettled state of the
country where it is situated. It is in a perfect state
of preservation, and both loftier and larger than
that of Manikyala. I also heard of eight or ten
towers of a like description towards the country of
the Kaffirs in Swat and Boonere. It seems very
probable that these buildings are the cemeteries of
kings, since they are all built with a chamber in
the midst of the pile. They may, however, be
Boodhist buildings.

A month had now elapsed since we arrived at
Peshawur, and the rapid approach of the hot weather
admonished us that we need not much longer fear
the snows of Cabool and Hindoo Koosh. The thermometer, which had stood at midday at 60° on our
arrival, now rose to 87°; the mulberries had ripened,
and the snow had entirely disappeared from the
hither range; yet the winter had been very severe;
and during our stay at Peshawur, hail-stones fell
which were fully as large as a musket ball. All was
therefore bustle for our departure; and our move-
ments were accelerated by the arrival of a letter
from Cabool, which begged us to advance without

delay. Yet it was no easy matter to bring the chief
to pronounce our leave, which was fixed for the 19th
of April, after much procrastination.

Among the inmates of Sooltan Mahommed Khan's
house, it would be unpardonable to omit the mention
of his " maître d'hôtel," Sutar Khan, a native of
Cashmeer, a stout good-humoured man, who so long
regaled us with his pilaos and other savoury dishes.
During the whole of our stay we were entertained
at the expense of the chief; and this person, a
merry-hearted good soul, with all the polish of his
countrymen, sought to gratify us in every way.
Though he did not figure in any high capacity, yet
his sister was married to the chief, and his influence
was considerable. He was a tall portly man, with
large black eyes, which I shall ever remember; for
they followed with delight every morsel of his
master's which he saw us eat. His appearance
showed that he liked the good things of this life,
and his disposition make him anxious to share them
with others. Such was Sutar Khan, the Cashmeeree
bulter : he pressed us for some recipes to improve
the gastronomic art, but we had no cook to tutor him.

CHAP. IV.

JOURNEY TO CABOOL.

On the 19th of April we took our leave of Sooltan
Mahommed Khan, and Peshawur. Nothing could
have surpassed the kindness of this nobleman; and
now that we were leaving him, he consigned us to a
Persian, one of his own officers, who was sent to Cabool on our account: he then produced a letter to his
brother at Candahar, as also to several persons in
Cabool; likewise six blank sheets bearing his seal,
which he begged we would fill up to any person of
his acquaintance whom we believed could avail us.
Such treatment, as may be imagined, called for our
gratitude; but it was with difficulty that I could
prevail on the chief to take a pair of pistols of small
value. I gave his son a musical box, and he regretted my doing so. As we left his house he saw
us mount, and wished us every success and prosperity; and would have accompanied us for some
distance, had we not objected. Several of the good
people about him, with whom we had become acquainted, came with us for the first march, and
among these were Gholam Kadir, and Meer Alum,
two sons of a Cazee, at Lodiana, to whose good
offices we were indebted on many occasions while
at Peshawur.

There are five different roads to Cabool; but we chose that which leads by the river, since the pass of Khyber is unsafe from the lawless habits of the people; and we therefore crossed the beautiful plain of Peshawur to Muchnee. At this city we had become intimate with one of the hill chiefs, who urged us to take the Khyber route; but no one trusts a Khyberee, and it was not deemed prudent. Nadir Shah paid a sum of money to secure his passage through the defile in that country, which is about eighteen miles in length, and very strong. I should have liked much to see these people in their native state; but our acquaintance, though a chief, was not to be depended on. He was a tall, bony, gaunt-looking man; like the rest of his tribe, much addicted to spirits; and, when speaking of his country, he called it " *Yaghistan*," or the land of the rebels. I accompanied this person to an orchard near Peshawur, where he wished us to join in a drinking party; but we considered him and his associates savage enough without intoxication.

We crossed the river of Cabool above Muchnee on a raft, which was supported on inflated skins, and but a frail and unsafe mode of transport. The river is only 250 yards wide, but runs with such rapidity, that we were carried more than a mile down before gaining the opposite bank. The horses and baggage ponies swam across. Muchnee is a straggling village, at the gorge of the valley where the Cabool river enters the plain. Below that place it divides into three branches in its course towards the Indus. It is usual to navigate this river on rafts; but there are likewise a few boats, and the pilgrims proceeding to Mecca often embark at Acora, and pass down the Indus in them to the sea. Merchandise is never sent by this route; but it is important to know there is a water channel of communication from near Cabool to the ocean.

On the 23d we had adjusted all matters for our advance, by conciliating the Momunds, a plundering tribe, somewhat less ferocious than their neighbours of Khyber, through whose country we were to pass. They demanded half a rupee of every Mahommedan, and double the sum of a Hindoo; but much less satisfied them, though they quarrelled about its distribution. We commenced our march, by scrambling over hills and rocks, and were soon satisfied of the influence of our friends, as we met some individual passengers, escorted by mere children, whose tribe was a sufficient protection for them. After a fatiguing march over mountain passes we found ourselves on the Cabool river, which was to be crossed a second time. We had now a full insight into our mode of travelling, and the treatment which we were to expect. We never moved but in a body; and when we got to the banks of the river under a scorching sun, had no means of crossing it till our friends the Momunds could be again appeased. We laid ourselves down in the shade of some rocks, which had fallen from precipices that rose in grandeur over us to the height of about 2000 feet, and before us the Cabool river rushed with great rapidity in its course on-

wards. Its breadth did not exceed 120 yards.
Towards afternoon our highlanders produced eight
or ten skins, and we commenced crossing ; but it
was night before we had all passed, and we then
set fire to the grass of the mountains to illuminate
our neighbourhood and ensure safety to the frail
raft. The passage of the river was tedious and
difficult : in some places the rapidity of the stream,
formed into eddies, wheeled us round, and we had
the agreeable satisfaction of being told that, if we
went some way down, there was a whirlpool, and,
if once enclosed in its circle, we might revolve in
hunger and giddiness for a day. This inconvenience we all escaped, though some of the passengers were carried far down the river, and we
ourselves had various revolutions in the smaller
eddies. There was no village or people on either
side of the river, and we spread our carpets on the
ground, and heartily enjoyed a cool night after the
day's fatigue. The noise of the stream soon lulled
most of us to sleep, and towards midnight nothing
was to be heard but the voices of the mountaineers,
who had perched themselves on a rock that pro-
jected over our camp, and watched till daylight.
A truly cut-throat band they appeared, and it was
amusing to observe the studied respect which all
of us paid them. Their chief, a ragged ruffian
without a turban, was mounted on a horse : his
praises were sung, and presents were given him :
but we had no sooner left the country, than every
one abused those whom he had been caressing.
The spirit of the party might be discovered by one

old man, who drove his horse into a wheat-field, on
the verge of the Momund country, calling out,
" Eat away, my good animal; the Momund scoun-
" drels have ate much of my wealth in their time."

After an exposure of about eight hours to a powerful sun, on the following morning we reached Duka
by a rocky and difficult road, and pushed on, in the
afternoon, to Huzarnow, a journey of upwards of
twenty miles. On reaching Duka, we had surmounted the chief part of our difficulties on the
road to Cabool. The view from the top of a mountain pass, before we descended into the valley of
the Cabool river, was very magnificent. We could
see the town of Julalabad, forty miles distant, and
the river winding its way in a snaky course through
the plain, and dividing it into innumerable fertile
islands as it passed. The Sufued Koh, or white
mountain, reared its crest on one side, and the
towering hill of Noorgil or Kooner on the other;
here the Afghans believe the ark of Noah to have
rested after the deluge, and this Mount Ararat of
Afghanistan, from its great height, is certainly
worthy of the distinction : it is covered with perpetual snow. There is an isolated rock not far from
this place, called Näogee, in Bajour, which answers,
in my mind, to Arrian's description of the celebrated rock of Aornus, which indubitably lay in
that neighbourhood. It is said to be inaccessible,
but by one road; to be strong and lofty; and large
enough to produce grain for the garrison, having
likewise an abundant supply of water; which is literally an account of Aornus. It is also within

twenty miles of Bajour; and we are informed that
the citizens of Bazaria (supposed to be Bajour) fled
to Aornus for safety in the night. I have not seen
the hill of Näogee.

At Muchnee, the hills are sandstone: on the
tops of the passes there are veins of quartz. In
the bed of the Cabool river the rocks are granite;
and over the village of Duka the formation is mica,
which occurs in vertical strata. A sweet aromatic
smell was exhaled from the grass and plants. One
shrub looked very like broom; another resembled
the flower-de-luce, and supplies the people with
mats to build their huts as well as sandals for their
feet, to which they are fixed by a string of the same
material. Our thirst and fatigue were much relieved by a plant of the sorrel kind, which we found
most grateful, and gathered and ate as we climbed
over the hills. The pasture is here favourable to
cattle, and the mutton used in Peshawur owes its
flavour to it.

Before leaving Duka we had a visit from the
chief of the Momunds, Sadut Khan, of Lalpoor,
a handsome man of about thirty, with a good-humoured countenance. We sat under a mulberry
tree, on a cot or bed, for half an hour; he pressed
us much to cross the river, and become his guests
for a few days, when he would entertain and amuse
us with his hawks, some of which were carried by
his attendants. We declined his civilities on the
excuse of our journey. I afterwards learned that
this smiling Momund had raised himself to the

chiefship of his clan by murdering two young nephews with their mother.

At Huzarnow, we met a Khyberee, with whom we had some acquaintance in the Punjab, where he had served as an hirkaru, or messenger, to Runjeet Sing. Immediately he heard of our arrival, he made his appearance; and, catching me by the feet, and then by the beard, intimated, in the little Persian which he could speak, that we were his guests, and must occupy his house in the village, which we gladly accepted. He was a most uncouth looking being, with a low brow and sunken eyes: he had two sons, neither of whom he had seen for fourteen years, till within a few days of our arrival. He had, nevertheless, twice carried expresses to Cabool; and though he had passed his native village and home, he had never stopped to make an inquiry. He had now returned for good to his country.

After a fatiguing march of twelve hours on the saddle, three of which were spent in waiting for stragglers, we reached Julalabad on the morning of the 26th. As we passed Soorkhdewar, where the caravans are sometimes plundered, our conductor, the Persian, whether to show his courage or the disordered state of his imagination, fancied himself attacked by robbers. He fired his carbine; and, by the time those in the rear came up, had completed a long story of his own daring bravery; how he had punished one of the robbers with the but end of his piece, and the danger which he had undergone from his antagonist's ball, that had whistled past his ear! His followers applauded his bravery, and I added my share of praise. It appeared singular that the Persian alone should have seen the highwaymen: but the whole matter was explained by a quiet remark from a member of the caravan; that the gentleman wished to give proof of his courage now that we were beyond danger.

Our route from Huzarnow to Julalabad lay through a wide stony waste, a part of which is known by the name of the "dusht," or plain of Butteecote, and famed for the pestilential wind or "simoom," that prevails here in the hot season, though the mountains on both sides are covered with perpetual snow. The natives of this country describe the simoom as generally fatal. Travellers who have recovered, say, that it attacks them like a dry wind, which makes them senseless. Water poured with great violence into the mouth sometimes recovers the patient; and a fire kindled near him has a good effect. Sugar and the dried plums of Bokhara are also given with advantage. Horses and animals are subject to the simoom as well as man; and the flesh of those who fall victims to it is said to become so soft and putrid, that the limbs separate from each other, and the hair may be pulled out with the least force. This pestilential wind is unknown in the high lands of Cabool, and principally confined to the plain of Butteecote now described. It is as malignant in its effects during night as in the day; and in summer no one ever thinks of travelling while the sun is above the horizon. In a party of thirty or forty individuals, one only may be attacked; nor are those who escape sensible of any change in the atmosphere. It may be simply the effects of heat on a certain state of the body.

We were not travelling in the season of hot and pestilential winds; but on this march we encountered one of these storms of wind and dust which are common in countries near the tropic. In the present instance, it was attended with rather a curious phenomenon: clouds of dust approached each other from *opposite* sides of the compass; and, when they met, took quite a different direction. It is, perhaps, to be accounted for, by the eddy of the wind in a low plain, about twelve or fifteen miles broad, with lofty mountains on either side. Julalabad, we found, had been deluged with rain, which we had entirely escaped.

In a hill north of the Cabool river and the village of Bussoul, we observed some extensive excavations in the rock, which are ascribed to the days of the Kaffirs, or infidels. These caves were hewn out in groups, the entrance to each being separate, and about the size of a common doorway. They may have formed so many villages, since it appears to have been common throughout Asia to dwell in such excavated places; as we learn in the account of the Trogdolites given by different historians. I do not suppose that we can draw an inference as to the people from the existence of this practice in different countries, since it would occur to most uncivilised nations, that a cave in the rock was a more safe residence, in a troubled society, than a hut on the plain. Near Julalabad there are seven round towers; but they differ in construction from the "topes" which I have described. They are said to be ancient, and very large; copper coins are found near them. In the country of Lughman, between Julalabad and the mountains, the people point out the tomb of Metur Lam, or Lamech, the father of Noah. Some refer the place to the age of the Kaffirs; but the good Mahommedans are satisfied to believe it the grave of a prophet, and that there are only three others on the earth.

We halted for a couple of days at Julalabad, which is one of the filthiest places I have seen in the East. It is a small town, with a bazar of fifty shops, and a population of about 2000 people; but its number increases tenfold in the cold season, as the people flock to it from the surrounding hills. Julalabad is the residence of a chief of the Barukzye family; who has a revenue of about seven lacs of rupees a year. The Cabool river passes a quarter of a mile north of the town, and is about 150 yards wide: it is not fordable. There are mountains of snow to the north and south of Julalabad, that run parallel with one another. The southern range is called Sufued Koh, but more frequently Rajgul. It decreases in size as it runs eastward, and loses its snow before reaching Duka. In the higher parts the snow never melts; which would give an elevation of about 15,000 feet in this latitude. To the north of Julalabad lies the famous Noorgil, before mentioned, about thirty miles distant ; and to the north-west the lofty peaks of Hindoo Koosh begin to show themselves.

We left the river of Cabool, and passed up a valley to Bala-bagh, and could now distinguish the rich gardens under the snowy hills, that produce the famous pomegranates without seed, which are exported to India. We halted in a vineyard. The vines of this country are not cut or pruned ; but allowed to ascend the highest trees, and were growing, at Bala-bagh, on lilyoaks, about eighty feet from the ground. The grapes so produced are inferior to those reared on a frame-work. It rained at Bala-bagh, and our quarters were more romantic than comfortable ; which led us, at dusk, to seek for shelter in the mosque. The people seemed too busy in the exercise of religious and worldly matters to mind us, and as yet we had not experienced the slightest incivility from any person in the country, though we strolled about every where. They do not appear to have the smallest prejudice against a Christian ; and I had never heard from their lips the name of dog or infidel, which figures so prominently in the works of many travellers. " Every country has its customs," is a proverb among them ; and the Afghan Mahommedans seem to pay a respect to Christians which they deny to their Hindoo fellow-citizens. Us they call " people of the book ;" while they consider them benighted and without a prophet.

At Gundamuk we reached the boundary of the hot and cold countries. It is said to snow on one side of the rivulet, and to rain on the other. Ve-

getable life assumes a new form; the wheat, which
was being cut at Julalabad, was only three inches
above ground at Gundamuk. The distance does
not exceed twenty-five miles. In the fields we
discovered the white daisies among the clover; and
the mountains, which were but ten miles distant,
were covered with forests of pine, that commenced
about a thousand feet below the limit of the snow;
we required additional clothing in the keen air.
Travellers are subject to a variety of little troubles,
which amuse or try the temper, according to the
disposition of the moment. A cat possessed itself
of my dinner this evening, as I was about to swallow
it; yet I satisfied the cravings of a hungry appetite
with bread and water, which, I may add, was ate
in a filthy stable; but we were fortunate in getting
such accommodation. I beg to add my praise of
the bread of this country, which they leaven and
bake much to the palate.

About three miles from Gundamuk we passed the
garden of Neemla, celebrated for the field of battle
in which Shah Shooja-ool Moolk lost his crown, in
the year 1809. The garden is situated in a highly
cultivated valley surrounded by barren hills. It is a
beautiful spot; the trees have all been pruned to,
or attained, the same height, and shade beneath
their boughs a variety of flowers, among which the
narcissus grows most luxuriantly. The spot, though
ornamented by art, is ill chosen for a battle; and
the fortune of war was here strangely capricious.
Shooja lost his throne, and his vizier, sustaining a
defeat from an army ten times inferior to his own

Never dreading such a result, he had brought his jewels and his wealth along with him, which he was happy to relinquish for his life. Futteh Khan, the vizier of Mahmood, who succeeded in gaining the day for his master, seated him on one of the state elephants, which had been prepared for the king, and took this mode to proclaim his victory. Shooja fled to the Khyber country, and has since failed in all his attempts to regain his kingdom.

Nothing strikes a stranger in this country more than the manner of keeping their horses, which differs so much from India. They never remove the saddle during the day; which they believe gives the horse a better rest at night. They never walk a horse up and down, but either mount him, or make him go round in a circle till he is cool. They give no grain, at this season, feeding them on green barley, which has not eared. They picket eight or ten horses to two ropes, which they fix in line parallel to one another. They always tie a knot on the tail. They keep the hind quarters of the horse covered at all times by a very neat felt, fringed with silk, which is held on by the crupper. They use the Uzbek saddle, which resembles that of our own hussars, and which I found agreeable enough, and always used. The riders tie their whip to the wrist. The Afghans take great care of their horses, but do not pamper them with spices, as in India, and always have them in excellent condition.

We continued our march to Jugduluk, and passed the Soorkh road, or red river, by a bridge, with a

variety of other small streams, which pour the
melted snow of the Sufued Koh into that rivulet.
The waters of all of them were reddish: hence
the name. The country is barren and miserable.
Jugduluk is a wretched place, with a few caves for
a village. There is a proverb which describes its
misery:—" When the wood of Jugduluk begins to
burn, you melt gold:" for there is no wood at hand
in the bleak hills. We halted under a grove of
trees, which is memorable as the spot where Shah
Zuman, one of the kings of Cabool, was blinded.

On our way we could distinguish that the road
had once been made, and also the remains of the
post-houses, which had been constructed every five
or six miles by the Mogul emperors, to keep up a
communication between Delhi and Cabool. They
may even be traced across the mountains to Balkh;
for both Humaioon and Aurungzebe, in their youth,
were governors of that country. What an opinion
does this inspire of the grandeur of the Mogul
empire! We have a system of communication
between the most distant provinces as perfect as
the posts of the Cæsars.

On our way to Cabool we met thousands of sheep
tended by the wandering Ghiljees, a tribe of Afghans; who now that the snow was off the ground,
were driving their flocks towards Hindoo Koosh,
where they pass the summer. Nothing could be
more pastoral. The grown up people followed the
sheep as they browsed on the margin of the hills,
and the boys and girls came up about a mile or two
in rear, in charge of the young lambs. An old

goat or sheep encouraged them to advance, and the young people assisted with switches of grass, and such ejaculations as they could raise. Some of the children were so young, that they could hardly walk; but the delight of the sport enticed them on. On the margin of the road we passed many encampments, where they were either moving or packing up. The Afghans have a low black, or rather, brown tent. The women did every thing for their lazy husbands, loaded the camels and drove them on: they are indeed swarthy dames, not very remarkable for beauty, with all their Arcadian life. They are well clad, and shod with broad iron nails fixed to their soles. The children were uncommonly healthy and chubby. It is said that these wandering people do not marry till they reach their twentieth year.

After passing the Soorkh road, we reached Ispahan, a village that marks another of Shooja's defeats, but before he gained the throne. A story is told of the vizier Futteh Khan, who was afraid of being supplanted on this field of battle by the Dooranee nobleman who aspired to the office of vizier. This individual, whose name was Meer Alum, had, on a former occasion, insulted Futteh Khan, and even knocked out one of his front teeth. The injury had to all appearance been forgiven, for he had since married a sister of the vizier; but the alliance had only been formed that Futteh Khan might easier accomplish his base intentions. The night before the battle he seized upon his brother-in-law and put him to death. A heap of stones, here called a

" toda," marks the scene of the murder. The vizier's sister threw herself at her brother's feet, and asked why he had murdered her husband? " What !" said he, " have you more regard for your husband, than your brother's honour? Look at my broken teeth; and know that the insult is now avenged. If you are in grief at the loss of a husband, I'll marry you to a mule driver." This incident is not a bad illustration of the boisterous manners and feelings of the Afghans. A saying among them tells one to fear the more, when an apparent reconciliation has taken place by an intermarriage.

By midnight on the 30th, we reached the pass of Luta-bund, from the top of which the city of Cabool first becomes visible, at a distance of twenty-five miles. The pass is about six miles long, and the road runs over loose round stones. We lay down at a spring called Koke Chushmu, or the Partridge Fountain, and slept without shelter through a bitterly cold night. Our conductor's hawks died from its effects, to his great grief. *Luta* means a shred or patch; and this pass is so called, from most travellers leaving some shred of their clothes on the bushes in the pass. In the winter the snow blocks up this road.

We rose with the morning star, and prosecuted our journey to Cabool, which we did not reach till the afternoon. The approach to this celebrated city is any thing but imposing; nor was it till under the shade of its fine bazar, that I believed myself in the capital of an empire. On our road we passed

the village of Bootkhak, where Mahmood of Ghuzni,
on his return from India, is said to have interred the
rich Hindoo idol which he brought from the famous
Somnat.   At Cabool, we proceeded straight to the
house of the Nawab Jubbar Khan, the brother of
the governor, who gave us a cordial welcome, and
sent to the bazar for a dinner, which I enjoyed.
Not so my unfortunate companion, whose health
forsook him immediately after crossing the Indus;
his strength was now completely undermined.   A
doubt arose as to the examination of our baggage at
the custom-house; but I judged it more prudent
to exhibit our poverty than allow the good people
to form designs against our supposed wealth.   We
were not, however, prepared for the search; and
my sextant and books, with the doctor's few bottles
and boxes, were laid out in state for the inspection
of the citizens.   They did them no harm, but set
us down without doubt as conjurors, after a display
of such unintelligible apparatus.

   Our worthy conductor, after he had safely delivered us into the hands of the Nawab, took his
leave to enjoy his native city, which he had not
seen for eight years.   Mahommed Shureef was
what might be termed a good fellow.   Though but
a young man, he had been a merchant, and realised
a fortune, which he now enjoyed in hunting and
hawking, with " a cup of good sack."   He was cor-
pulent and dropsical, but might be seen every
morning with his hawks and pointer at his heels.
He kept his revels more secretly.   I never saw a
boy more delighted than was this person as we

entered Cabool; had it been Elysium, he could not
have said more in its praise. He had been a most
companionable traveller, and added the address of a
Persian to the warmth and good feeling of an
Afghan.   An incident occurred on our entering
Cabool, which would have delighted other men than
him. A beggar had found out who he was, and
within half a mile of the city gate began to call
down every blessing on his head, and welcomed
him by name to his home, in a strain of great adu-
lation. "Give the poor man some money," said
Mahommed Shureef to his servant, with a significant nod of the head; and it would have been a
difficult manner to determine whether the merchant
or the beggar seemed most delighted. Our conductor then bade us adieu, with a recommendation
that we should trust any body but those who volun-
teered their services; as he did not give his countrymen credit for a high standard of morality.
He exacted a promise that we would dine with
him, and I thanked him for his advice and attentions.

CHAP. V.

CABOOL.

WE had not been many hours in Cabool before we heard of the misfortunes of Mr. Wolff, the missionary of the Jews, who was now detained at a neighbouring village. We lost no time in despatching assistance to him. He joined us the following day, and gave a long and singular account of his escape from death and slavery. This gentleman, it appears, had issued forth, like another Benjamin of Tudela, to inquire after the Israelites, and entered Tartary as a Jew, which is the best travelling character in a Mahommedan country. Mr. Wolff, however, is a convert to Christianity, and he published his creed to the wreck of the Hebrew people. He also gave himself out as being in search of the lost tribes; yet he made but few inquiries among the Afghans of Cabool, though they declare themselves to be their descendants. The narration of Mr. Wolff's adventures excited our sympathy and compassion: and, if we could not coincide in many of his speculations regarding the termination of the world, we made the reverend gentleman most welcome, and found him an addition to our society in Cabool. He had been in Bokhara, but had not ventured to preach in that centre of Islam. His after misfortunes had originated from his denominating himself a Hajee, which implies a *Mahommedan* pilgrim, and for which he had been plundered and beaten.

We had previously heard of the amiable character of our host, Nawab Jubbar Khan; and even found him, on personal acquaintance, to be quite a patriarch. He heals every difference among his many and turbulent brothers: himself the eldest of his family, he entertains no ambitious views, though he once held the government of Cashmeer and other provinces of the Dooranee empire. His brother, the present chief of Cabool, has requited many services by confiscating his estate; but he speaks not of his ingratitude. He tells you that God has bestowed on him abundance for his wants, and to reward those who serve him; that there are few pleasures equal to being able to give to those around, and to enjoy this world without being obliged to govern. I discovered, during my stay at Cabool, that the Nawab * assumes no false character, but expresses himself, as he feels, with sincerity. Never was a man more modest, and more beloved: he will permit but a single attendant to follow him; and the people on the high and by ways stop to bless him; the politicians assail him at home to enter into intrigues, and he yet possesses the respect of the whole community, and has, at the present moment, a greater moral influence than any of the

* Jubbar Khan has the title of Nawab, from having been governor of an Indian province of the Dooranee kingdom. Nawab is purely an Indian title.

Barukzye family in Afghanistan. His manners are remarkably mild and pleasing; and from his dress one would not imagine him to be an influential member of a warlike family. It is delightful to be in his society, to witness his acts, and hear his conversation. He is particularly partial to Europeans, and makes every one of them his guest who enters Cabool. All the French officers in passing to the Punjab lived with him, and still keep up a friendly intercourse. Such is the patriarch of Cabool; he is now about fifty years of age; and such the master of the house in which we were so fortunate as to dwell.

Our first object, after arrival, was to be introduced to the chief of Cabool, Sirdar Dost Mahommed Khan. The Nawab intimated our wishes, and we were very politely invited to dine with the governor on the evening of the 4th of May. Dr. Gerard was unable to attend from sickness; but Mr. Wolff and myself were conducted, in the evening, to the Bala Hissar, or Palace of the Kings, where the governor received us most courteously. He rose on our entrance, saluted in the Persian fashion, and then desired us to be seated on a velvet carpet near himself. He assured us that we were welcome to his country; and, though he had seen few of us, he respected our nation and character. To this I replied as civilly as I could, praising the equity of his government, and the protection which he extended to the traveller and the merchant. When we sat down, we found our party consist of six or eight native gentlemen, and three sons of the chief.

We occupied a small but neat apartment, which had
no other furniture than the carpet. The conversa-
ation of the evening was varied, and embraced so
many topics, that I find it difficult to detail them;
such was the knowledge, intelligence, and curiosity
that the chief displayed. He was anxious to know
the state of Europe, the number of kings, the
terms on which they lived with one another; and,
since it appeared that their territories were adjacent,
how they existed without destroying each other.
I named the different nations, sketched out their
relative power, and informed him that our advancement in civilisation did no more exempt us from
war and quarrels than his own country; that we
viewed each other's acts with jealousy, and endeavoured to maintain a balance of power, to prevent
one king from overturning another. Of this, however, there were, I added, various instances in
European history; and the chief himself had heard
of Napoleon. He next requested me to inform
him of the revenues of England; how they were
collected; how the laws were enacted; and what
were the productions of the soil. He perfectly
comprehended our constitution after a brief explanation; and said that there was nothing wonderful in our universal success, since the only revenue
which we drew from the people was to defray the
debts and expenses of the state. " Your wealth,
then," added he, "must come from India." I
assured him that the revenues of that country were
spent in it; that the sole benefits derived from its
possession consisted in its being an outlet to our

commerce; and that the only wealth sent to the mother country amounted to a few hundred thousand pounds, in addition to the fortunes taken away by the servants of the government. I never met an Asiatic who credited this fact before. Dost Mahommed Khan observed, "This satisfactorily accounts for the subjection of India. You have left much of its wealth to the native princes; you have not had to encounter their despair, and you are just in your courts." He enquired into the state of the Mahommedan principalities in India, and the exact power of Runjeet Sing, for sparing whose country he gave us no credit. He wished to know if we had any designs upon Cabool. He had been told by some Russian merchants of the manner of recruiting the armies by conscription in that country, and wished to know if it were general in Europe. He had also heard of their foundling hospitals, and required an explanation of their utility and advantage. He begged that I would inform him about China; if its people were warlike, and if their country could be invaded from India; if its soil were productive, and its climate salubrious; and why the inhabitants differed so much from those of other countries. The mention of Chinese manufactures led to a notice of those in England; he inquired about our machinery and steam-engines, and then expressed his wonder at the cheapness of our goods. He asked about the curiosities which I had seen, and which of the cities in Hindoostan I had most admired. I replied, Delhi. He then questioned me if I had seen the rhinoceros,

and if the Indian animals differed from those of
Cabool. He had heard of our music, and was
desirous of knowing if it surpassed that of Cabool.
From these matters he turned to those which con-
cerned myself; asked why I had left India, and the
reasons for changing my dress.   I informed him
that I had a great desire to see foreign countries,
and I now purposed travelling *towards* Europe by
Bokhara; and that I had changed my dress to prevent my being pointed at in this land; but that I
had no desire to conceal from him and the chiefs of
every country which I entered, that I was an Englishman, and that my entire adoption of the habits
of the people had added to my comfort.   The chief
replied in very kind terms, applauded the design,
and the propriety of changing our dress.

Dost Mahommed Khan then turned to Mr. Wolff
for an explanation of his history; and, as he was
aware of the gentleman's vocations, he had assembled among the party several Mahommedan doctors,
who were prepared to dispute on points of religion.
Since I often acted as Mr. Wolff's interpreter, I
might proceed to make mention of the various arguments which were adduced on either side; but I
do not anticipate what the reverend gentleman will,
no doubt, give to the world.   As is usual on such
subjects, the one party failed to convince the other;
and, but for the admirable tact of the chief himself,
the consequences might have been disagreeable.
The Mahommedans seemed to think that they had
gained the day, and even referred it for my decision; but I excused myself from the difficult task,

on the grounds of my being no moollah (priest).
As these reverend doctors, however, appeared to
found their creed upon reason, I thought the opportunity too favourable to let them escape, though
the argument I intended to use could not boast of
being original. I asked them to state their time of
prayers ; and, among others, they named before
sunrise, and after sunset. " Such are the hours,"
said I, " rigidly enjoined by the Koran ?"—" Yes,"
replied the priest ; " and every one is an infidel who
neglects them." These premises being given, I
begged the doctor to inform me how these prayers
could be performed in the Arctic circle, where the
sun neither rose nor set for five or six months in
the year. The divine had not before heard the
argument : he stammered out various confused
sentences ; and at last asserted that prayers were
not required in those countries, where it was sufficient to repeat the " Culuma," or creed of the
Mahommedans. I immediately required the divine
to name the chapter of the Koran on which he
founded his doctrine, since I did not remember to
have seen it in the book. He could not, for the
Koran does not contain it. A sharp dispute now
arose among the Afghans ; nor was the subject
renewed, but changed to more intelligible matters.
Before we withdrew, the chief made a very friendly
tender to assist us in our journey, and offered us
letters to the chiefs on the Oxus, and the King of
Bokhara. He also requested that we should frequently visit him while in Cabool, as he liked to
hear of other countries, and would always make

us welcome. We left at midnight, quite charmed
with our reception, and the accomplished address
and manners of Dost Mahommed Khan.

I lost no time in making excursions near Cabool,
and chose the earliest opportunity to visit the tomb
of the Emperor Baber, which is about a mile from
the city, and situated in the sweetest spot of the
neighbourhood. The good Nawab was my conductor in the pilgrimage. I have a profound respect
for the memory of Baber, which had been increased
by a late perusal of his most interesting Commentaries. He had directed his body to be interred in
this place, to him the choicest in his wide dominions. These are his own words regarding Cabool:
—"The climate is extremely delightful, and there
" is no such place in the known world."—" Drink
" wine in the citadel of Cabool, and send round the
" cup without stopping: for there is at once mountains and streams, town and desert."*

The grave is marked by two erect slabs of white
marble; and, as is common in the East, the different
letters of a part of the inscription indicate the
number of the year of the Hegira in which the
Emperor died. The device in the present instance
seems to me happy: " When in heaven, Roozvan
" asked the date of his death. I told him that
" heaven is the eternal abode of Baber Badshah."
He died in the year 1530. Near the Emperor,
many of his wives and children have been interred;
and the garden, which is small, has been once surrounded by a wall of marble. A running and clear

* Erskine's Translation of Baber.

stream yet waters the fragrant flowers of this cemetery, which is the great holiday resort of the
people of Cabool.   In front of the grave, there is a
small but chaste mosque of marble ; and an inscription upon it sets forth that it was built in the year
1640, by order of the Emperor Shah Jehan, after
defeating Mahommed Nuzur Khan in Balkh, and
Budukhshan, "that poor Mahommedans might
here offer up their prayers."   It is pleasing to see
the tomb of so great a man as Baber honoured by
his posterity.

There is a noble prospect from the hill which
overlooks Baber's tomb, and a summer-house has
been erected upon it by Shah Zuman, from which
it may be admired.   The Nawab and myself climbed
up to it, and seated ourselves. If my reader can
imagine a plain, about twenty miles in circumference, laid out with gardens and fields in pleasing
irregularity, intersected by three rivulets, which
wind through it by a serpentine course, and wash
innumerable little forts and villages, he will have
before him one of the meadows of Cabool. To the
north lie the hills of Pughman, covered half way
down with snow, and separated from the eye by a
sheet of the richest verdure. On the other side,
the mountains, which are bleak and rocky, mark
the hunting preserves of the kings; and the gardens
of this city, so celebrated for fruit, lie beneath, the
water being conducted to them with great ingenuity.
I do not wonder at the hearts of the people being
captivated with the landscape, and of Baber's ad-

miration; for, in his own words, " its verdure and flowers render Cabool, in spring, a heaven."

Our intercourse with the people was on a much better footing in Cabool than at Peshawur; for we were no longer in the house of a chief, and not troubled by too many visiters. The Nawab occupied one side of a large mansion, and left the other part to us. He, however, rallied round him many good sort of people, with whom we became acquainted: he brought them over in person, and we passed to and fro between each other's apartments during the whole day. The habits which we had adopted, now gave us many advantages in our communications with the natives. We sat with them on the same carpet, ate with them, and freely mingled in their society. The Afghans are a sober, simple people. They always interrogated me closely regarding Europe, the nations of which they divide into twelve " *koollahs*," or crowns, literally hats. It was delightful to see the curiosity of even the oldest men. The greatest evil of Mahommedanism consists in its keeping those who profess it within a certain circle of civilisation. Their manners never appear to alter. They have learning, but it is of another age, and any thing like philosophy is unknown in their history. The language of the Afghans is Persian, but it is not the smooth and elegant tongue of Iran. Pooshtoo is the dialect of the common people, but some of the higher classes cannot even speak it. The Afghans are a nation of children; in their quarrels they fight, and become friends without any ceremony. They cannot conceal their feelings from one another, and a person with any discrimination may at at all times pierce their designs. If they themselves are to be believed, their ruling vice is envy, which besets even the nearest and dearest relations. No people are more incapable of managing intrigue. I was particularly struck with their idleness; they seem to sit listlessly for the whole day, staring at each other; how they live it would be difficult to discover, yet they dress well, and are healthy and happy. I imbibed a very favourable impression of their national character.

Cabool is a most bustling and populous city. Such is the noise in the afternoon, that in the streets one cannot make an attendant hear. The great bazar, or "Chouchut," is an elegant arcade, nearly 600 feet long, and about 30 broad: it is divided into four equal parts. Its roof is painted; and over the shops are the houses of some of the citizens. The plan is judicious: but it has been left unfinished; and the fountains and cisterns, that formed a part of it, lie neglected. Still there are few such bazars in the East; and one wonders at the silks, cloths, and goods, which are arrayed under its piazzas. In the evening it presents a very interesting sight: each shop is lighted up by a lamp suspended in front, which gives the city an appearance of being illuminated. The number of shops for the sale of dried fruits is remarkable, and their arrangement tasteful. In May, one may purchase the grapes, pears, apples, quinces, and even the melons of the by-gone season, then ten months

old. There are poulterers' shops, at which snipes,
ducks, partridges, and plovers, with other game,
may be purchased. The shops of the shoemakers
and hardware retailers are also arranged with singular neatness. Every trade has its separate bazar,
and all of them seem busy. There are booksellers
and venders of paper, much of which is Russian,
and of a blue colour. The month of may is the
season of the "falodeh," which is a white jelly
strained from wheat, and drunk with sherbet and
snow. The people are very fond of it, and the
shopkeepers in all parts of the town seem constantly at work with their customers. A pillar of
snow stands on one side of them, and a fountain
plays near it, which gives these places a cool and
clean appearance. Around the bakers' shops,
crowds of people may be seen, waiting for their
bread. I observed that they baked it by plastering
it to the sides of the oven. Cabool is famed for its
kabobs, or cooked meats, which are in great request :
few cook at home. "*Rhuwash*" was the dainty of
the May season in Cabool. It is merely blanched
rhubarb, which is reared under a careful protection
from the sun, and grows up rankly under the hills
in the neighbourhood. Its flavour is delicious.
"*Shabash rhuwash!*" ("Bravo rhuwash!") is the cry
in the streets; and every one buys it. In the most
crowded parts of the city there are story-tellers
amusing the idlers, or dervises proclaiming the
glories and deeds of the prophets. If a baker
makes his appearance before these worthies, they
demand a cake in the name of some prophet; and,

to judge by the number who follow this occupation, it must indeed be a profitable one. There are no wheeled carriages in Cabool : the streets are not very narrow ; they are kept in a good state during dry weather, and are intersected by small covered aqueducts of clean water, which is a great convenience to the people. We passed along them without observation, and even without an attendant. To me, the appearance of the people was more novel than the bazars. They sauntered about, dressed in sheep-skin cloaks, and seemed huge from the quantity of clothes they wore. All the children have chubby red cheeks, which I at first took for an artificial colour, till I found it to be the gay bloom of youth. The older people seem to lose it. Cabool is a compactly built city, but its houses have no pretension to elegance. They are constructed of sun-dried bricks and wood, and few of them are more than two stories high. It is thickly peopled, and has a population of about sixty thousand souls. The river of Cabool passes through the city ; and tradition says that it has three times carried it away, or inundated it. In rain, there is not a dirtier place than Cabool.

It is in the mouth of every one, that Cabool is a very ancient city ; they call it 6000 years old. It formed once, with Ghuzni, the tributary cities of Bameean. Strange has been the reverse of circumstances ; — Ghuzni, under Mahmood, in the eleventh century, became a great capital ; and Cabool is now the metropolis both over it and Bameean. It is said that Cabool was formerly named

Zabool, from a Kaffir, or infidel king, who founded
it ; hence the name of Zaboolistan. Some authors
have stated, that the remains of the tomb of Cabool, or Cain, the son of Adam, are pointed out in
the city ; but the people have no such traditions.
It is a popular belief in Cabool, however, that the
devil fell here when cast out of heaven. In Cabool
itself there are not exactly traditions of Alexander,
but both Herat and Lahore are said to have been
founded by slaves of that conqueror, whom they
call a prophet. Their names were Heri (the old
name of Herat) and Lahore. Candahar is believed
to be an older city than either of these.   While
at Cabool, I made every attempt to procure coins ;
but without success, excepting a Cufic one of Bokhara, which was 843 years old.   Among the rarities
brought to the Cabool mint, I heard of a coin of the
shape and size of a sparrow's egg — a whimsical
model. Triangular and square coins are common ;
the latter belong to the age of Akbar.

In the number of our visiters was an Armenian,
of the name of Simon Mugurditch, commonly called
Sooliman, who gave us a sad account of the disper-
sion of his tribe.   There are but twenty-one persons now remaining, from a colony of some hundreds
introduced by Nadir and Ahmed Shah from Joolfa
and Meshid in Persia. By inscriptions in their
burying-ground, it would appear that Armenian
merchants settled in Cabool even before that period.
During the Dooranee monarchy, they held offices
under the government, and were respected till the
time of Timour Shah's death. In the disputes

about the succession, they have gradually withdrawn their families to other countries; and the present chief of Cabool, with the best intentions, has utterly ruined the Armenian colony, by prohibiting them from preparing wine and spirits, by which they gained their livelihood. He has also forbidden dice, with every description of incontinence, and likewise threatened to grill some of the bakers in their ovens for light weights. After a life by no means temperate, this chief has renounced wine, and commands, under the severest penalties, that his subjects should be equally abstemious. The Armenians and Jews of Cabool have, therefore, fled to other lands, as they had no means of support but in distilling spirits and wine. There are but three Jewish families in Cabool, the wreck of a hundred which it could last year boast. If Dost Mahommed Khan can succeed in suppressing drunkenness by the sacrifice of a few foreign inhabitants, he is not to be blamed; since forty bottles of wine, or ten of brandy, might be purchased from them for a single rupee. As the chief in person shows so good an example to his people, we shall not criticise his motives, nor comment on the inconsistency of a reformed drunkard. Cabool seems to have been always famed for its revels.

The Armenians clung to us as if we had been an addition to their colony, and we breakfasted with Simon Mugurditch and his family, where we met all the members of it. The little children came running out to meet us, kissed our hands, and then placed their foreheads upon them. They are a

very handsome people.   We saw their church — a
small building, which could never have contained a
hundred people.   Our host Simon gave us a very
comfortable entertainment, and laid it out on a cloth
covered with sentences of the Koran.   " It was an
Afghan cloth," said he, " and Christians are not
injured by these sentences, nor do they eat a less
hearty meal."   The Armenians have adopted all the
customs and manners of Mahommedans, and take
off both shoes and turbans on entering their church.
They are a harmless inoffensive people, but fond of
money.

Since our departure, we had been travelling in a
perpetual spring.   The trees were blossoming as we
left Lahore, in February ; and we found them full
blown in March, at Peshawur.   We had now the
same joyous state of the season in Cabool, and
arrived at an opportune time to see it.   This state
of the spring will give a good idea of the relative
height of the different places, and of the progress
of their seasons. Cabool is more than 6000 feet above
the level of the sea.   I passed some delightful days
in its beautiful gardens.   One evening I visited a
very fine one, in company with the Nawab, about
six miles from the city.   They are tastefully laid
out and well kept ; the fruit trees are planted at
regular distances ; the most of the gardens rise
with the acclivity of the ground in plateaus, or
shelves, over one another.   The ground was covered
with the fallen blossoms, which had drifted into the
corners, like so much snow.   The Nawab and myself seated ourselves under a pear tree of Samar-

cand, the most celebrated kind in the country, and
admired the prospect.   Great was the variety and
number of fruit trees.   There were peaches, plums,
apricots, pears, apples, quinces, cherries, walnuts,
mulberries, pomegranates, and vines, all growing in
one garden.   There were also nightingales, black-
birds, thrushes, and doves, to raise their notes, and
chattering magpies, on almost every tree, which
were not without their attraction, as reminding me
of England.   I was highly pleased with the nightingale; and, on our return home, the Nawab sent
me one in a cage, which sang throughout the night.
It is called the " Boolbool i huzar dastan," or, the
nightingale of a thousand tales; and it really seemed
to imitate the song of every bird.   The cage was
surrounded by cloth; and it became so noisy a
companion, that I was obliged to send it away before
I could sleep.   This bird is a native of Budukhshan.
The finest garden about Cabool is that called the
king's garden, laid out by Timour Shah, which lies
north of the town, and is about half a mile square.
The road which leads to it is about three miles
long, and formed the royal race-ground.   There is
a spacious octagon summer-house in the centre,
with walks that run up from each of its sides, shaded
with fruit trees, having a very pretty effect.   A
marble seat in front shows where the kings of Cabool sat in their prosperity, among

> ———— " the pears
> And sunniest apples that Cabool,
> In all its thousand gardens, bears."

The people are passionately fond of sauntering in these gardens, and may be seen flocking to them every evening. The climate of Cabool is most genial. At mid-day the sun is hotter than in England; but the nights and evenings are cool, and in August only do the people find it necessary to sleep on their balconies. There is no rainy season, but constant showers fall as in England. The snow lasts for five months in winter. During May, the thermometer stood at 64° in the hottest time of the day; and there was generally a wind from the north, cooled by the snow that covers the mountains. It must usually blow from that quarter, since all the trees of Cabool bend to the south.

Cabool is particularly celebrated for its fruit, which is exported in great abundance to India. Its vines are so plentiful, that the grapes are given, for three months of the year, to cattle. There are ten different kinds of these: the best grow on frameworks; for those which are allowed to creep on the ground are inferior. They are pruned in the beginning of May. The wine of Cabool has a flavour not unlike Madeira; and it cannot be doubted, that a very superior description might be produced in this country with a little care. The people of Cabool convert the grape into more uses than in most other countries. They use its juice in roasting meat; and, during meals, have grape powder as a pickle. This is procured by pounding the grapes before they get ripe, after drying them. It looks like Cayenne pepper, and has a pleasant acid taste. They also dry many of them as raisins, and use much grape syrup. A pound of grapes sells for a halfpenny. I have already mentioned the " rhuwash," or rhubarb of Cabool: it grows spontaneously under the snowy hills of Pughman; and Cabool has a great celebrity from producing it. The natives believe it exceedingly wholesome, and use it both raw, and cooked as vegetables. They tell an anecdote of some Indian doctors, who practised for a short time at Cabool, and waited for the fruit season, when the people would probably be unhealthy. Seeing this rhubarb in May and June, these members of the faculty abruptly left the country, pronouncing it a specific for the catalogue of Cabool diseases. This, at all events, proves it to be considered a healthy article of food. When the rhubarb is brought to market, the stalks are about a foot long, and the leaves are just budding. They are red; the stalk is white: when it first appears above ground, it has a sweet taste like milk, and will not bear carriage. As it grows older, it gets strong, stones being piled round to protect it from the sun. The root of the plant is not used as medicine. There are no date trees in Cabool, though they are to be found both east and west of it—at Candahar and Peshawur. There the people are ignorant of the art of extracting an intoxicating juice from them, as in India. Peshawur is celebrated for its pears; Ghuzni for its plums (which are sold in India under the name of the plum of Bokhara); Candahar for its figs, and Cabool for its mulberries; but almost every description, particularly stone fruit, thrives in Cabool. Fruit is more

plentiful than bread, and is considered one of the
necessaries of human life.   There are no less than
fourteen different ways of preserving the apricot of
Cabool : it is dried with and without the stone ; the
kernel is sometimes left, or an almond is substituted
in its stead ; it is also formed into cakes, and folded
up like paper.   It is the most delicious of the dried
fruits.

Among the public buildings in Cabool, the Bala
Hissar, or citadel, claims the first importance ; but
not from its strength.   Cabool is enclosed to the
south and west by high rocky hills ; and at the
eastern extremity of these the Bala Hissar is
situated, which commands the city.   It stands on a
neck of land, and may have an elevation of about
150 feet from the meadows of the surrounding
country.   There is another fort under it, also called
the Bala Hissar, which is occupied by the governor
and his guards.   The citadel is uninhabited by the
present chief ; but his brother built a palace in it
called the " Koollah i Firingee," or the Europeans'
Hat, which is the highest building.   Dost Mahommed Khan captured the Bala Hissar, by blowing up
one of its towers : it is a poor, irregular, and dilapidated fortification, and could never withstand a
siege.   The upper fort is small, but that below will
contain about five thousand people.   The king's
palace stands in it.   The Bala Hissar was built by
different princes of the house of Timour, from Baber
downwards.   Aurungzebe prepared extensive vaults
under it, to deposit his treasure, which may yet be
seen.   While it formed the palace of the kings of

Cabool, it was also the prison of the younger branches of the royal family, where they were confined for life. They tell a story, that, when set free from it, after murdering their keeper, they looked with astonishment at seeing water flow — so close had been their confinement in this walled abode. It is difficult to say, whether these unfortunate men were not happier than in their present state, which is that of abject poverty. Many of the sons of Timour Shah came in absolute hunger to solicit alms from us. I advised them to make a petition to the chief for some permanent relief; but they said that they had no mercy to expect from the Barukzye family, now in power, who thirsted after their blood.

Near the Bala Hissar, and separated from it and every part of the city, the Persians, or Kuzzilbashes, as they are called, reside. They are Toorks, and principally of the tribe of Juwansheer, who were fixed in this country by Nadir Shah. Under the kings of Cabool they served as body-guards, and were a powerful engine of the state. They yet retain their language, and are attached to the present chief, whose mother is of their tribe. I had an opportunity of seeing these people to advantage; being invited to a party given by our conductor from Peshawur, the jolly Naib Mahommed Shureef. I met the whole of the principal men, and their chief, Sheereen Khan. The entertainment was more Persian than Afghan. Among them, I could discover a new people, and a new mode of thinking; for they have retained some of the wit that marks their countrymen. As the evening was drawing to a close, the chief called on a person to display his powers, not in a tale, but in depicting the peculiarities of the neighbouring nations. He began with the Afghans; and, after an amusing enough exordium, which excepted the Dooranees or chiefs, (who, he said, were not like other Afghans,) he described the entry of some twenty or thirty nations into paradise. When the turn of the Afghans came, he went on blasphemously to relate, that their horrid language was unintelligible, and that, as the prophet had pronounced it to be the dialect of hell, there was no place in heaven for those who spoke it. The fellow had humour, and brought in some Afghan phrases, much to the amusement of the company. He then attacked the Uzbeks for their peculiar way of making tea, and uncouth manners. He now levelled his batteries against the whining, cheating, and deceitful Cashmeerian; and these people must be belied indeed, if they be not masters in vice.* All parties, however, admit their talents and ingenuity, which is a considerable counterbalance. The natives of Herat, and their peculiar dialect, exercised the powers of this loquacious Meerza: he imitated the roguery of their custom-house; and allowed himself, as the officer

---

* A Persian couplet runs thus : —

" Dur juhan ust do taefu be peer;
    Soonee i Balk, Shiah i Cashmeer: "

which may be translated, that there is not an honest man among the Soonees of Balkh or the Shiahs of Cashmeer.

on duty, to be bribed out of his due, by accepting some wine, which he pretended was not for himself.

The difference between Eastern manners and those of Europe is nowhere more discernible than in their manner of saying good things. An European enjoys an anecdote; but he would be very much surprised to be called on in a company to tell one for its amusement. In the East, there are professional anecdote makers; in the West, we are content with a *bon mot* as it flows in the course of conversation. Both may be traced to the government: for, in the East, though there is much familiarity, there is little social intercourse; and, in Europe, good manners teach us to consider every one at the same board on an equality.

During our stay, the "Eed" occurred, which is the festival kept in commemoration of Abraham's intention to sacrifice his son Isaac. It was observed with every demonstration of respect: the shops were shut; and the chief proceeded to prayer at an appointed place, with a great concourse of persons. In the afternoon, every one was to be seen flocking to the gardens; nor could I resist the impulse, and followed the crowd. In Cabool, you no sooner leave the bazar, than you find yourself on the banks of the river, which are beautifully shaded by trees of mulberry, willow, and poplar. Almost all the roads round the city lead by the verge of aqueducts or running water. They are crossed by bridges: and the large river has three or four of these edifices; but they cannot boast of architec-

tural beauty. The finest gardens of Cabool lie
north of the city; and they, again, are far surpassed
by those beyond, in the district of Istalif, under the
first snow-clad mountains, towards Hindoo Koosh.
Their site is to be seen from Cabool. I was conducted to the tomb of Timour Shah, which stands
outside the city, and is a brick building of an octagon shape, rising to the height of 50 feet. The
interior of it is about 40 feet square, and the architecture resembles that of Delhi. The building is
unfinished. A lamp was formerly lighted on this
sepulchre; but the sense of this king's favours, like
that of many others, has faded. Timour Shah made
Cabool his capital, and here is his tomb. His father
is interred at Candahar, which is the native country
of the Doorances.

I moved about every where during the day, and
had the pleasure of many sociable evenings with
our host the Nawab, whom I found, like many of
his countrymen, in search of the philosopher's stone.
Such an opportunity as our arrival seemed to promise him a rich harvest. I soon undeceived him,
and laughed at the crucibles and recipes which he
produced. I explained to him, that chemistry had
succeeded alchymy, as astronomy had followed as-
trology; but as I had to detail the exact nature of
these sciences, my asseverations of being no alchy-
mist had little effect. He therefore applied himself
to the doctor, from whom he requested recipes for
the manufacture of calomel and quinine, plasters
and liniments; which it was no easy matter to furnish. He could not credit that the arts of giving

and manufacturing medicines were distinct; and
set us down as very ignorant or very obstinate.
He would not receive the prepared medicines, as
they would be of no use to him after we had left.
We found this feeling generally prevalent; and woe
be to the doctor in these parts who gives medicines
which he cannot make. We kept the Nawab in
good humour, though we would not believe that he
could convert iron into silver. We heard from him
the position of many metallic veins in the country.
He produced, among other curiosities, some asbestos,
here called cotton-stone (sung i poomba), found
near Julalabad. The good man declared that he
must have some of our knowledge in return for
what he told so freely. I informed him that I belonged to a sect called Freemasons, and gave some
account of the craft. It was an institution, I said,
where, though we did not change the baser metals
into gold, we sought to transform the baser and
blacker passions of man into philanthropy and
charity: he particularly requested that he might be
admitted into the fraternity without delay. But as
the number of brethren must be equal to that of the
Pleiades, I put it off to a convenient opportunity.
He confidently believed that he had at last got
scent of magic in its purest dye; and had it been
in my power, I would have willingly initiated him.
He made me promise to send some flower-seeds of
our country, which he wished to see in Cabool;
and I faithfully forwarded them. I cut the plates
out of Mr. Elphinstone's History of Cabool, and
gave them to the Nawab at a large party: not only

is the costume exact, but in some of the figures, to their great delight, they discovered likenesses. Pictures are forbidden among the Soonee Mahommedans; but in the present instance they proved very acceptable. Among the Nawab's friends we met a man 114 years old, who had served with Nadir Shah. He had been upwards of eighty years in Cabool, and seen the Doorance dynasty founded and pass away. This venerable person walked up stairs to our rooms.

From the crowd of people which we constantly met at the house of our host, I was resolved on gathering some information on the much disputed point of the Afghans being Jews. They brought me all their histories; but I had no time to examine them, and wished for oral information. The Afghans call themselves " Bin i Israeel," or children of Israel; but consider the term of " Yahoodee," or Jew, to be one of reproach. They say that Nebuchadnezzar, after the overthrow of the temple of Jerusalem, transplanted them to the town of Ghore, near Bameean; and that they are called Afghans, from their chief Afghana, who was a son of the uncle of Asof (the vizier of Solomon), who was the son of Berkia. The genealogy of this person is traced from a collateral branch, on account of the obscurity of his own parent; which is by no means uncommon in the East. They say that they lived as Jews, till Khaleed (called by the title of Caliph) summoned them, in the first century of Mahommedanism, to assist in the wars with the infidels. For their services on that occasion, Kyse, their leader,

got the title of Abdoolrusheed, which means the
Son of the mighty.   He was also told to consider
himself the " butan" (an Arabic word) or mast of
his tribe, on which its prosperity would hinge, and
by which the vessel of their state was to be governed.
Since that time, the Afghans are sometimes called
Putan, by which name they are familiarly known
in India.   I never before heard this explanation of
the term.   After the campaign with Khaleed, the
Afghans returned to their native country, and were
governed by a king of the line of Kyanee, or Cyrus,
till the eleventh century, when they were subdued
by Mahmood of Ghuzni.   A race of kings, sprung
from Ghore, subverted the house of Ghuzni, and
conquered India.   As is well known, this dynasty
was divided, at the death of its founder, into the
divisions east and west of the Indus ; a state of
things which lasted till the posterity of Timourlane
reduced both to a new yoke.

Having precisely stated the traditions and history
of the Afghans, I can see no good reason for dis-
crediting them, though there be some anachronisms,
and the dates do not exactly correspond with those
of the Old Testament.   In the histories of Greece
and Rome we find similar corruptions, as well as in
the later works of the Arab and Mahommedan
writers.   The Afghans look like Jews : they say
they are descended from Jews ; and the younger
brother marries the widow of the elder, according
to the law of Moses.   The Afghans entertain strong
prejudices against the Jewish nation ; which would
at least show that they had no desire to claim,

without a just cause, a descent from them. Since
some of the tribes of Israel came to the East, why
should we not admit that the Afghans are their descendants, converted to Mahommedanism?   I am
aware that I am differing from a high authority *,
but I trust that I have made it appear on reasonable
grounds.

As the chief desired, I passed another evening
with him; and the doctor, being convalescent, accompanied me: Mr. Wolff had proceeded on his
journey to India. Dost Mahommed Khan pleased
us as much as ever; he kept us till long past midnight, and gave us a full insight into the political
affairs of his country, and the unfortunate differ-
ences that exist between him and his brothers. He
expressed hopes of being able to restore the monarchy, evinced a cordial hatred towards Runjeet
Sing, and seemed anxious to know if the British
Government would accept his services as an auxi-
liary to root him out; but I replied, that he was
our friend. He then promised me the command of
his army, if I would remain with him; an offer
which he afterwards repeated. " Twelve thousand
horse and twenty guns shall be at your disposal."
When he found that I could not accept the honour,
he requested me to send some friend to be his
generalissimo. On this occasion, we had some
highly interesting conversation regarding the Kaffirs, who live in the hills north of Peshawur and
Cabool, and are supposed to descend from Alex-

*See Mr. Elphinstone's Caubul, vol. i. p. 244. et seq.

ander. The Chief, on the former occasion, had
produced a young Kaffir boy, one of his slaves,
about ten years old, who had been captured for two
years. His complexion, hair, and features were
quite European; his eyes were of a bluish colour.
We made him repeat various words of his language,
some of which were Indian. The Kaffirs live in a
most barbarous state, eating bears and monkeys.
There is a tribe of them called " Neemchu Moos-
sulman," or half Mahommedans, who occupy the
frontier villages between them and the Afghans, and
transact the little trade that is carried on between
them. It is curious to find a people so entirely
distinct from the other inhabitants ; but, unfortunately, every thing that regards them rests in obscurity. I have hereafter stated the particulars
which I collected regarding the Kaffirs, whom I
take to be the aborigines of Afghanistan, and in nowise connected with the reputed descendants of
Alexander the Great, as has been stated by some
authors.

We had passed nearly three weeks in Cabool;
which appeared as a few days. It was now necessary to prepare for our journey, which did not seem
an easy matter. No caravan was yet ready ; and it
was even doubtful if the roads were passable, as
snow had fallen during the month. It occurred to
me that our best plan would be to hire a Cafila-
bashee, a conductor of one of the great caravans,
as our own servant ; and we might thus proceed at
once, without the delay attendant upon a caravan,
and, I hoped, with equal safety. The Nawab did
not altogether relish the plan, nor our precipitate

departure.   He would have willingly kept us for
months.   We however, entertained one Hyat, a
hale old man, who had grown grey in crossing the
Hindoo Koosh.   When the Nawab found our de-
termination to depart, he urged his relative, the
Ameen ool Moolk, a nobleman of the late Shah
Mahmood, who carries on commercial transactions
with Bokhara and Russia, to despatch one of his
trusty persons with us.   It was therefore determined
that a brother of his nazir, or steward, named Doulut, a respectable Afghan, also styled the Nazir,
should proceed with us.   He had business in Bokhara, and was even going on to Russia : our move-
ments expedited his departure.   Every thing looked
well, and we were furnished, by the Nawab's kindness, with letters to the Afghans in Bokhara.   The
most influential of these was Budr-oo-deen.   His
agent in Cabool, who brought me the letters, was
resolved on being rewarded for doing so by an enjoyment of our society.   His name was Khodadad,
and he was a moollah.   He stopped and dined with
us on boiled fowl and rice; but he declared that,
whatever might be our wisdom as a nation, we had
no correct ideas of good living.   He did not like
our English fare, which was cooked with water, he
said, and only fit for an invalid.   Khodadad was a
very intelligent man, who had travelled in India
and Tartary, and was well read in Asiatic lore.
He had also studied Euclid, whom his countrymen,
he said, nicknamed " Uql doozd," or wisdom-stealer,
from the confusion he had produced in men's heads.
He was not fond of mathematics, and wished to
know our motive for studying them: he had not

heard that it improved the reasoning faculties ; and only considered the persons versed in Euclid as deeper read than others. The chief also prepared his letters ; but there is little communication between the Afghans and Uzbeks, and we found them of no service ; that for the King of Bokhara was lost or stolen. One of Dost Mahommed Khan's court, however, the governor of Bameean, Hajee Kauker, furnished us with letters, which were of real use, as will afterwards appear. This man, though serving under the chief of Cabool, is more friendly to his brother of Peshawur, by whom we were introduced to him. I held my intercourse with him secret, and he tendered the services of fifty horsemen, which it was prudent to decline.

Before our departure from Cabool, I made the acquaintance of many of the Hindoo or Shikarpooree merchants. The whole trade of Central Asia is in the hands of these people, who have houses of agency from Astracan and Meshid to Calcutta. They are a plodding race, who take no share in any business but their own, and secure protection from the government by lending it money. They have a peculiar cast of countenance, with a very high nose : they dress very dirtily. Few of them are permitted to wear turbans. They never bring their families from their country, which is Upper Sinde, and are constantly passing to and from it, which keeps up a national spirit among them. In Cabool, there are eight great houses of agency belonging to these people, who are quite separate from the other Hindoo inhabitants. Of them, there are about three hundred families. I met one of these Shikarpooree merchants on the Island of Kisham, in the Gulf of Persia ; and were Hindoos tolerated in that country, I feel satisfied that they would spread all over Persia, and even Turkey.

With such an extensive agency distributed in the parts of Asia which we were now about to traverse, it was not, as may be supposed, a very difficult task to adjust our money matters, and arrange for our receiving a supply of that necessary article, even at the distance which we should shortly find ourselves from India. Our expenses were small, and golden ducats were carefully sewed up in our belts and turbans, and sometimes even transferred to our slippers ; though, as we had to leave these at the door of every house, I did not always approve of such stowage. I had a letter of credit in my possession for the sum of five thousand rupees, payable from the public treasuries of Lodiana or Delhi; and the Cabool merchants did not hesitate to accept it. They expressed their readiness either to discharge it on the spot with gold, or give bills on Russia at St. Macaire (Nijnei Novogorod), Astracan, or Bokhara, which I had no reason to question : I took orders on the latter city. The merchants enjoined the strictest secrecy ; and their anxiety was not surpassed by that of our own to appear poor ; for the possession of so much gold would have ill tallied with the coarse and tattered garments which we now wore. But what a gratifying proof have we here of the high character of our nation, to find the bills of those who almost appeared as beggars cashed, without hesitation, in a foreign and far distant capital!   Above all, how much is our wonder excited to find the ramifications of commerce extending uninterruptedly over such vast and remote regions, differing as they do from each other in language, religion, manners, and laws!

CHAP. VI.

JOURNEY OVER THE HINDOO KOOSH, OR SNOWY MOUNTAINS.

If we had quitted Peshawur with the good wishes of the chief, we were now accompanied by those of his brother, the Nawab. On the 18th of May, which happened on a Friday, we quitted Cabool after noontide prayers, according to the usual custom of travellers, that we might not offend the prejudices of the people, who also consider that hour auspicious. We thought we had parted from the good Nawab at the door of his house, when he gave us his blessing; but before leaving the city, he once more joined us, and rode out for two or three miles, when this worthy man left us, much to our regret. He seemed to live for every one but himself. He entertained us with great hospitality during our stay; and had, day by day, urged us to take any other road than that of Toorkistan, prognosticating every evil to us. He now took leave of us with much feeling; nor was it possible to suppress a tear as we said adieu. Though his brother, the chief, had not caressed us as he of Peshawur, he had yet shown great politeness and attention, of which we expressed ourselves most sensible before taking our departure.

We halted for the night at a small village called
Killa-i-Kazee, and, at the first outset, experienced
the influence and utility of our Cafila-bashee. He
cleared out a house for us, by bribing a moollah to
leave it; and we found the quarters very snug, for
it was piercingly cold. Our friend Hyat was a
good-humoured man, and we made the reasonable
bargain with him, that he was to be rewarded according to his merits, of which we were to be the
judges. We committed ourselves to him as a bale
of goods, and desired him to march as he thought
best. I gave him my few books and instruments,
which he passed off as part of the property of the
Jewish families who had left Cabool in the preceding year. Prudence dictated our proceeding very
quietly in this part of our journey; and we were
now designated " Meerza," or secretary, a common
appellation in these countries, which we ever after
retained. The doctor allowed his title to slumber;
but it was soon apparent that we should have been
helpless without our conductor; for, on the following
morning, a fellow, possessing some little authority,
seized my horse's bridle, and demanded a sight of
the contents of my saddle-bags. I was proceeding
with all promptness to display my poverty, when a
word from the Cafila-bashee terminated the investigation. We were not now recognised as Europeans by any one, which certainly gave a pleasing
liberty to our actions. Among the contraband
goods, for which the officers of the Custom-house
were desired to search, was the singular article of
Korans; for it appeared that the traders had ex-

ported so many of these good books beyond Hindoo Koosh, that the "Faithful" in Afghanistan were likely to be robbed of the whole of them. The suppression of the trade was a highly popular act on the part of the chief of Cabool; since they are very expensive works, written with great pains and labour, and most valuable.

We left the road which leads to Candahar on our left, and proceeded up the valley of the Cabool river to its source at Sirchushma. Our first halting-place was Julraiz, which is so called from two Persian words that signify running water; and near the village there were two beautifully clear brooks, the banks of which were shaded by trees. It is these running rivulets that make this country so enchanting, in spite of its bleak rocks. The valley was not above a mile in breadth, and most industriously cultivated; the water being in some places conducted for a hundred feet up hill. In the lower lands, the rice fields rose most picturesquely in gradation above each other, and the hills on either side were topped with snow. The thermometer stood at 60°.

At Sirchushma, which literally means the fountain-head, we visited two natural ponds, the sources of the river of Cabool, replenished by springs, and formed into preserves for fish, which are kept with great care. It is a place of pilgrimage sacred to Ali, who is said to have visited it,—a "pious lie," which is not supported by any authority, since the son-in-law of Mahommed never saw Cabool, though his reputed deeds in this neighbourhood be both

numerous and wonderful. We fed the fish with
bread, which disappeared in a moment, torn from
our hands by some thousands of them : they are
molested by no one, since it is believed that a curse
rests on the head of an intruder.

Before entering the valley of the river, we left
the famous Ghuzni to the south : it is only sixty
miles from Cabool. This ancient capital is now a
dependency on that city, and a place of small note :
it contains the tomb of the great Mahmood, its
founder. There is a more honourable monument
to his memory in a magnificent dam, which he constructed at great expense, and the only one of seven
now remaining. It is worthy of remark, that the
ruler of the Punjab, in a negotiation which he
lately carried on with the ex-King of Cabool, Shooja
ool Moolk, stipulated, as one of the conditions of
his restoration to the throne of his ancestors, that
he should deliver up the sandal-wood gates at the
shrine of the Emperor Mahmood, — being the same
which were brought from Somnat, in India, when
that destroyer smote the idol, and the precious
stones are said to have fallen from his body. Upwards of eight hundred years have elapsed since the
spoliation, yet the Hindoo still remembers it, though
these doors have so long adorned the tomb of the
Sultan Mahmood. Baber expresses his wonder that
so great a monarch should have ever made Ghuzni
his capital; but the natives will tell you that the
cold renders it inaccessible for some months in the
year, which gave him greater confidence while de-
solating Hindoostan and the land of the infidels.

We wound up the valley, which became gradually narrower, till we reached a level tract on the mountains, — the pass of Oonna, — the ascent to which is guarded by three small forts. Before reaching the summit, we first encountered the snow, with which I was too happy to claim acquaintance after a separation of a dozen winters; though there were no companions with whom I could renew the frolics of youth. It snowed as we crossed the pass, which is about 11,000 feet high; and at length we found ourselves, with pleasure, at a small village, free from the chilling wind which blew all day. We had already made considerable progress in our mountain journey: the rivers now ran in opposite directions; and our advance had brought us into the cold country of the Huzaras, where the peasants were only ploughing and sowing, while we had seen the harvest home at Peshawur, and the grain in ear at Cabool.

We continued our mountain journey by the base of the lofty and ever-snow-clad mountain of Koh i Baba, which is a remarkable ridge, having three peaks that rise to the height of about 18,000 feet. On the evening of the 21st of May, we reached the bottom of the pass of Hajeeguk, half dead with fatigue, and nearly blind from the reflection of the snow. For about ten miles we had travelled in the bed of a rivulet, that was knee deep, fed by melting snow, which we crossed more than twenty times. We then entered the region of the snow, which still lay deep on the ground: by noon it became so soft that our horses sunk into it, threw their burdens and riders, and in several places were with the utmost difficulty extricated. That part of the ground which was free from snow had become saturated with the melted water, and a quagmire; so that we alternately waded through mud and snow. The heat was oppressive,—I imagine from reflection; I had almost lost the use of my eyes, and the skin peeled from my nose, before we reached a little fort under the pass, at which we alighted in the evening with a Huzara family.

We had here an opportunity of seeing the Huzaras in their native state among the mountains; and were received by an old lady, in a miserable flat-roofed house, partly below ground, with two or three openings in the roof, as windows. She was taking care of her grandchild, and bade us welcome, by the lordly name of " Agha." I called her " Mother;" and the old dame chatted about her house and family matters. We were taken for Persians; and, since the Huzaras are of the same creed as that nation, were honoured guests. Our mendicant garb could lead to no discovery that we were Europeans. The old woman assured us that the snow prevented them from stirring out of their houses for six months in the year (for it never rains), and that they sowed the barley in June, and reaped it in September. These people have no money, and are almost ignorant of its value. We got every thing from them by barter, and had no occasion to show them gold, by which Englishmen are so soon found out in every country. A traveller among them can only obtain the necessaries of life by giving a few yards of coarse cloth, a little tobacco, pepper, or sugar, which are here appreciated far above their value. The Huzaras are a simple-hearted people, and differ much from the Afghan tribes. In physiognomy, they more resemble Chinese, with their square faces and small eyes. They are Tartars by descent, and one of their tribes is now called Tatar Huzara. There is a current belief that they bestow their wives on their guests, which is certainly erroneous. The women have great influence, and go unveiled: they are handsome, and not very chaste; which has perhaps given rise to the scandal among their Soonee neighbours, who detest them as heretics. Were their country not strong, they would soon be extirpated; for they have enemies in every direction. The good matron, who gave us an asylum from the snow and frost, tendered also her advice for my eyes, which she said had been *burned* by the snow. She recommended the use of antimony, which I applied with the pencil, much to the improvement of my appearance, as she informed me; but I can more surely add, to my relief and comfort when I again encountered the snow.

I observed that these mountaineers, though some of them were living at elevations of 10,000 feet, were altogether free from that unseemly disease, the goitre, which I had observed in the Himalaya, eastward of the Indus, even below 4000 feet. Perhaps bronchocele is a disease confined to the lesser altitudes; an opinion held by members of the faculty of the first eminence on the Continent, as I find

from a paper in the Transactions of the Medical
Society of Calcutta, by Dr. M. J. Bramley, of the
Bengal army. That gentleman, however, in his
treatise on the disease, which is founded on personal experience during a residence in the mountainous regions of Nipal, adduces facts that would
lead to a contrary conclusion regarding its locality,
which he states to be more general on the crest of
a high mountain than in the valley of Nipal.

One would have imagined that, in these elevated
and dreary regions, the inhabitants would be engaged with other subjects than abstruse points of
theology. A moollah, or priest, however, had lately
appeared among them to proclaim some novel doc-
trines; and, among others, that Ali was the Deity,
and greater than Mahommed himself. He had
found some hundred followers, whom this fanatic
had impressed with such an opinion of his power,
that they believed he could raise the dead, and pass
through fire without injury. One of the Huzara
chiefs, who was shocked at the blasphemy of this
false prophet, had preached a crusade against him
for misleading the faithful; and many of the people
accompanied him to assist in reclaiming the deluded
to Islam. They informed us that this sect was styled
" Ali Illahi," and had adopted many odious customs;
among others, that of the community of women:
they also held bacchanalian orgies in the dark, from
which they were named " Chiragh Koosh," or lamp-
killers, in allusion to the darkness which concealed
their iniquities. Such a sect, I am assured, is not
at all novel, since the Mogots of Cabool have long

since professed some of its tenets, and still secretly practise them. It is also known in several parts of Persia and Turkey; but the march of intellect had not hitherto extended it to the gelid regions of Hindoo Koosh.

The crusade of the Huzaras proved a fortunate circumstance for us, as the chieftain of 12,000 families, and of these passes, by name Yezdan Bukhsh, was absent upon it; and he is a person who acknowledges but a doubtful allegiance to Cabool. By the kindness of Hajee Khan Kauker, we were introduced to him; but the report of his character did not lead us to hope for more than common civility, if we even received that. We escaped, however, in the religious turmoil, after waiting for an hour at the door of the fort, and each of us paying a rupee as tax to his deputy, since we were not Mahommedans. Our letter might, perhaps, have prevailed on the Huzaras to let us pass at this cheap rate; but it was long before they adjusted the demand with the Cafila-bashee, who gave me many a significant glance during the treaty. The doctor and myself sought no closer connection than a look at these mountaineers; but, as it appeared, we were altogether unworthy of their notice.

After a night's rest, and the friendly advice of the Huzara matron, we commenced the ascent of the pass of Hajeeguk, which was about 1000 feet above us, and 12,400 feet from the sea. We took our departure early in the morning of the 22d of May; the frozen snow bore our horses, and we

reached the summit before the sun's influence had
softened it. The thermometer fell 4 degrees below
the freezing point; the cold was very oppressive,
though we were clad in skins with the fur inside.
I often blessed the good Nawab of Cabool, who had
forced a pelisse of otter skin upon me, that proved
most useful. The passage was not achieved without adventure, for there was no road to guide us
through the snow; and the surveyor, Mahommed
Ali, along with his horse, went rolling down a declivity, one after the other, for about thirty yards.
This exhibition in front served to guide the rear to
a better path; but it was impossible to resist laughing at the Jack and Jill expedition of the poor surveyor and his horse; he, a round figure wrapped
up in fur, and far outstripping his long-shanked
animal, which made deeper indentations in the snow.
We were now about to commence the ascent of the
pass of Kaloo, which is still 1000 feet higher than
that of Hajeeguk; but our progress was again arrested by snow. We doubled it, by passing round
its shoulder, and took a side path through a valley,
watered by a tributary of the Oxus, which led us to
Bameean.

Nothing could be more grand than the scenery
which we met in this valley. Frightful precipices
hung over us; and many a fragment beneath informed us of their instability. For about a mile it
was impossible to proceed on horseback, and we
advanced on foot, with a gulf beneath us. The dell
presented a beautiful section of the mountains to

the eye of a geologist *; and, though a by-path,
appeared to have been fortified in former years, as
innumerable ruins testified.   Some of these were
pointed out as the remnants of the post-houses of
the Mogul emperors; but by far the greater number
were assigned to the age of Zohak, an ancient king
of Persia.   One castle in particular, at the northern
termination of the valley, and commanding the
gorge, had been constructed with great labour on
the summit of a precipice, and was ingeniously
supplied with water.   It would be useless to record all the fables of the people regarding these
buildings.

Bameean is celebrated for its colossal idols and
innumerable excavations, which are to be seen in
all parts of the valley, for about eight miles, and
still form the residence of the greater part of the
population.   They are called " Soomuch" by the
people.   A detached hill in the middle of the valley
is quite honeycombed by them, and brings to our re-
collection the Troglodytes of Alexander's historians.
It is called the city of Ghoolghoola, and consists of
a continued succession of caves in every direction,
which are said to have been the work of a king named
Julal.   The hills at Bameean are formed of indurated
clay and pebbles, which renders their excavation a
matter of little difficulty ; but the great extent to
which it has been carried excites attention.   Caves
are dug on both sides of the valley, but the greater
number lie on the northern face, where we found the
great idols : altogether they form an immense city.

* See Vol. III. book i. ch. 7.

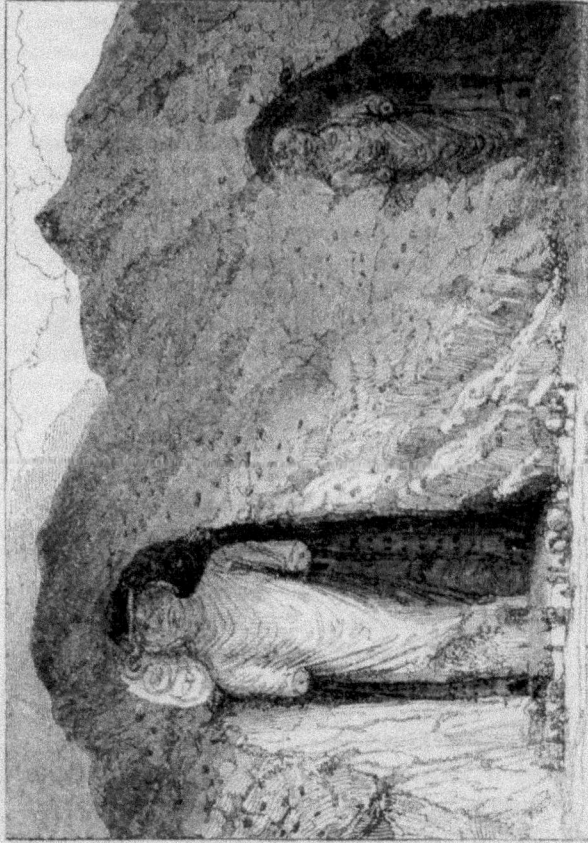

IDOLS OF BAMEEAN.

Labourers are frequently hired to dig in them; and
their trouble is rewarded by rings, relics, coins, &c.
They generally bear Cufic inscriptions, and are of a
later date than the age of Mahommed.   These excavated caves, or houses, have no pretensions to
architectural ornament, being no more than squared
holes in the hill.   Some of them are finished in the
shape of a dome, and have a carved frieze below the
point from which the cupola springs.   The inhabitants tell many remarkable tales about the caves
of Bameean; one in particular — that a mother had
lost her child among them, and recovered it after a
lapse of twelve years!   The tale need not be believed; but it will convey an idea of the extent of
the works.   There are excavations on all sides of
the idols; and below the larger one, half a regiment
might find quarters. Bameean is subject to Cabool:
it would appear to be a place of high antiquity;
and is, perhaps, the city which Alexander founded
at the base of Paropamisus, before entering Bactria.
The country, indeed, from Cabool to Balkh, is yet
styled " Bakhtur Zumeen," or Bakhtur country.
The name of Bameean is said to be derived from
its elevation, — " bam" signifying balcony, and the
affix " eean" country.   It may be so called from
the caves rising one over another in the rock.

There are no relics of Asiatic antiquity which
have roused the curiosity of the learned more than
the gigantic idols of Bameean.   It is fortunately in
my power to present a drawing of these images.
They consist of two figures, a male and a female;
the one named Silsal, the other Shahmama.   The

figures are cut in alto relievo on the face of the hill,
and represent two colossal images. The male is
the larger of the two, and about 120 feet high. It
occupies a front of 70 feet; and the niche in which
it is excavated extends about that depth into the
hill. This idol is mutilated; both legs having been
fractured by cannon; the countenance above the
mouth is also destroyed. The lips are very large;
the ears long and pendent; and there appears to
have been a tiara on the head. The figure is covered
by a mantle, which hangs over it in all parts, and
has been formed of a kind of plaster; the image
having been studded with wooden pins in various
places to assist in fixing it. The figure itself is
without symmetry, nor is there much elegance in
the drapery. The hands, which held out the mantle,
have been both broken. The female figure is more
perfect than the male, and has been dressed in the
same manner. It is cut in the same hill, at a distance of 200 yards, and is about half the size. The
annexed sketch will convey better notions of
these idols than a more elaborate description. The
square and arched apertures which appear in the
woodcut represent the entrance of the different
caves or excavations; and through these there is a
road which leads to the summit of both the images.
In the lower caves, the caravans to and from Cabool
generally halt; and the upper ones are used as gra-
naries by the community.

I have now to note the most remarkable curiosity
in the idols of Bameean. The niches of both have
been at one time plastered, and ornamented with

paintings of human figures, which have now disappeared from all parts but that immediately over
the heads of the idols. Here the colours are as
vivid, and the paintings as distinct, as in the Egyp-
tian tombs. There is little variety in the design of
these figures; which represent the bust of a woman,
with a knob of hair on the head, and a plaid thrown
half over the chest; the whole surrounded by a
halo, and the head again by another halo. In one
part, I could trace a group of three female figures
following each other. The execution of the work
was indifferent, and not superior to the pictures
which the Chinese make in imitation of an European
artist.

The traditions of the people regarding the idols
of Bameean are vague and unsatisfactory. It is
stated, that they were excavated about the Christian
era, by a tribe of Kaffirs (infidels), to represent a
king, named Silsal, and his wife, who ruled in a
distant country, and was worshipped for his greatness. The Hindoos assert that they were excavated by the Pandoos, and that they are mentioned
in the great epic poem of the Mahabarat. Certain
it is, that Hindoos, on passing these idols, at this
day, hold up their hands in adoration : they do not
make offerings ; though this custom may have fallen
into disuse since the rise of Islam. I am aware
that a conjecture attributes these images to the
Boodhists ; and the long ears of the great figure
render the surmise probable. I did not trace any
resemblance to the colossal figures in the caves of
Salsette, near Bombay ; but the shape of the head

is not unlike that of the great trifaced idol of Ele-
phanta. At Manikyala, in the Punjab, near the
celebrated " tope," I found a glass or cornelian
antique, which exactly resembles this head. In the
paintings over the idols I observed a close resemblance to the images of the Jain temples in Western
India, on Mount Aboo, Girnar, and Palitana in
Kattywar. I judge the figures to be female ; but
they are very rude; though the colours in which
they are sketched are bright and beautiful. There
is nothing in the images of Bameean to evince any
great advancement in the arts, or what the most
common people might not have easily executed.
They cannot, certainly, be referred to the Greek
invasion ; nor are they mentioned by any of the
historians of Alexander's expedition. I find in the
history of Timourlane, that both the idols and excavations of Bameean are described by Sherif o deen,
his historian. The idols are there stated to be so
high that none of the archers could strike the head.
They are called Lat and Munat ; two celebrated
idols which are mentioned in the Koran : the writer
also alludes to the road which led up to their summit from the interior of the hill. There are no inscriptions at Bameean to guide us in their history;
and the whole of the later traditions are so mixed
up with Ali, the son-in-law of Mahommed, who, we
well know, never came into this part 'of Asia, that
they are most unsatisfactory. It is by no means
improbable that we owe the idols of Bameean to the
caprice of some person of rank, who resided in this
cave-digging neighbourhood, and sought for an

immortality in the colossal images which we have now described.

After a day's delay at Bameean, where we could not boast of much hospitality — since we procured a house with difficulty, and were obliged to quit several that we entered — we set out for Syghan, a distance of thirty miles. At the pass of Akrobat, which we crossed half way, we left the dominions of modern Cabool. Following the geography of our maps, I had expected to find the great snowy mountains beyond us; but we now looked upon them in range behind. The "Koh i Baba" is the great continuation of Hindoo Koosh. In our front we had yet to cross a wide belt of mountains; but they were almost free from snow, and much lower than those which we had traversed. We were conducted to the pass of Akrobat by twenty horsemen, which a letter of introduction to the governor of Bameean from Hajee Khan of Cabool had procured as a protection from the Dih Zungee Huzaras, who plunder these roads. The escort was mounted on fine Toorkmun horses, and accompanied by some native greyhounds — a fleet sort of dog, with long shaggy hair on the legs and body. The party took their leave on the pass, where we bade farewell to them and the kingdom of Cabool.

At Syghan we found ourselves in the territory of Mahommed Ali Beg, an Uzbek, who is alternately subject to Cabool and Koondooz as the chiefs of these states respectively rise in power. He satisfies the chief of Cabool with a few horses, and his Koon-

dooz lord with a few men, captured in forays by his
sons and officers, who are occasionally sent out for
the purpose.   Such is the difference between the
taste of his northern and southern neighbours. The
captives are Huzaras, on whom the Uzbeks nomi-
nally wage war for their Shiah creed, that they may
be converted to Soonees and good Mahommedans.
A friend lately remonstrated with this chief for his
gross infringement of the laws of the Prophet, in the
practice of man-stealing.   He admitted the crime;
but as God did not forbid him in his sleep,
and his conscience was easy, he said that he
did not see why he should desist from so profitable
a traffic.   I should have liked an *opportunity* to ad-
minister a sleeping draught to this conscience-
satisfied Uzbek.   He is nowise famed for justice, or
protection of the traveller: a caravan of Jews passed
his town last year, on route to Bokhara; he detained
some of their women, and defended the outrage, by
replying to every remonstrance, that their progeny
would become Mahommedan, and justify the act.
So this wretch steals men, and violates the honour
of a traveller's wife, because he believes it acceptable conduct before his God, and in consonance
with the principles of his creed.   Our Cafila-bashee
waited on this person, to report our arrival; and
told him, it seems, that we were poor Armenians.
He jested with him, and said we might be Europeans; but our conductor appealed to a letter of introduction from Cabool, in which we had not been
so denominated.   A nankeen pelisse, with eight or
nine rupees (the usual tax on a caravan), satisfied

this man-selling Uzbek, and we passed a comfortable night in a very nicely carpeted "mihman
khana," or public-house of guests, which is situated
at the verge of the village; the chief himself sending us a leg of venison, as we were known to his
friends in Cabool.   We were already in a different
country; the mosques were spread with felts, which
indicated greater attention to matters of religion,
and they were also much better buildings.   We
were instructed not to sleep with our feet towards
Mecca; which would be evincing our contempt for
that holy place; and I ever after observed the
bearings of the compass in-doors, as attentively as I
had hitherto done outside.   I also cut the central
portion of the hair of my mustachios; since the
neglect of such a custom would point me out as a
Shiah, and consequently an infidel.   We made all
these arrangements in Syghan; which is a pretty
place, with fine gardens, though situated in a dreary
valley, destitute of all vegetation beyond its immediate precincts.   When we left it next morning, a
man came about five hundred yards from the village
to give us the "fatha" or blessing, as is usual in this
country; and we departed, and stroked down our
beards with gravity at the honour.

Seeing this rigid adherence to the laws of Mahommed, and the constant recurrence to the practice of the Koran in every act of life, I was not
disposed to augur favourably for our comfort, or the
reliance which we could place upon the people with
whom we were now to mingle.   I thought of the
expeditions of Prince Beckevitch, and our own un-

fortunate predecessors, poor Moorcroft and his party. The fate of the Russian Count and his little army is well known; they were betrayed, and barbarously massacred. The lot of Moorcroft was equally melancholy; since he and his associates perished of fever, and not without suspicions of some more violent death. I shall have occasion to speak of them hereafter. We could not, however, but persuade ourselves, that a more encouraging field lay before us. We had not come, as the Russian, to search for gold, nor to found a settlement; and we had none of the wealth of the English traveller, which, I do not hesitate to say, proved his ruin. We appeared even without presents to the chiefs; for it was better to be thought mean, than to risk our heads by exciting the cupidity of avaricious men. It may be imagined that our feelings at this moment were not of an agreeable nature; but fuller experience dissipated many of our fears. The notions even of our conductor were singular. Shortly after leaving Cabool, I took up a stone by the road-side, to examine its formation; and the Cafila-bashee, who observed me, asked with anxiety, " Have you found it ?"—" What ?"—" Gold." I threw away the stone, and became more cautious in my future observations.

From Syghan we crossed the pass of "Dundan Shikun," or the Tooth-breaker, which is aptly named from its steepness and difficulty. We here found the assafœtida plant in exuberance, which our fellow travellers ate with great relish. This plant, I believe, is the silphium of Alexander's historians;

for the sheep cropped it most greedily, and the people consider it a nutritious food. We now descended into a narrow valley, with a beautiful orchard of apricots, that extended for some miles beyond the village of Kamurd. The rocks rose on either side to a height of three thousand feet, frequently precipitous; nor was the dell any where more than three hundred yards wide. We could not see the stars, to take an observation at night: the whole scene was most imposing.

At Kamurd we passed the seat of another petty chief, Ruhmut oollah Khan, a Tajik deeply addicted to wine. He had been without a supply for ten days, and gave vent to such ejaculations and regrets as amused our party for the remainder of the march. Heaven and earth were the same to him, he said, without his dose; and he produced a flaggon, with an earnest request that the Cafila-bashee would replenish it at Khoolloom, and send it to him by the first opportunity. A coarse loongee, coupled with a promise of the wine, satisfied this chief; for he also claims a tax on the traveller, though he is but a tributary of Koondooz. His power is limited, and it is curious to observe how he keeps on terms with his master, Mahommed Moorad Beg. Unable to make "chupaos," or forays, and capture human beings, like his neighbour of Syghan, he, last year, deliberately seized the whole of the inhabitants of one of his villages, and despatched them, men, women, and children, as slaves, to Koondooz. He was rewarded by three additional villages for his allegiance and services; yet we here hired a son of this man to escort us on our travels; and it was well we did so.

The chief of Kamurd, in a quarrel which he had some years since with one of his neighbours, unfortunately lost his wife, who was captured. She was immediately transferred to his rival's seraglio, and in time bore him a numerous family. After a lapse of years, circumstances restored her to her husband; but the propriety of receiving her into his family was referred to the Mahommedan doctors. As the woman had been carried off without her consent, it was decided that she should be taken back, with all her family. It is common among the Toorks to marry the wives of their enemies captured in battle; but the custom is barbarous, and appears to contradict the nice principles of delicacy regarding women, which are professed by all Mahommedans.

I have hitherto forgotten to mention, that our companion the Nazir was accompanied by a person named Mahommed Hoosein, an amusing character, who had travelled into Russia, and often entertained us with an account of that country, and the metropolis of the Czars. It appeared to him, and several other Asiatics whom I afterwards met, a very close approximation, in wine and women, to the paradise of their blessed Prophet. A Mahommedan, who is transported from a country where females are so much secluded, would at all times be struck with the great change in an European country; but in Russia, where the moral tone of society appears to be rather loose, their amazement is great indeed. The foundling hospitals and their inmates are a sub-

ject of perpetual remark; and however much the
Arabian prophet may have condemned the use of
intoxicating fluids, I could discover, from those who
had visited Russia, that the temptations of the gin
and punch shops had not been resisted. Many of
the Asiatics, too, become gamblers; and commerce
has imported cards into the holy city of Bokhara.
The pack consists of thirty-six cards, and the games
are strictly Russian. In describing the feelings of
an Asiatic on the subject of Europe, there must be
much sameness; but it is at all times most interesting to listen to their tales. Particulars which quite
escape us, and a multiplicity of trifles, are noticed
with great gravity. Nothing is so wonderful to him
as the European notions of military discipline and
drill, which he considers to be a description of tor-
ture and despotism. I had to answer reiterated and
endless questions on the utility of making a man
look always one way, march off always with one foot,
and hold his hands in certain positions on a parade
ground. As they had not heard of the great Fre-
derick, I could not refer to his high name for an
example; but I pointed to India and Persia as sure
proofs of the advantage of disciplined over undis-
ciplined valour. The Asiatics, however, have a far
higher opinion of European wisdom than valour;
and truly, since dependence on mere bodily strength
has ceased, wisdom is bravery.

On the 26th of May, we crossed the last pass of
the Indian Caucasus—the Kara Koottul, or Black
Pass—but had yet a journey of ninety-five miles
before we cleared the mountains. We descended

at the village of Dooab into the bed of the river of
Khooloom, and followed it to that place among
terrific precipices, which at night obscured all the
stars but those of the zenith. On this pass we had
an adventure, which illustrates the manners of the
people among whom we were travelling, and might
have proved serious. Our Cafila-bashee had intimated to us that we had reached a dangerous neighbourhood, and consequently hired an escort, headed,
as I have stated, by the son of Ruhmut oollah Khan.
In ascending the pass, we met a large caravan of
horses, *en route* to Cabool; and, on reaching the
top, descried a party of robbers advancing over a
ridge of hills, and from the direction of Hindoo
Koosh. The cry of " Allaman, Allaman !" which
here means a robber, soon spread; and we drew up
with our escort to meet, and, if possible, fight the
party. The robbers observed our motions, and
were now joined by some other men, who had lain
in ambush, which increased their party to about
thirty. Each of us sent on two horsemen, who
drew up at a distance of an hundred yards, and
parleyed. The robbers were Tatar Huzaras, commanded by a notorious freebooter named Dilawur,
who had come in search of the horse caravan. On
discovering that it had passed, and that we were in
such good company as the son of the chief of Kamurd, they gave up all intentions of attack, and we
pushed on without delay; immediately we had
cleared the pass, they occupied it; but the whole
of their booty consisted of two laden camels of the
caravan, which had loitered behind. These they

seized in our view, as well as their drivers, who
would now become slaves for life; and had we not
hired our escort, we should have perhaps shared a
similar fate, and found ourselves next day tending
herds and flocks among the mountains. The party
was well mounted, and composed of desperate men:
disappointed of their prey, they attacked the village
of Dooab at night, where we first intended to halt.
We had luckily pushed on three miles farther, and
bivouacked in the bed of a torrent in safety. The
incidents of our escape furnished some room for reflection; and we had to thank the Cafila-bashee for
his prudence, which had cleared us of the danger.
The old gentleman stroked down his beard, blessed
the lucky day, and thanked God for preserving his
good name and person from such scoundrels.

The life which we now passed was far more
agreeable than a detail of its circumstances would
lead one to believe, with our dangers and fatigues.
We mounted at daylight, and generally travelled
without intermission till two or three in the afternoon. Our day's progress averaged about twenty
miles; but the people have no standard of measure;
and miles, coses, and fursukhs, were equally unknown, for they always reckon by the day's journey.
We often breakfasted on the saddle, on dry bread
and cheese; slept always on the ground, and in the
open air; and after the day's march, sat down cross-
legged, till night and sleep overtook us. Our caravan was every thing that could be wished, for the
Nazir and his amusing fellow-traveller were very
obliging: there were only eight persons in our

party, and three of these were natives of the country : two others were instructed to pretend that they were quite distinct from us; though one of them noted the few bearings of the compass, which I myself could not conveniently take without leading to discovery. We were quite happy in such scenes, and at the novelty of every thing; it was also delightful to recognise some old friends among the weeds and shrubs. The hawthorn and sweet brier grew on the verge of the river; and the rank hemlock, that sprung up under their shade, now appeared beautiful from the associations which it awakened. Our society, too, was amusing; and I took every favourable occasion of mingling with the travellers whom we met by the way, and at the halting-places.

I found nothing more puzzling than the different modes of salutation among the Afghans, with which time only can familiarise a foreigner. When you join a party, you must put your right hand on your heart, and say " Peace be unto you!" (*Sulam Aliakoom.*) You are then told you are welcome; and when you depart, you repeat the ceremony, and are again told you are welcome. On the road a traveller salutes you with " May you not be fatigued!" (*Mandunu bashee*;) to which you reply, " May you live long !" (*Zindu bashee.*) If acquainted, the salutations become more numerous. Are you strong? are you well? are you free from misfortunes? &c.: to all of which, you must answer, " Thanks be to God!" (*Shookur.*) On parting, your friend will tell you that your journey is not a tedious one, and consign you to God's keeping (*bu uman i Khooda*). If invited to dinner, you must reply to the civility, " May your house be peopled !" (*Khana i to abad ;*) and if you be complimented on any occasion, you must answer that " I am not worthy of you ; it is your greatness." Every person, high and low, you must address by the title of Khan or Agha, to gain his good graces. If he is a moollah or priest, you must call him Akhoond or teacher, if a moollah's son, Akhoondzada. A secretary is called Meerza ; which is, however, a cognomen for all nondescript characters, in which class we were numbered. Intimate acquaintances call each other " lalu" or brother. The Afghans must have learned all this ceremony from the Persians, for there is not a more unsophisticated race of people in Asia. It was quite entertaining to hear the various salutations which were addressed to our Cafila-bashee : every person on the road seemed to know him ; and, as we passed along, he used to teach us lessons of good breeding, which I took every occasion, as his apt scholar, to display.

We continued our descent by Khoorrum and Sarbagh to Heibuk, which is but a march within the mountains ; and gradually exchanged our elevated barren rocks for more hospitable lands. Our road led us through tremendous defiles, which rose over us to a height of from two to three thousand feet, and overhung the pathway, while eagles and hawks wheeled in giddy circles over us : among them we distinguished the black eagle, which is a

noble bird.   Near Heibuk, the defile becomes so
narrow, that it is called the " Dura i Zindan," or
Valley of the Dungeon ; and so high are the rocks,
that the sun is excluded from some parts of it at
mid-day.   There is a poisonous plant found here,
which is fatal even to a mule or a horse : it grows
something like a lily ; and the flower, which is about
four inches long, hangs over and presents a long
seed nodule.   Both it and the flower resemble the
richest crimson velvet.   It is called " zuhr boota"
by the natives, which merely expresses its poisonous
qualities.   I brought a specimen of this plant to
Calcutta, and am informed by Dr. Wallich, the intelligent and scientific superintendent of the Company's botanic garden, that it is of the Arum species.
We now found vast flocks browsing on the aromatic
pastures of the mountains, and passed extensive
orchards of fruit trees.   Herds of deer might be
seen bounding on the summits of the rocks ; and in
the valleys, the soil was every where turned up by
wild hogs, which are here found in great numbers.
The people also became more numerous as we approached the plains of Tartary, and at Heibuk we
had to encounter another Uzbek chief named Baba
Beg, a petty tyrant of some notoriety.

As we approached his town, a traveller informed
us that the chief was anticipating the arrival of the
Firingees (Europeans), whose approach had been
announced for some time past.   This person is a
son of Khilich Ali Beg, who once ruled in Khooloom
with great moderation ; but the child has not imitated the example of his parent.   He poisoned a

brother at a feast, and seized upon his father's
wealth before his life was extinct. He had greatly
augmented the difficulties of Mr. Moorcroft's party;
and was known to be by no means favourable to
Europeans. His subjects had driven him from his
native town of Khooloom for his tyranny, and he
now only possessed the district of Heibuk. We saw
his castle about four in the afternoon, and approached
with reluctance; but our arrangements were conducted with address, and here also we escaped in
safety. On arrival, our small caravan alighted outside Heibuk, and we lay down on the ground as fatigued travellers, covering ourselves with a coarse
horse blanket till it was night. In the evening, the
chief came in person to visit our Cabool friend the
Nazir, to whom he offered every service; nor did
he appear to be at all aware of our presence. Baba
Beg, on this occasion, made an offer to send the
party, under an escort of his own, direct to Balkh,
avoiding Khooloom — an arrangement which I
heard with pleasure, and, as it will soon appear, that
might have saved us a world of anxiety. Our fellow-travellers, however, declined the proffered kindness, and vaunted so much of their influence at
Khooloom, that we had no dread in approaching a
place where we were ultimately ensnared. While
this Uzbek chief was visiting the Nazir, we were
eating a mutton chop by the fireside within a few
yards and near enough to see him and hear his
conversation. He was an ill-looking man, of de-
bauched habits. He was under some obligation to
our fellow-travellers; and we and our animals fared

well on the flesh and barley which he sent for their
entertainment. Our character was never suspected;
and so beautiful a starlight night was it, that I did
not let this, the first opportunity, pass without observing our latitude north of Hindoo Koosh. We
set out in the morning before the sun had risen, and
congratulated ourselves at having passed with such
success a man who would have certainly injured us.

Heibuk is a thriving village, with a castle of sun-
dried brick, built on a commanding hillock. For the
first time among the mountains, the valley opens,
and presents a sheet of gardens and most luxuriant
verdure. The climate also undergoes a great change;
and we find the fig tree, which does not grow in
Cabool, or higher up the mountains. The elevation
of Heibuk is about 4000 feet. The soil is rich, and
the vegetation rank. We had expected to be rid of
those troublesome companions of a tropical climate,
snakes and scorpions; but here they were more numerous than in India, and we disturbed numbers of
them on the road. One of our servants was stung
by a scorpion; and as there is a popular belief that
the pain ceases if the reptile be killed, it was put to
death accordingly. The construction of the houses
at Heibuk arrested our attention: they have domes
instead of terraces, with a hole in the roof as a chim-
ney; so that a village has the appearance of a clus-
ter of large brown beehives. The inhabitants adopt
this style of building, as wood is scarce. The
people, who were now as different as their houses,
wore conical skull-caps, instead of turbans, and almost every one we met, whether traveller or villager,

appeared in long brown boots. The ladies seemed to select the gayest colours for their dresses ; and I could now distinguish some very handsome faces, for the Mahommedan ladies do not pay scrupulous attention to being veiled in the villages. They were much fairer than their husbands, with nothing ungainly in their appearance, though they were Tartars. I could now, indeed, understand the praises of the Orientals as to the beauty of these Toorkee girls.

On the 30th of May we made our last march among the mountains, and debouched into the plains of Tartary at Khooloom, or Tash Koorghan, where we had a noble view of the country north of us, sloping down to the Oxus. We left the last hills about two miles from the town, rising at once in an abrupt and imposing manner ; the road passing through them by a narrow defile, which might easily be defended. Khooloom contains about ten thousand inhabitants, and is the frontier town of Moorad Beg of Koondooz, a powerful chief, who has reduced all the countries north of Hindoo Koosh to his yoke. We alighted at one of the caravansarais, where we were scarcely noticed. A caravansary is too well known to require much description ;—it is a square, enclosed by walls, under which are so many rooms or cells for accommodation. The merchandise and cattle stand in the area. Each party has his chamber, and is strictly private ; since it is contrary to custom for one person to disturb another. All are travellers, and many are fatigued. If society were every where on as good a footing as in a caravansary, the world would be spared the evils of calumny.

We here rested after our arduous and fatiguing journey over rocks and mountains; and were, indeed, refreshed by the change. Since leaving Cabool, we had slept in our clothes, where we could seldom or ever change them. We had halted among mud, waded through rivers, tumbled among snow, and for the last few days been sunned by heat. These are but the petty inconveniences of a traveller; which sink into insignificance, when compared with the pleasure of seeing new men and countries, strange manners and customs, and being able to temper the prejudices of one's country, by observing those of other nations.

CHAP. VII.

SERIOUS DIFFICULTIES. — A JOURNEY TO
KOONDOOZ.

WE had entered Khooloom with an intention of setting out next day on our journey to Balkh ; placing
implicit reliance on the assertion of our friends,
that we had nothing to apprehend in doing so.
Judge, then, of our surprise, when we learned that
the officers of the custom-house had despatched a
messenger to the chief of Koondooz, to report our
arrival, and request his instructions as to our disposal. We were, meanwhile, desired to await the
answer. Our companion, the Nazir, was much cha-
grined at the detention ; but it was now useless to
upbraid him for having ever brought us to Khooloom.
He assured us that it was a mere temporary inconvenience ; and likewise despatched a letter to the
minister at Koondooz, requesting that we might not
be detained, since his business in Russia could not
be transacted without us. The minister was a friend
of the Nazir's family; and since we had plunged
ourselves into difficulties, matters seemed at least to
look favourable for our safe conduct through them.
I could not but regret that I had ever allowed myself to be seduced by the advice of any one ; and
would, even at this late period, have endeavoured to

escape to Balkh, had not the Cafila-bashee, and
every one, pronounced it headstrong and imprac-
ticable. At one time, indeed, about midnight, the
Cafila-bashee acceded to our proposals for escaping
to Balkh in the course of the next night, and even
said the first verse of the Koran as his oath and
blessing. I did not, however, understand that the
plan was to be kept secret from the Nazir, to whom
I revealed it next day, to the great dissatisfaction
and dismay of the Cafila bashee, who was visited
with a due share of his wrath. " Wait," said the
Nazir to us, " for a reply from Koondooz, and we
cannot doubt its favourable nature." We did wait;
and at midnight, on the 1st of June, received a summons to repair to Koondooz with all despatch; while
the minister, in reply to our conductor's letter,
begged he would not allow himself to be detained on
our account, but proceed on his journey to Bokhara!
Our surprise may be better imagined than described.
It was now too late to make our escape, for we were
watched in the caravansary, and the officers would not
even allow my horse to be taken into the town and shod.
It might have been accomplished on our first arrival,
but then it was deemed injudicious, and it only remained, therefore, for us to face the difficulties of
our situation in a prompt and becoming manner. I
urged an immediate departure for Koondooz, leaving
Dr. Gerard, and all the party, except two, at Khooloom. I was now resolved on personating the character of an Armenian, and believed that despatch
would avail me and allay suspicion. I had letters
from the saint at Peshawur, which would bear me

out, as I thought, in the new character, since we were there denominated Armenians; but my fellow-travellers assured me that the very possession of such documents would prove our real condition, and I destroyed them all, as well as the letters of the Cabool chief, which were alike objectionable. I divested myself, indeed, of all my Persian correspondence, and tore up among the rest many of Runjeet Sing's epistles, which were now in my eyes less acceptable than I thought they would ever prove. During these arrangements, I discovered that the Nazir had no relish for a journey to Koondooz, and seemed disposed to stay behind, almost frantic with despair; but shame is a great promoter of exertion, and I begged he would accompany me, to which he agreed.

The better to understand the critical situation in which we were now placed, I shall give a brief sketch of the disasters which befell Mr. Moorcroft in this part of the country, in the year 1824, from the very personage who now summoned us to Koondooz. On that traveller crossing the mountains, he proceeded to wait on the chief, and having made him some presents suitable to his rank, returned to Khooloom. He had no sooner arrived there, than he received a message from the chief, saying, that some of his soldiers had been wounded, and requesting that he would hasten his return, and bring along with him his medical instruments, and Mr. Guthrie, an Indo-Briton, who had accompanied Mr. Moorcroft as a surgeon. Mr. Moorcroft's own abilities in that capacity were also known, for he had already

given proofs of great skill to these people.   He set
out for Koondooz without suspicion, but found, on
his arrival there, that his surgical services were not
wanted, and it was merely a plan to ensnare him.
The chief ordered him to send for all his party and
baggage, which he did; and, after a month's delay,
he only succeeded in liberating himself, by comply-
ing with the most extravagant demands of Moorad
Beg.   By one means or another, he possessed himself of cash to the value of 23,000 rupees, before
Mr. Moorcroft was permitted to depart; and it
would have been well had the matter here terminated; but the cupidity of the chief had been excited.
It is also said, that he entertained some dread of
Moorcroft's designs, from the arms and two small
field-pieces, which he carried with him for purposes
of protection.   The party prepared to quit Khooloom for Bokhara, but, on the very eve of departure,
were surrounded by 400 horsemen, and again summoned to Koondooz.   It was not now concealed,
that the chief was resolved on seizing the whole of
the property, and putting the party to death.   Mr.
Moorcroft took the only course which could have
ever extricated his party and himself.   In the disguise of a native he fled at night, and after a surprising journey, at length reached Talighan, a town
beyond Koondooz, where a holy man lived, who was
reputed to possess much influence over the conscience of Moorad Beg.   He threw himself at the
feet of this saint, seized the hem of his garment, and
sued for his protection.   " Rise up," said he, " it is
granted; fear nothing."   This good man imme-

diately sent a messenger to Koondooz, to summon
the chief, who appeared in person with the answer.
At his peril, he could not now touch a hair of the
traveller's head; Moorad Beg obeyed, and the holy
man declined to receive the smallest reward for his
services.   After Mr. Moorcroft's flight, the Uzbeks
marched his fellow-traveller, Mr. George Trebeck,
with all the party and property, to Koondooz. Their
anxiety was not allayed till their arrival at that
place, when they heard of the success of Moorcroft,
his safety, and their own.   After these disasters,
Moorcroft pursued his journey into Bokhara, but
unfortunately died on his return, in the following
year, at Andkhooee, about eighty miles from Balkh.
His fellow-traveller, Mr. Trebeck, was unable to
force his way beyond Muzar, in the neighbourhood
of that city, since the chief of Koondooz was resolved on waylaying the party on its return, and
the only safe road to Cabool led by Khooloom,
where they had already encountered such difficulties.   He lingered about Balkh for four or five
months, and died of fever, from which he had been
suffering during the whole of that time.   The Indo-
Briton, Mr. Guthrie, was previously cut off by the
same disease, to which most of their followers also
fell victims. Thus terminated their unfortunate
expedition into Tartary.

On the evening of the 2d of June, I set out on
my journey to Koondooz, which lies higher up the
valley of the Oxus, having previously prevailed on
the custom-house officer, who was a Hindoo, to accompany me. I did not leave Khooloom under

very encouraging circumstances, having just discovered that a Hindoo of Peshawur had *kindly* ap-
prised the authorities of many of our acts, circumstances, and condition, since leaving Hindoostan;
adding, indeed, numerous exaggerations to the narration, in which we were set forth as wealthy individuals, whose bills had even affected the money
market. When beyond the town, we found our
caravan to consist of eight or ten tea merchants, of
Budukhshan and Yarkund, who had disposed of their
property, and were returning to their country. In
our own party there was the Nazir, Cafila-bashee, and
myself, with the Hindoo, whose name was Chumun-
dass, who came unattended. I discovered that this
latter person had a pretty correct knowledge of
our affairs, but I did not assist to fill up the thread
of his discourse, and boldly denominated myself a
Hindoostan Armenian. The name of Englishman,
which had carried us through safely in all other
places, was here replete with danger; since it not
only conveyed notions of great wealth, but a belief
that that can be renewed from the inferior metals.
I had, however, discovered that the Hindoo was a
good man, for his easy manner in searching our
baggage at the caravansary, after our first arrival,
left a favourable impression on my mind; and he
himself declared to the Nazir, that it was no fault
of his that we were dragged to Koondooz, since he
was but a custom-house officer, and obliged to report our arrival. It was evident to me, that an impression might be made on such a person by persuasion and gold, and from his very presence with

us, I construed that money might be his god.   He
and I soon fell into conversation, and I found him
to be a native of Mooltan, who had long resided in
these countries.   I spoke much of India, and its
people and customs; told him that I had seen his
native town, using as much eloquence as I was possessed of to praise its people, and every thing connected with it.   It would have been difficult to
discover, from the varied topics of our conversation,
that the time was one of most anxious suspense.
I ran over the gods of the Hindoo catalogue as far as
I remembered, and produced almost a fever of delight in my associate, who had long ceased to hear
them named in aught but terms of deep reproach.
It was now time to turn my persuasion to account,
and as we talked in the language of India, our conversation was conducted in a dialect foreign to most of
our party, and unheeded by them.   I pointed out
in plain terms to the Hindoo, our forlorn and hope-
less condition, when in the power of a person like
the chief of Koondooz; and I put it to himself, if
our baggage did not testify our poverty.   I then
showed him, that as I belonged to India, I might
one day serve him in that country, and finally
offered to give him a reward in money, and con-
jured him by all his Pantheon to aid us in our difficulties.   When about twelve miles from Khooloom,
we alighted at a village called Ungaruk, to feed our
horses, and it now occurred to me that a truly favourable opportunity to make an escape presented
itself.   There was no guard or escort to attend us,
and the honest Hindoo was far from Khooloom, and

without the means of giving an alarm, whilst the
most moderate speed would carry us beyond Moorad
Beg's frontier, and even to the city of Balkh, before
morning. This feasible plan, however, could not
evidently be put into execution, since Dr. Gerard
would be left at Khooloom, and his safety more than
ever endangered; and it could only now be regretted, that the scheme had not sooner presented
itself. The tone of the Hindoo had, however, reconciled me in a great degree to my situation, and
we again prosecuted our midnight journey, and
renewed our conversation. Before the sun had
risen, I was satisfied that if more honourable motives
had not opened this man's heart, the baser metals
had, and I almost then believed, that we should
triumph over our misfortunes. A new dilemma,
however, now overtook us.

We journeyed till within an hour of dawn by a
dreary road, over two low passes among hills, not
enlivened by a single tree, nor blessed with a drop
of fresh water for forty-five miles. In this dismal
waste, our attention was roused by some lighted
matches in front, that appeared to cross our path,
and which we could not but conclude were robbers,
since this country is infested by banditti. One of
the tea merchants busied himself in tearing up rags,
rubbing them with gunpowder, and lighting them,
literally as *demonstrations* of our force; and judging
by the number of lights that appeared from the
opposite party, they must have done the same,
which might have been amusing enough had we not
construed them into real matchlocks. We had but

one piece, and five or six swords, and could have
made but a sorry resistance; but generalship may
be shown with a small as well as a large band, and
the tea merchant, who seemed accustomed to such
scenes, called on us to dismount, and prepare for the
attack. I will not conceal my feelings at this moment, which were those of vexation and irritability
at so many succeeding disasters. At length we
approached within speaking distance, and one forward youth in our party challenged in Persian, but
he was instantly silenced by an elderly man, who
spoke out in Turkish. The Persian, being the language of commerce, would at once betray our character, and it was proper that we should at least
appear as soldiers. The other party gave no reply,
but veered off towards Khooloom, and we ourselves
took the road of Koondooz, mutually glad, I suppose, to be rid of each other. At the town we discovered that we had drawn up against peaceable
travellers, who must have been as glad as we were to
escape. About eleven in the forenoon we reached
the first fields, and alighted in an orchard of apricots, about twelve miles distant from Koondooz, and
stole a few hours' rest after the night's journey. I
found myself near a hedge of honeysuckles, a bush
that delighted me, and which I had never before
seen in the East. We reached Koondooz at night-
fall, after performing a journey of more than seventy
miles.

We were received on our arrival at the house of
Atmaram, the minister, or, as he is styled, the Dewan
Begee, of Moorad Beg, and sat in his doorway till

he came out. I shall long remember the silent
look which passed between him and the Nazir.
The reception augured well, for the minister conducted us to his house of guests, and fine beds were
brought for our use, but he said nothing on the
subject which most interested us, and we were left
to think about our own affairs. I was now to personate the character of a very poor traveller, and as
it behoved me to act as such, I looked demure, took
up my seat in a corner, fared with the servants, and
treated the Nazir, my master, with great respect;
and evinced, on every occasion, as much humility
as possible. It was prudent, however, that when
questioned we should all tell the same story, and
in a quiet hour, before going to sleep, I gave out
my character as follows. That I was an Armenian
from Lucknow, Sikunder Alaverdi, by profession a
watchmaker, and that, on reaching Cabool, I had
procured intelligence from Bokhara regarding my
relatives in that country, which led me to take a
journey to it, and that I was the more induced to
do so from the protection I should receive from the
Nazir, to whose brother in Cabool I was, in some
manner, a servant. We discarded the subject of
my accompanying the Nazir to Russia, as it might
lead to unpleasant inquiries. I then went on to
state, that Dr. Gerard was a relative of my own,
and that he was left sick at Khooloom, and thus
brought within a short space as much evasion as my
ingenuity could invent. All our party agreed, that
it would be most advisable to take the name of an
Armenian, and entirely discard that of European;

but the Cafila-bashee wished to know how far it was proper to deal in such wholesale lies, which had excited his merriment. I replied in the words of Sady,

> " Durogh i musluhut amez
> Bih uz rastee bu fitna ungez."

" An untruth that preserves peace is better than truth that stirs up troubles." He shook his head in approbation of the moralist's wisdom, and I afterwards found him the most forward in the party to enlarge on my pretended narrative and circumstances. It was agreed that we should first tell the consistent tale to the Hindoo of the custom-house, and then adopt it generally; and the Nazir promised in the course of to-morrow to unfold it to the minister.

The 4th of June slipped away without any adjustment of our concerns, and the Nazir now evinced an imbecility and weakness of intellect, which there was no tolerating. At one moment he was whining out to the visiters a sorrowful detail of our disasters, half in tears; at another time he was sitting erect, with all the pride and self-sufficiency of a man of consequence. In the afternoon he retired to a garden, and returned with a train of followers, as if he had been a grandee instead of a prisoner; nor had he even visited the minister during the day, so that our affairs were no further advanced at night than in the morning. As soon as it was dark, I took an opportunity of pointing out to my friend the great impropriety of such conduct, for

which I encountered, at first, a good share of his
indignation. I told him that his grief and pride
were equally ill-timed and impolitic; that every
hour added to the danger of our situation; and, if
he acted rightly, he would immediately seek an interview with the minister, and endeavour either to
convince or deceive him. You are in the house of
a Hindoo, I added, and you may effect any thing
by throwing yourself upon him, and sitting in
" *dhurna*," that is, without food, till your request is
granted. Your course, continued I, is now the reverse, as you appear to prefer parading in his gardens, and devouring the savoury viands which he
sends us. The earnestness with which I enforced
these views produced a good effect, and the Nazir
sent a messenger to the minister to say, that if he
were the friend of his family, he would not detain
him in this manner, for he had not come as a dog,
to eat his bread, but as an acquaintance, to solicit a
favour. I rejoiced at the decision which he was
now displaying, and called out in accents of delight
from my corner of the apartment, but the Nazir here
requested me to conduct myself with greater dis-
cretion, and remain more peaceable. I deserved the
rebuke, and was thus glad to compromise matters
between us. When the minister received the
message, he called the Nazir to him, and a long
explanation ensued regarding our affairs, which, as
far as I could gather, had left him bewildered as to
their reality. It now appeared, however, that we
were to have his good offices, for it was settled
that we should set out early next morning to the

country seat of the chief, where we should see that personage. The Nazir, as being a man of consequence, was instructed not to appear empty-handed, and the minister, with great kindness, returned a shawl which he had presented to him on his arrival, and desired him to give it and another to the chief of Koondooz.

During the day I had seen a good deal of the people, for there were many visiters, and though most of them courted the great man, a few found their way to me in the corner. Nothing is done in this country without tea, which is handed round at all times and hours, and gives a social character to conversation, which is very agreeable. The Uzbeks drink their tea with salt instead of sugar, and sometimes mix it with fat; it is then called "*keimuk chah*." After each person has had one or two large cups, a smaller one is handed round, made in the usual manner, without milk. The leaves of the pot are then divided among the party, and chewed like tobacco. Many of the strangers evinced an interest in the affairs of Cabool; some spoke of Runjeet Sing, and a few of the English in India. Most of them were merchants, who trade between this and China. They spoke much of their intercourse with that singular nation, and praised the equity and justice that characterised their commercial transactions. These merchants were Tajiks, and natives of Budukhshan, a country on which we now bordered. From these people I heard a variety of particulars regarding the reputed descendants of Alexander the Great, who are yet said to exist in this neighbourhood, and the

valley of the Oxus, as well as the countries near the
head of the Indus.   The subject had occupied much
of my attention, and a tea merchant of our small
caravan had amused me on the road from Khooloom,
with the received lineage of these Macedonians.
He was a priest, and believed Alexander the Great
to be a prophet, which, in his eyes, satisfactorily accounted for the uninterrupted progeny of Greeks,
since no human being could injure so holy a race.
In Koondooz I heard the traditions, which I have
stated at length in the next volume.

Early on the morning of the 5th, we set out on
our journey to Moorad Beg. We found him at the
village of Khanu-abad, which is about fifteen miles
distant, and situated on the brow of the hills above
the fens of Koondooz, enlivened by a rivulet, which
runs briskly past a fort, shaded by trees of the
richest verdure.   We crossed this stream by a
bridge, and found ourselves at the gate of a small,
but neatly fortified dwelling, in which the chief was
now holding his court.   There were about five hundred saddled horses standing at it, and the cavaliers
came and returned in great numbers.   All of them
were booted, and wore long knives, stuck into the
girdle, for swords, some of which were richly
mounted with gold.   We sat down under the wall,
and had ample time to survey the passing scene,
and admire the martial air and pomp of these warlike Uzbeks.   None of the chiefs had more than a
single attendant, and there was great simplicity in
the whole arrangements.   A Hindoo belonging to
the minister went inside to announce our arrival,

and, in the mean time, I rehearsed my tale, and drew on a pair of boots, as well for the uniformity as to hide my provokingly white ankles. My face had long been burned into an Asiatic hue, and from it I feared no detection. The custom-house officer stood by, and I had taken care to have him previously schooled in all the particulars above related. We were summoned, after about an hour's delay, and passed into the first gateway. We here found an area, in which stood the attendants and horses of the chief. Six or eight " yessawuls" or doorkeepers then announced our approach, as we entered the inner building. The Nazir headed the party, and marching up to the chief kissed his hand, and presented his shawls. The Hindoo of the custom-house followed, with two loaves of Russian white sugar, which he gave as his offering; and, in my humble capacity, I brought up the rear, and advanced to make my obeisance, sending forth a loud " sulam alaikoom," and placing my hands between those of the chief, kissed them according to custom, and exclaimed "tukseer," which literally means *offence* or *crime*, and is the usual mode of expressing inferiority. The Uzbek gave a growl of approbation, and rolling on one side, said, " Ay, ay, he understands the sulam." The "yessawul" then gave a signal for my retreat, and I stood at the portal with my hands crossed, among the lower domestics. Moorad Beg was seated on a tiger skin, and stretched out his legs covered with huge boots, in contempt of all Eastern rules of decorum. He sat at the door, for, contrary to the custom of other Asiatic courts,

an Uzbek there takes up his position, and his visiters
pass into the interior of the apartment.   The chief
was a man of tall stature, with harsh Tartar features;
his eyes were small to deformity, his forehead broad
and frowning, and he wanted the beard which
adorns the countenance in most Oriental nations.
He proceeded to converse with the Nazir ; and put
several questions regarding Cabool, and then on his
own affairs, during which he spoke of our poverty
and situation.   Then came the Hindoo of the custom-house with my tale.   " Your slave," said he,
" has examined the baggage of the two Armenians,
and found them to be poor travellers. It is in every
person's mouth that they are Europeans (Firingees),
and it would have placed me under your displeasure
had I let them depart ; I have, therefore, brought
one of them to know your orders."   The moment was
critical ; and the chief gave me a look, and said in
Turkish,— " Are you certain he is an Armenian?"
A second assurance carried conviction, and he issued
an order for our safe conduct beyond the frontier.
I stood by, and saw his secretary prepare and seal
the paper ; and I could have embraced him when he
pronounced it finished.

It was now necessary to retreat with caution, and
evince as little of the joy which we felt as possible.
The chief had not considered me even worthy of a
question ; and my garb, torn and threadbare, could
give him no clue to my condition.   His attendants
and chiefs, however, asked me many questions ; and
his son, a youth with the unpromising name of
Atalik, sent for me to know the tenets of the Ar-

menians — if they said prayers, believed in Mahommed, and would eat with the " Faithful." I replied, that we were "people of the book," and had our prophets; but to the home question of our credence in Mahommed, I said, that the New Testament had been written before that personage (on whom be peace) had appeared on earth. The lad turned to the Hindoos who were present, and said, "Why, this poor man is better than you." I then narrated my story to the prince with more confidence, and kissed the young chief's hand for the honour he had done in listening to it.

We were soon outside the fortification, and across the bridge; but the heat of the sun was oppressive, and we alighted at a garden to pass a few hours. The Hindoos got us refreshment; and, yet enacting the part of a poor man, I had a portion of the Nazir's pillao sent to me, and ate heartily by myself. In the afternoon we returned to Koondooz; and the good Hindoo of the custom-house told me by the way, that the Uzbeks were bad people, and did not deserve truth. " Whoever you be, therefore, you are now safe." I did most sincerely rejoice at the success of the journey; for if the chief had suspected our true character for a moment, we should have been deprived of all our money, subjected to great vexation, and, perhaps, been confined for months in the unhealthy climate of Koondooz. We must, at all events, have abandoned every hope of prosecuting our journey; and assumed poverty would have soon availed us little; since there were not wanting persons who had a shrewd guess at our concerns. The

whole affair exhibits a simplicity on the part of the
Uzbeks which is hardly to be credited; but no
people are more simple. The veteran Cafila-bashee
who accompanied me, was taken for my fellow-
traveller, Dr. Gerard, though a grave, grey-bearded,
demure Moslem; and the whole court of Moorad
Beg were left in ignorance of what many of the
Hindoo community knew as well as ourselves,—
that we were Europeans.

At Koondooz we alighted in our old quarters, at
the house of the minister. The town is situated
in a valley, surrounded on all sides by hills, except
the north, where the Oxus flows at a distance of
about forty miles. It is watered by two rivers,
which join north of the town. The climate is so
insalubrious, that there is a proverb among the
people, which runs as follows:—"If you wish to
die, go to Koondooz." The greater part of the
valley is so marshy, that the roads are constructed
on piles of wood, and run through the rankest
weeds; yet wheat and barley are produced, as also
rice, in the places which are not entirely inundated.
The heat is described as intolerable, yet snow lies
for three months in the year. Koondooz has at
one time been a large town, but its population does
not now exceed 1500 souls; and no person makes
it a residence who can live in any other place,
though it be yet the market town of the neighbourhood. The chief never visits it but in winter. It
has a fort, surrounded by a ditch, which is a place
of strength: the walls are constructed of sun-dried
brick; and such is the heat, that they crumble

under the sun's rays, and require constant repair. The great mountains of Hindoo Koosh lie in sight, south of Koondooz, covered with snow: the neighbouring hills are low, creeping ridges, covered with grass and flowers, but destitute of trees or brushwood. A little further up the valley the climate becomes much more genial; and the people speak in raptures of the groves and rivulets, the fruits and flowers, of Budukhshan. The ruler of Koondooz, Mahommed Moorad Beg, is an Uzbek of the tribe of Kudghun, who has but lately risen into power. He is now encroaching in every direction, and possesses all the valley of the Oxus; and very lately had sovereignty over Balkh. He yet stamps his coin with the general appellation of that capital, the " Mother of Cities." He is quite independent, and now rules all the countries immediately north of Hindoo Koosh.

We could not quit Koondooz without the formal sanction of the minister; and waited for his pleasure till three in the afternoon. He then sent a *khillut*, or dress of honour, to the Nazir; and a tunic, with some other articles of dress, to me and the Cafila-bashee; for we could not, it seems, leave the house of guests of so great a person without some mark of his favour. I, however, discovered that the Nazir, now that he had recovered from his fright, was resolved on profiting to the utmost by the minister's bounty; and had set on foot a negotiation, by means of one of his servants, to get as large a present as possible. I was horrified at

such conduct, as it might again involve us in difficulty; but the mean fellow succeeded, and we
were all clothed in dresses of honour, as I have
stated.   He, indeed, got a horse in addition.   It is
necessary to mention, that the minister was con-
templating a journey to Cabool, where he hoped
for some good offices from the Nazir's family.   I,
who was but a spectator of events, enjoyed the
display of character which they brought forth.   We
dressed ourselves in our new robes, and saddled at
three P. M.; nor did we halt till we reached Khooloom on the following morning,—a distance of more
than seventy miles,—worn out with fatigue, after
being seated on one horse for twenty hours.   It is
singular, that I rode the very same animal which
had been given to me by the brother of the Peshawur chief; and which, it will be remembered, he
had forced upon me, as it might prove of service
in my difficulties among the Uzbeks; a horse of the
same breed having formerly availed Mr. Moorcroft
when he escaped to Talighan.   How singular the
coincidence! how much more singular the gift!
It was with heartfelt satisfaction that I again found
myself with Dr. Gerard and our own party, and
witnessed the universal joy.   I could detail to them
my adventures at Koondooz, but could not relieve
myself by sleep from the fatigue which I had undergone.   I have found that, after a certain period,
the frame is beyond sleep, which only returns to
refresh and recruit the system after the body has
been rubbed and rested, and the stomach refreshed
by tea, the most cheering beverage to the way-

worn traveller.   Among the Uzbeks, we frequently lived upon it.

Khooloom is a much more pleasant place than Koondooz, and has many beautiful gardens, and fine fruit. Its apricots, cherries, and mulberries, were now ripe and tempting; but it was not prudent to incur further risks, with such an example as that of poor Moorcroft before us, and we prepared for a start on the following morning.   We showed the order of Moorad Beg to the Wallee, or governor, and he appointed the prescribed escort to attend us. During night, I transferred a portion of my gold to the Hindoo of the custom-house, for his eminent services; and, to elude discovery, paid it through the hands of the Nazir: but my astonishment may be conceived, when I discovered in the morning, that, out of twenty gold pieces, he had pocketed fifteen, and put off the Hindoo with five! It was no time for explanation, and, after ascertaining the correctness of the fact, I paid it a second time, and left Khooloom in the company of our avaricious friend the Nazir. This *honest* person made us stop by the way, to give him an opportunity of reading a chapter of the Koran, with which he always travelled; suspending it in a bag from the pommel of his saddle, and pulling it forth at stated hours. Dr. Gerard and myself preceded our people, who followed with a caravan, and reached Muzar in the afternoon of the 8th, a distance of thirty miles beyond Khooloom.

The country between these places is barren and dreary; and the road leads over a low pass, called

Abdoo, which is the resort of robbers from every quarter; since the whole of the neighbouring chiefs plunder on it. Our escort of Uzbeks reconnoitred the pass, from which Muzar is visible about fifteen miles off, and then left us to journey by ourselves. These men were speaking of the spoil which they themselves had captured a few days before, and I cannot say that I regretted their departure. The ruins of aqueducts and houses prove that this country has been at one time peopled; but it is now destitute of water, and, consequently, of inhabitants. On our route we saw a very magnificent *mirage* on our right hand, — a snaky line of vapour, as large as the Oxus itself, and which had all the appearance of that river. It mocked our parched tongues; for we had expended the contents of the leathern bottles which we always carried, long before we reached the village.

Muzar contains about 500 houses, and is within the limits of the canal of Balkh. It can muster about 1000 horse, and is independent of that city and Khooloom. It belongs to a priest, or Mootuwullee, who superintends the worship at a shrine of great sanctity, which is here dedicated to Ali. Muzar means a tomb; and that of this place consists of two lofty cupolas, built by Sultan Ali Meerza of Herat, about 350 years ago. I visited the shrine, went round it as a pilgrim, and gave my mite in that character. If I could not believe the legends of this pretended sanctuary, and join in the devotions of the people, I could offer up thanks in my own way for our late escape. The congregation at evening prayers was numerous; and the priests sat at the door of the shrine, and divided the proceeds of the day, copper by copper, among certain families, who are entitled to it by hereditary right. A priest came up, and asked me why I did not pray with the rest. I told him I was not a Mahommedan; yet they did not object to my entering the shrine; though I ought not to have risked a trial. There was no object of curiosity to be seen that differed from similar Mahommedan buildings. In the evening, it is illuminated by lights from brass chandeliers.

Muzar is the place where Mr. Trebeck, the last of Moorcroft's unfortunate party, expired. One of our companions, a Hajee, attended him on his death-bed, and conducted us to the spot in which he is laid; which is in a small burying-ground, westward of the town, under a mulberry tree, that was now shedding its fruit upon the grave. This young man has left a most favourable impression of his good qualities throughout the country which we passed; and I could not but feel for his melancholy fate. After burying his two European fellow travellers, he sank, at an early age, after four months' suffering, in a far distant country, without a friend, without assistance, and without consolation. The whole of his property was either embezzled by a priest who accompanied the party, or confiscated by *the holy men* of this sanctuary, who yet retain it: it consisted of some valuable horses, camp equipage, money, and a few printed books. All the manuscripts of Moorcroft's journey into

Bokhara have been fortunately recovered; and, in justice to an amiable man, who devoted his life to a passion for travel and research, they ought, long ere this, to have been published. The money did not fall into the hands of the people of Muzar: it may be traced, but I cannot say found.

On the morning of the 9th of June, we entered the ancient city of Balkh, which is in the dominions of the King of Bokhara; and wound among its extensive ruins for nearly three miles before reaching a caravansary in the inhabited corner of this once proud "Mother of Cities" (Am ool Bulad). On the way we were met by two police officers, Toork-muns, who searched us for our money, that they might tax it. I told them at once that we had twenty gold tillas* each; and they demanded one in twenty, according to their law, since we were not Mahommedans. We complied, and took a sealed receipt; but they returned in the evening, and demanded as much more, since we avowed ourselves as Europeans, and were not subject to a Mahommedan ruler. I discovered that their position was legal, and paid the sum; but I had a greater store of gold than that about my own person. The people gave us no molestation; and our baggage and books were freely submitted to the eye and astonishment of the police. We should, of course, have concealed them, had it been in our power. One of the most satisfactory feelings which we experienced on our arrival at Balkh, was the

* A tilla is worth 13s.

sure relief from the hands of our enemy at Koondooz, and, I may now add, from the tricks of our
conductor, the Nazir; for he had lately adopted so
unworthy a line of conduct, that we resolved no
longer to place reliance upon him. As we were
now in the territories of a king, we could tell him
our opinions; though it had, perhaps, been more
prudent to keep them to ourselves. If experience
had proved the Nazir unworthy of our confidence,
Hyat, the Cafila-bashee, had fully established himself in our good graces by his sensible and faithful
conduct. He deprecated the meanness of the
Nazir, and evinced more detestation of it than ourselves. Hyat was a man of no small penetration;
and I was a little staggered at a conversation which
passed between us as we approached Balkh, when
discussing the motives which had led to our undertaking such a journey. I stated that Bokhara lay
on the road to Europe: but Hyat rejoined, that
the Firingees sought for information on all countries, and that the untimely death of Mr. Moorcroft had withheld any correct knowledge of Toorkistan; and we had, probably, been despatched, in
a quiet way, to procure it, as much of that gentleman's misfortunes were to be referred to the
mode in which he had travelled. I smiled at the
shrewd guess of the man, gave an ironical shout of
" Barikilla!" (Bravo!), and praised his sagacity:
but Hyat and I had become good friends; and we
had not only nothing to fear, but much to hope,
from his kind offices.

CHAP. VIII.

BALKH, — AND CONTINUATION OF THE JOURNEY TO BOKHARA.

WE continued at Balkh for three days, to examine the remains of this once proud city. Its ruins extend for a circuit of about twenty miles, but present no symptoms of magnificence ; they consist of fallen mosques and decayed tombs, which have been built of sun-dried brick ; nor are any of these ruins of an age prior to Mahommedanism, though Balkh boasts an antiquity beyond most other cities in the globe. By the Asiatics it is named the " Mother of Cities," and said to have been built by Kyamoors, the founder of the Persian monarchy. After the conquest of Alexander the Great, it flourished under the name of Bactria, with a dynasty of Grecian kings. In the third century of the Christian era, " Artaxerxes had his authority solemnly acknowledged in a great assembly held at Balkh, in Khorasan." * It continued subject to the Persian empire, and the residence of the Archimagus, or head of the Magi, till the followers of Zoroaster were overthrown by the inroads of the caliphs. Its inhabitants were butchered in cold blood by

* Gibbon, c. viii.

Jenghis Khan; and, under the house of Timour, it became a province of the Mogul empire. It formed the government of Aurungzebe in his youth; and was at last invaded by the great Nadir. On the establishment of the Dooranee monarchy, after his death, it fell into the hands of the Afghans, and within the last eight years has been seized by the King of Bokhara, whose deputy now governs it. Its present population does not amount to 2000 souls; who are chiefly natives of Cabool, and the remnant of the Kara noukur, a description of militia established here by the Afghans. There are also a few Arabs. The Koondooz chief has marched off a great portion of its population, and constantly threatens the city; which has driven the inhabitants to the neighbouring villages. In its wide area, the city appears to have enclosed innumerable gardens; which *increased its size without adding to its population*: and from the frail materials of which its buildings are constructed, the foundations being only brick, I doubt if Balkh ever were a substantial city. There are three large colleges, of a handsome structure, now in a state of decay, with their cells empty. A mud wall surrounds a portion of the town; but it must be of a late age, since it excludes the ruins on every side for about two miles. The citadel, or *ark*, on the northern side, has been more solidly constructed; yet it is a place of no strength. There is a stone of white marble in it, which is yet pointed out as the throne of Kai Kaoos, or Cyrus. Balkh stands on a plain, about six miles from the hills, and not upon them, as is

erroneously represented. There are many ine-
qualities in the surrounding fields, which may arise
from ruins and rubbish. The city itself, like Ba-
bylon, has become a perfect mine of bricks for the
surrounding country. These are of an oblong
shape, rather square. Most of the old gardens are
now neglected and overgrown with weeds; the
aqueducts are dried up; but there are clumps of
trees in many directions. The people have a great
veneration for this city; believing that it was one
of the earliest peopled portions of the earth, and
that the re-occupation of it will be one of the signs
of the approaching end of the world. The fruit
of Balkh is most luscious; particularly the apricots,
which are nearly as large as apples. They are
almost below value, for 2000 of them were to be
purchased for a rupee; and, with iced water, they
are indeed luxuries, though dangerous ones. Snow
is brought in quantities from the mountains south
of Balkh, about twenty miles distant, and sold for a
trifle throughout the year.

The climate of Balkh is very insalubrious, but
not disagreeable. In June, the thermometer did
not rise above 80°, and the next month is the
hottest in the year. The wheat ripens in that
month, which makes the harvest fifty days later
than Peshawur. Its unhealthiness is ascribed to
the water, which is so mixed up with earth and
clay as to look like a puddle after rain. The soil
is of a greyish colour, like pipe-clay, and very rich;
when wet, it is slimy. The crops are good; the
wheat stalks grow as high as in England, and do

not present the stunted stubble of India. In Balkh, the water has been distributed, with great labour, by aqueducts from a river. Of these there are said to be no less than eighteen; but many are not now discoverable. They frequently overflow, and leave marshes, which are rapidly dried up under the sun's rays. This seems to account for the diseases of the place. All old cities and ruins are, perhaps, more or less unhealthy. It is not probable, however, that so many kings and princes would have patronised a site which was always unfavourable to the health of man; and Balkh itself is not situated in a country naturally marshy, but on a gentle slope which sinks towards the Oxus, about 1800 feet above the level of the sea. All the water of its river is lost long before reaching that stream.

At Balkh, I used every endeavour to collect ancient coins, which could not fail to be valuable in such classic ground. They brought me several copper ones, similar to those which I found at Manikyala in the Punjab, representing a full-length figure, holding a censer or pot in his right hand, and dressed in a high cap; this, I believe, determines the whole series of them to be Persian. It is well known that India formed one of the satrapies of Darius; and we read of a connexion between it and Persia in ancient times, which will perhaps clear up the history of these coins. The execution is rude; and, as they differ from one another, it would appear they are rather medals than coins. I have, in the succeeding volume, given accurate engravings of these relics. Those

who feel interested in the subject will find that
some of a like description have been discovered in
India, and mentioned in the Transactions of the
Asiatic Society of Bengal. Among the coins which
I examined at Balkh, there were many Cufic and
Arabic, and a whole series of those of the emperors
of Hindostan. One gold piece of Shah Jehan spoke
well for the execution of his age. It is remarkable,
that, in the countries north of Hindoo Koosh, the
current coinage of the present time is that of the
emperors of Delhi, who ruled prior to the age of
Nadir.

On the 12th of June, the caravan arrived from
Khooloom with our people, and we prepared to accompany it in its onward journey to Bokhara. For
three days we had been living with our friend the
Cafila-bashee, who managed to get rice and meat
for us from the bazaar; but we made a bungling
matter of our cookery. This was but a minor inconvenience, and not without a hope of remedy.
It was now necessary, however, to give our Cafila-
bashee leave to return to Cabool; since an Afghan
would be of little use among Uzbeks. I was, indeed, sorry to part with Hyat, as his temper and
disposition were admirably fitted for managing the
people, and he had friends every where who es-
teemed and respected him. I feared we should
miss the man who used to get us food and lodging,
when procurable, and tell lies by wholesale regarding our character when necessary. We made him
presents in return for his good offices;—their
value far surpassed his expectations; so that he

was more than happy. I gave him a note of hand
expressive of our sense of his services; and he ran
about in every direction to assist us when setting
out, took the Cafila-bashee of the new caravan aside,
and pointed out to him how much it would be his
interest to serve us: he waited till the caravan departed; and seeing us in our panniers (the new
mode of travelling on camels), he bade us farewell,
consigned us to God, and left us to plod our way.
As some proof of this man's honesty, I may mention, that on his return to Cabool he found a knife,
which we had left in a caravansary; this he despatched by a trusty man who was coming to
Bokhara, along with a letter expressive of his remembrance of us, and thanks for our kindness.

The caravan assembled outside the city, and near
to another melancholy spot, the grave of poor
Moorcroft, which we were conducted to see. Mr.
Guthrie lies by his side. It was a bright moonlight
night, but we had some difficulty in finding the spot.
At last, under a mud wall which had been purposely
thrown over, our eyes were directed to it. The
bigoted people of Balkh refused permission to the
travellers being interred in their burial-ground;
and only sanctioned it near the city, upon condition
of its being concealed, lest any Mahommedan
might mistake it for a tomb of one of the true believers, and offer up a blessing as he passed it. It
was impossible to view such a scene at the dead of
night, without many melancholy reflections. A
whole party buried within twelve miles of each
other, held out small encouragement to us, who

were pursuing the same track, and led on by nearly similar motives. It was fortunate that the living experienced no such contempt as the dead, for we received no slight from any one, though our creed and our nation were not concealed. The corpse of Moorcroft was brought from Andkhooee, where he perished, at a distance from his party. He was attended by a few followers, all of whom were plundered by the people. If he died a natural death, I do not think he sank without exciting suspicions; he was unaccompanied by any of his European associates or confidential servants, and brought back lifeless on a camel, after a short absence of eight days; the health of Mr. Trebeck did not admit of his examining the body.

We left Balkh at midnight, with a small caravan of twenty camels; and now exchanged our horses for these useful animals. Two panniers, called "*kujawas*," are thrown across each camel: the Doctor weighed against an Afghan; and I was balanced by my Hindoostanee servant. At first, this sort of conveyance was most inconvenient; for the panniers were but four feet long and two and a half wide, and it required some suppleness and ingenuity to stow away a body of five feet nine inches in such a space, tumbled in like a bale of goods. Custom soon reconciled us to the jolting of the camels and the smallness of the conveyance; and it was a great counterbalance to discover that we could read and even note without observation.

A march of thirty miles brought us to the limits of the water of Balkh, through a rich country, every where intersected by canals. Such is their effect on the temperature, that the thermometer fell below 52° in the morning; though more than two thirds of the land lay waste. Our camels revelled on a thorny shrub called "chooch" or "zooz" by the natives. The language of the most graphic writer could not delineate this country with greater exactness than Quintus Curtius has done, and I marked the following passage on the spot:—" The face of Bactriana is contrastingly diversified: in many places, luxuriant trees and vines yield fruit of fine growth and flavour; numerous springs (canals?) irrigate a rich soil. The more generous land is sowed with corn; other fields afford pasturage. Further, great part of the country is deformed by tracts of barren sand, in which a mournful absence of vegetation refuses nourishment to man. When the winds blow from the Indian Ocean, the floating dust is swept into masses. The cultivated portion of the country is crowded with inhabitants, and well stocked with horses. Bactra, the capital, is situated under Mount Paropamisus. The river Bactrus, which washes its walls, gives name to the city and province." * The trees, fruit, and corn of Balkh have a great celebrity; its horses are equally well known. Though it has no springs, and a river does not now pass its walls, the country is intersected by the canals of one that flows from the neighbouring mountains, the water of which is artificially divided before reaching the town.

* Quintus Curtius, lib. vii. cap. 4.

On the 14th of June we entered the desert, and
travelled all night on our way to the Oxus. We
left the great high road from Balkh to Kilef, the
usual ferry, from a fear of robbers, and journeyed
westward. At daylight we halted, and had an insight of what we were to expect in the deserts of
Tartary. The mountains of Hindoo Koosh had entirely disappeared below the horizon, and a wide
plain like an ocean of sand surrounded us on all
sides. Here and there were a few round huts, or,
as they are called, "*khirghas*," the abode of the
erratic Toorkmuns. The inhabitants were few in
number; at first sight, they present a fierce and ter-
rible aspect to a stranger. We alighted near one
of their settlements; and they strutted about, dressed in huge black sheepskin caps, but did not molest
us; and I have now only to introduce our new acquaintances, since we shall have ample opportunities
to speak of them hereafter. We pitched our camp
in their desert, and found a scanty supply of water
that had trickled down thus far from the canals of
Balkh. We had now no tent, nor shelter of any
kind, but a coarse single blanket, which we used to
stretch across two sets of panniers. Even this
flimsy covering sheltered us from the sun's rays;
and at night we had it removed, and slept in the
open air. Our food now consisted of bread and tea;
for the Toorkmuns often object to dispose of their
sheep, since it injures their estate; and we could
only look on their countless flocks with a desire to
possess a single lamb, which often could not be gratified. Europeans, who are so much accustomed to

animal food, are sensible of the change to a diet of bread; but we found it tolerably nutritive, and had much refreshment from tea, which we drank with it at all hours. I found that abstinence from wine and spirits proved rather salutary than otherwise; and I doubt if we could have undergone the vicissitudes of climate, had we used such stimulants.

It appeared that we had not altogether escaped the tracks of plunderers by our diversion from the main road, and we therefore hired a guard of Toorkmuns to escort us to the Oxus, now only a march distant. We saddled at sunset; and after a journey of fifteen hours, and a distance of thirty miles, found ourselves on the banks of that great river, which I gazed on with feelings of pure delight. It now ran before us in all the grandeur of solitude, as a reward for the toil and anxiety which we had experienced in approaching it. It might not have been prudent to commit ourselves to a guard of Toorkmuns in such a desert; but they conducted us in safety, and made few or no inquiries about us. They spoke nothing but Turkish. They rode good horses, and were armed with a sword and long spear. They were not encumbered with shields and powder-horns, like other Asiatics; and a few only had matchlocks. They beguiled the time by singing together, in a language that is harsh but sonorous. They appeared to me the *beau idéal* of light dragoons; and their caps gave to the whole of them a becoming uniformity. They never use more than a single rein, which sets off their horses to advantage. Some of the Toorkmun chiefs, I afterwards observed, had rosettes and loose pieces of leather ornamented with gold and silver, which fell behind the ear of the animal, giving his head a showy and becoming appearance. Till within a mile and a half of the river, we had traversed a peculiarly inhospitable and unpromising country, quite destitute of water; and its stunted herbage either protruded from mounds of loose drifting sand, or made its appearance through sheets of hard clay. I shall long remember our dreary advance on the Oxus, and the wild society in which it was performed,

> ———— " of those
> Who dwell beyond the everlasting snows
> Of Hindoo Koosh, in stormy freedom bred."

We halted on the banks of the river, near the small village of Khoju Salu. The vicinity of the Oxus is intersected by aqueducts for nearly two miles, but by no means industriously cultivated; it was a better sign of a more tranquil country, to see each peasant's house standing at a distance from that of his neighbour, and in the midst of his own fields. We were detained for two days on the banks of the river, till it came to our turn of the ferry-boat; which transferred our caravan, on the 17th, to the northern bank, or the country of Mawurool nuhr, a part of Tartary (Tatary, according to our nomenclature), but, more correctly speaking, Toorkistan. The river was upwards of 800 yards wide, and about 20 feet deep. Its waters were loaded with clay, and the current passed on at the rate of about three

miles and a half an hour. This river is called Ji-
hoon and Amoo by the Asiatics.

The mode in which we passed the Oxus was singular, and, I believe, peculiar to this part of the
country. We were drawn by a pair of horses, who
were yoked to the boat, on each bow, by a rope
fixed to the hair of the mane. The bridle is then
put on as if the horse were to be mounted ; the boat
is pushed into the stream, and, without any other
assistance than the horses, is ferried directly across
the most rapid channel. A man on board holds the
reins of each horse, and allows them to play loosely
in the mouth, urging him to swim ; and, thus guided,
he advances without difficulty. There is not an oar
to aid in impelling the boat ; and the only assistance
from those on board consists in manœuvring a rude
rounded pole at the stern, to prevent the vessel
from wheeling in the current, and to give both horses
clear water to swim. They sometimes use four
horses ; and in that case, two are fixed at the stern.
These horses require no preparatory training, since
they indiscriminately yoke all that cross the river.
One of the boats was dragged over by the aid of
two of our jaded ponies ; and the vessel which attempted to follow us without them, was carried so
far down the stream as to detain us a whole day on
the banks, till it could be brought up to the camp
of our caravan. By this ingenious mode, we crossed
a river nearly half a mile wide, and running at the
rate of three miles and a half an hour, in fifteen
minutes of actual sailing ; but there was some detention from having to thread our way among the sand-

banks that separated the branches. I see nothing to prevent the general adoption of this expeditious mode of passing a river, and it would be an invaluable improvement below the Ghats of India. I had never before seen the horse converted to such a use; and in my travels through India I had always considered that noble animal as a great incumbrance in crossing a river.

After our passage of the Oxus, we commenced our journey towards Bokhara, and halted at Shorkudduk, where there were no inhabitants, and about fifteen or twenty brackish wells. The water was clear, but bitter and ill tasted. Our manner of journeying now became more agreeable. We started about five or six P. M., and travelled till eight or nine next morning. The stages exceeded twenty-five miles; but camels cannot march for a continuance beyond that distance, on account of heat. At night, they move steadily forward at the rate of two miles an hour, and are urged on by a pair of tinkling bells hung from the breast or ears of the favourite, that precedes each " *kittar*," or string. The sound is enlivening and cheerful; and when their jingle ceases by a halt of the caravan, the silence which succeeds, in the midst of an uninhabited waste, is truly striking. At the setting and rising of the sun, the caravan halts to admit of the performance of prayers; and the sonorous sound of " Ullaho Akbar" summons all "true believers" to the presence of God. They stroke down their beards, and, with their eyes turned towards Mecca, perform the genuflexions prescribed by their creed. We sat and looked at the solemnity, without suf-

fering either taunts or abuse; and experienced a
toleration that would have done credit to the most
civilised country of Europe. In the society of a
caravan, there is much good fellowship, and many
valuable lessons for a selfish man. It levels all
distinctions between master and servant; and where
both share every thing, it is impossible to be singular. Our servants now ate from the same dishes
as ourselves. An Asiatic will never take a piece
of bread, without offering a portion of it to those
near him. The Indian Mahommedans were surprised at their brethren in the faith, who gave us a
share of their food, and freely partook of our own.

We next reached Kiz Kooduk, or the Maiden's
Well, as the words signify in Turkish. I blessed
the young lady who had dug it; for we had suffered much from the want of water, and now found
a beautiful well in the midst of some hundred
others, all of which, as well as the springs we met
on the road, were salt. It is said to have been dug
by a virgin. Yesterday we had no water; to-day
we had no wood; and it was only by collecting the
dung of the camels that we could boil the water
for our tea. Who could have imagined that we
were approaching those paradises of the East, Samarcand and Bokhara? We had been travelling
among low waving hills, or rather ridges, destitute
of trees or wood; covered with a dry kind of grass,
growing on a soil that was hard and gravelly. The
wells were about eighteen feet deep. At different
intervals on the road, we saw *robats* or caravansaries, which have been constructed with large

covered cisterns, called " surdabas," or water-coolers, to collect the rain water in behalf of travellers. The whole of these were now empty. The climate was dry and variable ; and the thermometer, which stood at 103° in the day, fell to 60° at night, which was cool and delightful. In this country, a steady wind generally blows from the north. Our day broke at twenty minutes after three, and we had a long and refreshing twilight, which compensated in some degree for the scorching heat of the sun.

One of the tea merchants of the caravan paid us frequent visits at our halting-ground, and we soon became intimate with him. He was a Khwaju, as the followers of the first caliphs are called, and was both a priest and a merchant. He appeared pleased with our society ; and we drank tea together on the banks of the Oxus. We told him our true story. From our intercourse with this Khwaju, I gained some insight into the state of literature among the Uzbeks. I gave him the perusal of a small Persian work, the " Memoirs of King Shooja of Cabool." The book was written by the King himself; and gives a detail of his life and adventures, in a simple style, free from extracts of the Koran, metaphors, and other extravagancies of Oriental authors. It also dispenses with any mention of those miracles which never fail to be wrought in favour of an Eastern despot, according to the accounts of historians. The work, in fact, was what would be called by us an interesting detail of events. The Khwaju returned it to me a few days after, saying that it was a dry production, not enlivened by the

fear of God, or a remembrance of the Prophet, but
entirely occupied with matters of a personal nature.
Since that was the object of the book, he could not
have given it higher praise. The Khwaju is not
the only person who has found such faults in similar
works; for a Right Reverend Divine *, who furnished us with so admirable and interesting a journal
of his travels in India, has been blamed by some
for its worldliness. Since literature among the
Mahommedans is exclusively confined to the moollahs, we should be the less surprised at their finding
fault with a work that had not a due sprinkling of
the literature of their order.

Near the country we now entered, there is a
tribe of Uzbeks, called Lakay, who are celebrated
for their plundering propensities. A saying among
them curses every one who dies in his bed, since a
true Lakay should lay down his life in a foray or
" chupao." I was told that the females sometimes
accompany their husbands on these marauding expeditions; but it is stated, with greater probability,
that the young ladies plunder the caravans which
pass near their home. This tribe lives near Hissar,
which is a romantic neighbourhood; since, besides
the Amazons of Lakay, three or four neighbouring
tribes claim a descent from Alexander the Great.

Our next march, to a place called Kirkinjuk,
brought us to a settlement of the Toorkmuns, and
the country changed from hillocks to mounds of
bare sand. The well water was now double the

* Bishop Heber.

depth, or about thirty-six feet from the surface.
The flocks of the Toorkmuns cropped the scanty
grass around us; and horses, camels, and sheep,
roamed about loose, as in a state of nature. A
shepherd who tended these flocks lingered long
near our encampment. He was an unfortunate
Persian, who had been captured about eight years
before near Meshid, along with 300 other persons,
and now sighed for his liberty, that he might visit
the famous shrine of Imam Ruza in his own holy
city. His name had been Mahommed; it was
changed to Doulut, or the Rich — a singular cognomen for a poor wretch who tended sheep in a
desert under a scorching sun. He gave us a favourable account of his treatment by his master,
who intended to purchase a wife for him; but he
had no hope of his liberty. The poor man prowled
all day about our caravan, and expressed many a
wish to accompany it; he had, however, been purchased for thirty pieces of gold, and if he had no
riches of his own, he yet formed a part of those of
his owner.

I overheard a controversy among some of the
merchants regarding Christians, whether they were
or were not infidels (Kaffirs), and, as may be imagined, was not a little anxious to hear the decision.
One person, who was a priest, maintained that they
could not be infidels, since they were " people of
the book." When it was asserted that they did
not believe in Mahommed, the subject became more
complicated. I learned, from their conversation,
that a universal belief prevails among the Mahom-

medans of the consummation of their creed by
Christians. Christ, they say, lives, but Mahommed
is dead; yet their deductions are curious, since
Jesus is to descend from the fourth heaven, and
the whole world will be *Mahommedanised!* A singular instance of blasphemy was related by this
party. " A native of Budukhshan blackened his
face, and sallied forth into the highway, telling all
the passengers that, as he had prayed to God
without any good effect for eight years, he now
appeared to disgrace the Creator in the eyes of
his creatures." Fanatical madman!

In the afternoon of the 20th, as we approached
the town of Kurshee, we descried at sunset, far to
the eastward of us, a stupendous range of mountains covered with snow. As this was in the
middle of summer, their elevation must be greater
than is assigned to any range north of Hindoo
Koosh. They were at a distance of perhaps 150
miles, and we could distinguish them but faintly
on the following morning, and never saw them
again. At daylight we came to the oäsis of Kurshee, a cheering scene, after having marched from
the Oxus, a distance of eighty-five miles, without
seeing a tree. On nearing this town, we entered a
flat and champaign country, which was entirely
desolate, till within the limits of the river: tortoises,
lizards, and ants, appeared to be its only inhabitants. As a welcome to this first Tartar town, one
of our friends in the caravan sent us, *as a delicacy,*
two bowls of " keimuk chah," or tea, on which the
fat floated so profusely that I took it for soup; but

it was really tea mixed with salt and fat, and is the morning beverage of the Uzbeks. Custom never reconciled me to this tea, but our Afghan fellow-travellers spoke of it in loud strains of praise; nor did the manner in which our gift speedily disappeared, when handed over to them, at all belie their taste.

We had looked forward to our arrival at an inhabited place with much delight, after our marches in the desert; but we here experienced that misfortune to which travellers are more liable than other people,—sickness. Some of us had been complaining for a few days previously, and immediately on our arrival I was prostrated by a severe attack of intermittent fever; the surveyor was seized at the same time; and, on the following day, the doctor and two others of our party were ill. The merchants and people of the caravan likewise suffered, and we came to the conclusion that we must have caught the disease at Balkh, or on the banks of the Oxus. The terror of the Balkh fever had vanished, and we had not feared the seeds of disease. We adopted the usual treatment of India,—taking emetics and medicine; and, in my own case, I followed them up with quinine, which had the most happy effect. In three days my teeth ceased to chatter, and my body to burn; but the doctor, who persisted in treating himself with calomel *secundum artem*, was not so fortunate, and he did not shake off the disease till long after we had left the country. One of our fellow-travellers, a merchant of Budukhshan, who had endeared himself to us, died on his reaching Bokhara. Our chances of life were far less than his: he offered up sacrifices, and refused quinine. Our stay at Kurshee was prolonged for three or four days, during which we lived in a garden under some trees, and without other shelter. It was a miserable hospital; but we quenched our parching thirst, under a thermometer at 108°, with sherbet of cherries, cooled by ice, which we here found in great plenty.

In the midst of our indisposition, we were disturbed by some vexatious rumours regarding ourselves. We were informed that the king had heard of our approach, and not only had prohibited our entering the city of Bokhara, but objected to our prosecuting the journey. This tale was further exaggerated by the mention of certain yessawuls or officers of the court having been sent to seize us, which we credited the more readily, since these persons paid us no less than three visits for the examination of our baggage, which in nowise contributed to our repose. We had become pretty well accustomed to rumours of every kind, for an European who travels in Eastern countries must expect many alarms. I resolved to take immediate steps to counteract any bad impression towards us, and forthwith addressed the minister of Bokhara, and despatched Sooliman, an Afghan, one of our own people, with the letter. I approached the minister with all the forms of Eastern etiquette and eloquence; and, as we were in a bigoted country, denominated him " the Tower of Islam; the Gem of the Faith, the Star of Religion, the Dispenser of

Justice, Pillar of the State," &c. &c.   I went on to
inform him particularly of our circumstances, and
of our having passed in safety through the dominions of other princes, and stated the delight which
we now felt at being in the neighbourhood of
Bokhara, " the citadel of Islam."   I concluded by
telling him, that in all countries we had considered
ourselves as the subjects of the ruler, and that we
now approached the capital of the Commander of
the Faithful (so the King of Bokhara is called),
whose protection of the merchant and the traveller
is known in the utmost corners of the East.   I had,
on former occasions, found the advantage of being
the first to convey information of our own approach,
nor did I doubt a good result from this communication.   We were not deceived, and before reaching
the city, discovered that a lying Persian in our
caravan had given currency to these rumours, which
were altogether destitute of foundation.   The minister sent back our servant to meet us, and say,
that we should be welcome in Bokhara.

Our halt at Kurshee gave us some opportunity
of seeing the place.   It is a straggling town, a mile
long, with a considerable bazar, and about 10,000
inhabitants.   The houses are flat-roofed, but mean.
A mud fort, surrounded by a wet ditch, forms a
respectable defence on the south-west side of the
town.   A river, which rises from Shuhur Subz,
about fifty miles distant, and famous as the birth-
place of Timour, passes north of Kurshee, and
enables its inhabitants to form innumerable gardens,
which are shaded by trees groaning under fruit,

and some lofty poplars. These trees have a tall
and noble aspect; and their leaves, when rustling
in the wind, assume a white silvery appearance,
though actually green, which has a curious and
pleasing effect on the landscape. Never were the
blessings of water more apparent than in this spot,
which must otherwise have been a barren waste.
On the banks of the rivulet and its branches, every
thing is verdant and beautiful; away from them, all
is sandy and sterile. Kurshee is the largest place
in the kingdom of Bokhara, next to the capital.
Its öasis is about twenty-two miles broad, but the
river expends itself in the surrounding fields.

We marched from Kurshee to Karsan, sixteen
miles distant, which is a thriving village, situated
on the extremity of this öasis. We arrived on the
market-day, for in the towns of Toorkistan they
hold their bazars on stated days, as in Europe.
We met many people proceeding to the throng,
but not a single individual on foot—all were eques-
trians. A stranger is amused at seeing a horse
literally converted into a family conveyance, and a
man jogging along with his wife behind him. The
ladies are of course veiled, like most females in
this country: they prefer blue cloths to white, as
in Cabool, and are sombre-looking figures. We
now found ourselves among the Uzbeks, a grave,
broad-faced, peaceable people, with a Tartar expression of countenance. They are fair, and some
of them are handsome; but the bulk of the people,
the men at least, are without personal beauty. I
was struck with the great number of old looking

men among them. We had now left the Toorkmun
tribes, who do not here extend much beyond the
Oxus.

In our second march from Kurshee, we halted at
Kuroul-tuppa, where there is a caravansary built
by Abdoolla, a king of Bokhara, who reigned in the
sixteenth century. It put me in mind of Hindostan and its monarchs. We also passed three large
reservoirs (surdabas), which were made by order
of this philanthropic prince. They had been
erected at great expense in a flat and desert country, and the rain water that falls is conducted to
them by ditches often from a great distance. The
king Abdoolla had made a pilgrimage to Mecca,
but imbibed an impression that it had not proved
acceptable in the sight of God. In the hope of
propitiating divine favour, he set about the construction of caravansarais and cisterns in all parts
of his dominions, acts more beneficial to mankind,
and therefore more acceptable, I venture to believe,
than pilgrimages to shrines or tombs.

At Kurshee, we were joined by some other travellers, among whom was a moollah from Bokhara,
who introduced himself to me: the people of this
country possess great affability of manner, and make
agreeable companions. The priest and I rode together on our last march to the city, being the
only persons on horseback. He gave me an account of the college to which he belonged in Bokhara, and requested me to visit it, which I did not
fail to do. My other friend, the Khwaju, at length
changed conveyances with the priest, and enter-

tained me for half the night, by repeating and explaining odes and lines of poetry, more to my amusement than edification, for they were all about nightingales and love. It is curious to find so much said on this passion, in a country where there is really so little of it. It does not appear to strike the people themselves; though some of their verses breathe a spirit which one might think would discover it to them, thus : —

> " Ashiq shood ba gubree ki deen nu darud,
>   Een kar kar i ishq ust dukhlee ba deen nu darud."

" I fell in love with an infidel girl, destitute of religion. This is love, what has it to do with religion?" Yet, after this, they marry without seeing each other, or knowing further than that they are of different sexes; nor is this all : a merchant, in a foreign land, marries for the time he is to continue in it, and dismisses the lady when he returns to his native country; when both of them seek for other alliances.

Our journey from the Oxus to Bokhara had been of a most fatiguing and trying nature. In Cabool, we had been chilled by cold, and were now almost burned up with heat. Our mode of travelling, too, had been extremely irksome, for camels only advance at half the pace of a horse, and we spent double the time on the march, which increased the fatigue. The only horse which accompanied us was so completely knocked up that he fell down in several places before entering Bokhara. We also travelled at night, and the rest which one gets on a camel is broken and disturbed. Our water had often been bad, and our food chiefly consisted of hard biscuit. All these inconveniences were, however, drawing to a close; and, before we had reached the gates of Bokhara, they had given rise to reflections of a more pleasing nature. At the outset of our journey we used to look forward with some anxiety to the treatment we might experience in that city; and, indeed, in many of the then remote places which we had already passed. As we advanced, these apprehensions had subsided, and we now looked back with surprise at the vast expanse of country which we had traversed in safety. Bokhara, which had once sounded as so distant from us, was now at hand, and the success which had hitherto attended our endeavours gave us every hope of bringing the journey to a happy termination. With these feelings, we found ourselves at the gates of this eastern capital, an hour after sunrise, on the 27th of June; but there was nothing striking in the approach to Bokhara. Though the country is rich, it is flat, and the trees hide the walls and mosques till close upon it. We entered with the caravan, and alighted in a retired quarter of the city, where our messenger had hired a house.

CHAP. IX.

BOKHARA.

OUR first care on entering Bokhara was to change our garb, and conform to the usages prescribed by the laws of the country. A petition to the minister might, perhaps, have relieved us from the necessity, but the measure was in consonance with our own principle, and we did not delay a moment in adopting it. Our turbans were exchanged for shabby sheep-skin caps, with the fur inside; and our "*kummurbunds*" (girdles) were thrown aside for a rude piece of rope or tape. The outer garment of the country was discontinued, as well as our stockings; since these are the emblems of distinction in the holy city of Bokhara between an infidel and a true believer. We knew also that none but a Mahommedan might ride within the walls of the city, and had an inward feeling which told us to be satisfied if we were permitted, at such trifling sacrifices, to continue our abode in the capital. A couplet*, which describes Samarcand as the paradise of the world, also names Bokhara as the strength of religion and of Islam; and, impious and powerless as

* Samarcand suequl-i-rooee zumeen ust
Bokhara qoowut-i-Islam wu deen ust.

we were, we could have no desire to try experiments among those who seemed, outwardly at least, such bigots. The dress which I have described is nowhere enjoined by the Koran; nor did it obtain in these countries for two centuries after the prophet, when the prejudice of some of the caliphs discovered that the " Faithful" should be distinguished from those who were not Mahommedans.

On entering the city, the authorities did not even search us; but in the afternoon an officer summoned us to the presence of the minister. My fellow-traveller was still labouring under fever, and could not accompany me; I therefore proceeded alone to the ark or palace, where the minister lived along with the king. I was lost in amazement at the novel scene before me, since we had to walk for about two miles through the streets of Bokhara, before reaching the citadel. I was immediately introduced to the minister, or as he is styled, the Koosh Begee, or Lord of all the Begs, an elderly man, of great influence, who was sitting in a small room that had a private court-yard in front of it. He desired me to be seated outside on the pavement, yet evinced both a kind and considerate manner, which set my mind at ease. The hardness of my seat, and the distance from the minister, did not overpower me with grief, since his son, who came in during the interview, was even seated farther off than myself. I presented a silver watch and a Cashmeer dress, which I had brought for the purpose; but he declined to receive any thing, saying, that he was but the slave of the king. He then interrogated me for about two hours as to my own affairs, and the objects which had brought me to a country so remote as Bokhara. I told our usual tale of being in progress *towards* our native country, and produced my passport, from the Governor-General of India, which the minister read with peculiar attention. I then added, that Bokhara was a country of such celebrity among Eastern nations, that I had been chiefly induced to visit Toorkistan for the purpose of seeing it. "But what is your profession?" said the minister. I replied, that I was an officer of the Indian army. "But tell me," said he, "something about your knowledge," and he here made various observations on the customs and politics of Europe, but particularly of Russia, on which he was well informed. In reply to some inquiries regarding our baggage, I considered it prudent to acquaint him, that I had a sextant, since I concluded that we should be searched, and it was better to make a merit of necessity. I informed him, therefore, that I liked to observe the stars and the other heavenly bodies, since it was a most attractive study. On hearing this, the Vizier's attention was roused, and he begged, with some earnestness, and in a subdued tone of voice, that I would inform him of a favourable conjunction of the planets and the price of grain which it indicated in the ensuing year. I told him, that our astronomical knowledge did not lead to such information; at which he expressed himself disappointed. On the whole, however, he appeared to be satisfied as to our character, and assured me of his protection. While in Bokhara, he said that he must prohibit our using pen and ink, since it might lead to our conduct being misrepresented to the king, and prove injurious. He also stated, that the route to the Caspian Sea, by way of Khiva, had been closed for the last year; and that if we intended to enter Russia, we must either pursue the northern route from Bokhara, or cross the Toorkmun desert, below Orgunje, to Astrabad on the Caspian.

Two days after this interview, I was again summoned by the Vizier, and found him surrounded by a great number of respectable persons, to whom he appeared desirous of exhibiting me. I was questioned in such a way as to make me believe that our character was not altogether free from suspicion; but the Vizier said jocularly, " I suppose you have been writing about Bokhara." Since I had in the first instance given so true a tale, I had here no apprehensions of contradiction; and freely told the party that I had come to see the world and the wonders of Bokhara, and that, by the Vizier's favour, I had been already perambulating the city, and seen the gardens outside its walls. The minister was the only person who appeared pleased with my candour, and said, that he would be always happy to see me in the evening. He enquired if I had any curiosity to exhibit to him either of India or my own country; but I regretted my inability to meet his wishes. On my return home, it struck me that the all-curious Vizier might be gratified by the sight of a patent compass, with its glasses,

screws, and reflectors ; but it also occurred that he
might regard my possession of this complicated
piece of mechanism in a light which would not be
favourable. I, however, sallied forth with the instrument in my pocket, and soon found myself again
in his presence. I told him, that I believed I had
a curiosity which would gratify him, and produced
the compass, which was quite new and of very
beautiful workmanship. I described its utility, and
pointed out its beauty, till the Vizier seemed quite
to have forgotten " that he was but a slave of the
king, and could receive nothing ;" indeed, he was
proceeding to bargain for its price, when I interrupted him by an assurance, that I had brought it
from Hindostan to present to him, since I had heard
of his zeal in the cause of religion, and it would
enable him to point to the holy Mecca and rectify
the " *kiblu*" of the grand mosque, which he was
now building in Bokhara. I could therefore receive
no return, since we were already rewarded above
all price by his protection. The Koosh Begee
packed up the compass with all the haste and
anxiety of a child, and said that he would take it
direct to his majesty, and describe the wonderful
ingenuity of our nation. Thus fell one of my com-
passes. It was a fine instrument by Schmalcalder,
but I had a duplicate, and I think it will be admitted that it was not sacrificed without an ample
return. Had we been in Bokhara in disguise, and
personating an assumed character, our feelings
would have been very different from what they now
were. Like owls, we should only have appeared at

night ; but, after this incident, we stalked abroad in
the noontide sun, and visited all parts of the city.

My usual resort in the evening was the Registan
of Bokhara, which is the name given to a spacious
area in the city, near the palace, which opens upon
it. On two other sides there are massive buildings,
colleges of the learned, and on the fourth side is a
fountain, filled with water, and shaded by lofty
trees, where idlers and newsmongers assemble round
the wares of Asia and Europe, which are here exposed for sale. A stranger has only to seat himself on a bench of the Registan, to know the
Uzbeks and the people of Bokhara. He may here
converse with the natives of Persia, Turkey, Russia,
Tartary, China, India, and Cabool. He will meet
with Toorkmuns, Calmuks, and Kuzzaks *, from the
surrounding deserts, as well as the natives of more
favoured lands. He may contrast the polished
manners of the subjects of the " Great King" with
the ruder habits of a roaming Tartar. He may see
the Uzbeks from all the states of Mawur-ool nuhr,
and speculate from their physiognomy on the
changes which time and place effect among any
race of men. The Uzbek of Bokhara is hardly to
be recognised as a Toork or Tartar from his inter-
mixture of Persian blood. Those from the neighbouring country of Kokan are less changed ; and
the natives of Orgunje, the ancient Kharasm, have
yet a harshness of feature peculiar to themselves.
They may be distinguished from all others by dark

* Cossacks.

sheep-skin caps, called " *tilpak*," about a foot high.
A red beard, grey eyes, and fair skin, will now and
then arrest the notice of a stranger, and his attention will have been fixed on a poor Russian, who
has lost his country and his liberty, and drags out a
miserable life of slavery. A native of China may
be seen here and there in the same forlorn pre-
dicament, shorn of his long cue of hair, with his
crown under a turban, since both he and the Russian
act the part of Mahommedans. Then follows a
Hindoo, in a garb foreign to himself and his country. A small square cap and a string, instead of a
girdle, distinguishes him from the Mahommedans,
and, as the Moslem tells you, prevents their pro-
faning the prescribed salutations of his language by
using them to an idolater. Without these distinctions, the native of India is to be recognised by his
demure look, and the studious manner in which he
avoids all communication with the crowd. He
herds only with a few individuals, similarly circum-
stanced with himself. The Jew is as marked a
being as the Hindoo: he wears a somewhat different dress, and a conical cap. No mark, however,
is so distinguishing as the well known features of
the Hebrew people. In Bokhara they are a race
remarkably handsome, and I saw more than one
Rebecca in my peregrinations. Their features are
set off by ringlets of beautiful hair hanging over
their cheeks and neck. There are about 4000
Jews in Bokhara, emigrants from Meshid, in Persia,
who are chiefly employed in dying cloth. They
receive the same treatment as the Hindoos. A

stray Armenian, in a still different dress, represents
this wandering nation; but there are few of them
in Bokhara. With these exceptions, the stranger
beholds in the bazars a portly, fair, and well dressed
mass of people, the Mahommedans of Toorkistan.
A large white turban, and a "*chogha*," or pelisse,
of some dark colour, over three or four others of
the same description, is the general costume; but
the Registan leads to the palace, and the Uzbeks
delight to appear before their king in a mottled
garment of silk, called "udrus," made of the
brightest colours, and which would be intolerable
to any but an Uzbek. Some of the higher persons
are clothed in brocade, and one may distinguish the
gradations of the chiefs, since those in favour ride
into the citadel, and the others dismount at the
gate. Almost every individual who visits the king
is attended by his slave; this class of people are for
the most part Persians, or their descendants, and
have a peculiar appearance. It is said, indeed, that
three fourths of the people of Bokhara are of slave
extraction; for of the captives brought from Persia
into Toorkistan, few are permitted to return, and,
by all accounts, there are many who have no inclination to do so. A great portion of the people
of Bokhara appear on horseback; but, whether
mounted or on foot, they are dressed in boots, and
the pedestrians strut on high and small heels, in
which it was difficult for me to walk or even stand.
They are about an inch and a half high, and the
pinnacle is not one third of that in diameter. This
is the national dress of the Uzbeks. Some men of

rank have a shoe over the boot, which is taken off
on entering a room. I must not forget the ladies
in my enumeration of the inhabitants. They generally appear on horseback, riding as the men; a
few walk, and all are veiled with a black hair-cloth.
The difficulty of seeing through it makes the fair
one stare at every one as in a masquerade. Here,
however, no one must speak to them; and if any of
the king's harem pass, you are admonished to look
in another direction, and get a blow on the head if
you neglect the advice. So holy are the fair ones
of the " holy Bokhara."

My reader may now, perhaps, form some idea of
the appearance of the inhabitants of Bokhara. From
morn to night the crowd which assembles raises a
humming noise, and one is stunned at the moving
mass of human beings. In the middle of the area
the fruits of the season are sold under the shade of
a square piece of mat, supported by a single pole.
One wonders at the never-ending employment of
the fruiterers, in dealing out their grapes, melons,
apricots, apples, peaches, pears, and plums, to a
continued succession of purchasers. It is with
difficulty that a passage can be forced through the
streets, and it is only done at the momentary risk
of being rode over by some one on a horse or
donkey. These latter animals are exceedingly fine,
and amble along at a quick pace with their riders
and burdens. Carts of a light construction are also
driving up and down, since the streets are not too
narrow to admit of wheeled carriages. In every
part of the bazar there are people making tea,

which is done in large European urns, instead of
teapots, and kept hot by a metal tube.   The love
of the Bokharees for tea is, I believe, without
parallel, for they drink it at all times and places,
and in half a dozen ways: with and without sugar,
with and without milk, with grease, with salt, &c.
Next to the venders of this hot beverage one may
purchase " *rahut i jan*," or the delight of life, —
grape jelly or syrup, mixed up with chopped ice.
This abundance of ice is one of the greatest luxuries
in Bokhara, and it may be had till the cold weather
makes it unnecessary.   It is pitted in winter, and
sold at a price within the reach of the poorest
people.   No one ever thinks of drinking water in
Bokhara without icing it, and a beggar may be seen
purchasing it as he proclaims his poverty and en-
treats the bounty of the passenger.   It is a refreshing sight to see the huge masses of it, with
the thermometer at 90°, coloured, scraped, and
piled into heaps like snow.   It would be endless to
describe the whole body of traders; suffice it to
say, that almost every thing may be purchased in
the Registan: the jewellery and cutlery of Europe,
(coarse enough, however,) the tea of China, the
sugar of India, the spices of Manilla, &c. &c.   One
may also add to his lore both Toorkee and Persian
at the book-stalls, where the learned, or would-be-
so, pore over the tattered pages.   As one with-
draws in the evening from this bustling crowd to
the more retired parts of the city, he winds his
way through arched bazars, now empty, and passes
mosques, surmounted by handsome cupolas, and

adorned by all the simple ornaments which are admitted by Mahommedans.   After the bazar hours,
these are crowded for evening prayers.   At the
doors of the colleges, which generally face the
mosques, one may see the students lounging after
the labours of the day ; not, however, so gay or so
young as the tyros of an European university, but
many of them grave and demure old men, with
more hypocrisy, but by no means less vice, than the
youths in other quarters of the world.   With the
twilight this busy scene closes, the king's drum
beats, it is re-echoed by others in every part of the
city, and, at a certain hour, no one is permitted to
move out without a lantern.   From these arrangements the police of the city is excellent, and large
bales of cloth are left on the stalls at night with
perfect safety.   All is silence until morning, when
the bustle again commences in the Registan.   The
day is ushered in with the same guzzling and tea-
drinking, and hundreds of boys and donkeys laden
with milk hasten to the busy throng.   The milk is
sold in small bowls, over which the cream floats : a
lad will bring twenty or thirty of these to market
in shelves, supported and suspended by a stick over
his shoulder.   Whatever number may be brought
speedily disappear among the tea-drinking population of this great city.

Soon after our arrival, I paid a visit to our late
travelling companions, the tea-merchants, who had
taken up their abode in a caravansary, and were
busy in unpacking, praising, and selling their tea.
They sent to the bazar for ice and apricots, which

we sat down and enjoyed together. One of the
purchasers took me for a tea-merchant, from the
society I was in, and asked for my investment. His
request afforded the merchants and myself some
amusement; but they did not undeceive the person as to my mercantile character, and we continued to converse together. He spoke of the
news of the day, the late conquests of the king at
Shuhr Subz, and of the threats of the Persians to
attack Bokhara, all without ever suspecting me to
be aught but an Asiatic. In return, we had visits
from these merchants, and many other persons, who
came to gratify curiosity at our expense. We were
not permitted to write, and it was an agreeable
manner of passing time, since they were very communicative. The Uzbeks are a simple people, with
whom one gets most readily acquainted, though
they speak in a curious tone of voice, as if they
despised or were angry with you. They never saluted us by any of the forms among Mahommedans;
but appeared to have another set of expressions, the
most common of which are, " May your wealth increase" (doulut zyadu), or (oomr duraz) " May your
life be long." They, nevertheless, always said the
" fatha," or prayer from the Koran, stretching out
their hands and stroking down their beards, in which
we joined, before they sat down with us. Many of
our visiters betrayed suspicions of our character;
but still evinced no unwillingness to converse on all
points, from the politics of their king to the state of
their markets. Simple people! they believe a spy
must measure their forts and walls; they have no

idea of the value of conversation. With such ready returns on the part of our guests, it was not irksome for me to explain the usages of Europe; but let me advise a traveller to lay in a good stock of that kind of knowledge before he ventures to journey in Eastern countries. One must have a smattering of trade, arts, science, religion, medicine, and, in fact, of every thing; and any answer is better than a negative, since ignorance, real or pretended, is construed into wilful concealment.

I took an early opportunity of seeing the slave-bazar of Bokhara, which is held every Saturday morning. The Uzbeks manage all their affairs by means of slaves, who are chiefly brought from Persia by the Toorkmuns. Here these poor wretches are exposed for sale, and occupy thirty or forty stalls, where they are examined like cattle, only with this difference, that they are able to give an account of themselves *vivâ voce*. On the morning I visited the bazar, there were only six unfortunate beings, and I witnessed the manner in which they are disposed of. They are first interrogated regarding their parentage and capture, and if they are Mahommedans, that is Soonees. The question is put in that form, for the Uzbeks do not consider a Shiah to be a true believer; with them, as with the primitive Christians, a sectary is more odious than an unbeliever. After the intended purchaser is satisfied of the slave being an infidel (kaffir), he examines his body, particularly noting if it be free from leprosy, so common in Toorkistan, and then proceeds to bargain for the price. Three of the Persian boys were for sale

at thirty tillas of gold apiece * ; and it was surprising
to see how contented the poor fellows sat under
their lot.   I heard one of them telling how he had
been seized south of Meshid, while tending his
flocks.   Another, who overheard a conversation
among the by-standers, regarding the scarcity of
slaves that season, stated, that a great number had
been taken.   His companion said with some feeling,
" You and I only think so, because of our own misfortune ; but these people must know better."
There was one unfortunate girl, who had been long
in service, and was now exposed for sale by her
master, because of his poverty.   I felt certain that
many a tear had been shed in the court where I
surveyed the scene ; but I was assured from every
quarter that slaves are kindly treated ; and the circumstance of so many of them continuing in the
country after they have been manumitted, seems to
establish this fact.   The bazars of Bokhara are
chiefly supplied from Orgunje.   Russians and Chinese are also sold, but rarely.   The feelings of an
European revolt at this most odious traffic ; but the
Uzbeks entertain no such notions, and believe that
they are conferring a benefit on a Persian when they
purchase him, and see that he renounces his here-
tical opinions.

From the slave market I passed on to the great
bazar, and the very first sight which fell under my
notice was the offenders against Mahommedanism
of the preceding Friday.   They consisted of four

* 200 rupees. — 20l.

individuals, who had been caught asleep at prayer time, and a youth, who had been smoking in public. They were all tied to each other, and the person who had been found using tobacco led the way, holding the hookah, or pipe, in his hand. The officer of police followed with a thick thong, and chastised them as he went, calling aloud, "Ye followers of Islam, behold the punishment of those who violate the law!" Never, however, was there such a series of contradiction and absurdity as in the practice and theory of religion in Bokhara. You may openly purchase tobacco, and all the most approved apparatus for inhaling it; yet if seen smoking in public you are straightway dragged before the Cazee, punished by stripes, or paraded on a donkey, with a blackened face, as a warning to others. If a person is caught flying pigeons on a Friday, he is sent forth with the dead bird round his neck, seated on a camel. If seen in the streets at the time of prayers, and convicted of such habitual neglect, fines and imprisonment follow; yet there are bands of the most abominable wretches, who frequent the streets at evening for purposes as contrary to the Koran as to nature. Every thing, indeed, presents a tissue of contrarieties; and none were more apparent to me than the punishment of the culprits who were marching, with all the pomp of publicity, past the very gateway of the court where human beings were levelled with the brutes of the earth, *no doubt* against the laws of humanity, but *as certainly* against the laws of Mahommed.

The Hindoos of Bokhara courted our society, for

that people seem to look upon the English as their
natural superiors. They visited us in every country
which we passed, and would never speak any other
language but Hindoostanee, which was a bond of
union between us and them. In this country they
appeared to enjoy a sufficient degree of toleration
to enable them to live happily. An enumeration of
their restrictions might make them appear a perse-
cuted race. They are not permitted to build temples, nor set up idols, nor walk in procession : they
do not ride within the walls of the city, and must
wear a peculiar dress. They pay the "*jizyu*," or
poll-tax, which varies from four to eight rupees a
year ; but this they only render in common with
others, not Mahommedans. They must never
abuse or ill-use a Mahommedan. When the king
passes their quarter of the city, they must draw up,
and wish him health and prosperity ; when on
horseback outside the city, they must dismount if
they meet his majesty or the Cazee. They are not
permitted to purchase female slaves, as an infidel
would defile a believer ; nor do any of them bring
their families beyond the Oxus. For these sacrifices the Hindoos in Bokhara live unmolested, and,
in all trials and suits, have equal justice with the
Mahommedans. I could hear of no forcible instance
of conversion to Islam, though three or four individuals had changed their creed in as many years.
The deportment of these people is most sober and
orderly ; — one would imagine that the tribe had
renounced laughter, judging by the gravity of their
countenances. They themselves, however, speak

highly of their privileges, and are satisfied at the celerity with which they can realise money, though it be at the sacrifice of their prejudices. There are about 300 Hindoos in Bokhara, living in a caravansary of their own. They are chiefly natives of Shikarpoor in Sinde, and their number has of late years rather increased. The Uzbeks, and, indeed, all the Mahommedans, find themselves vanquished by the industry of these people, who will stake the largest sums of money for the smallest gain.

Among the Hindoos we had a singular visiter in a deserter from the Indian army at Bombay. He had set out on a pilgrimage to all the shrines of the Hindoo world, and was then proceeding to the fire temples on the shores of the Caspian! I knew many of the officers of the regiment (the 24th N. I.) to which he had belonged, and felt pleased at hearing names which were familiar to me in this remote city. I listened with interest to the man's detail of his adventures and travels, nor was he deterred by any fear that I would *lodge information* against him, and secure his apprehension. I looked upon him as a brother in arms, and he amused me with many a tale of *my friend* Moorad Beg of Koondooz, whom he had followed in his campaigns, and served as a bombardier. This man, when he first showed himself, was disguised in the dress of a pilgrim ; but the carriage of a soldier is not to be mistaken, even if met at Bokhara.

The house in which we lived was exceedingly small, and overlooked on every side, but we could

not regret it, since it presented an opportunity of
seeing a Toorkee beauty, a handsome young lady,
who promenaded one of the surrounding balconies,
and *wished to think* she was not seen.   A pretended
flight was not even neglected by this fair one,
whose curiosity often prompted her to steal a
glance at the Firingees. Since we had a fair exchange, she was any thing but an intruder, though
unfortunately too distant for us to indulge " in the
sweet music of speech." The ladies of Bokhara
stain their teeth quite black ; they braid their hair,
and allow it to hang in tresses down their shoulders.
Their dress differs little from the men : they wear
the same pelisses, only that the two sleeves, instead of
being used as such, are tucked together and tied behind. In the house even they dress in huge Hessian
boots made of velvet, and highly ornamented. What
a strange taste for those who are for ever concealed,
to choose to be thus booted as if prepared for a
journey ! On the head they wear large white turbans, but a veil covers the face, and many a lovely
countenance blooms unseen. The exhibition of
beauty, in which so much of a woman's time is
spent in more favoured countries, is here unknown.
A man may shoot his neighbour if he sees him on
a balcony, at any but a stated hour.   Assassination
follows suspicion ; for the laws of the Koran, regarding the sex, are most strictly enforced. But
jealousy is not the worst vice of the Uzbeks.

   In my travels through Cabool, I had often enjoyed
the luxuries of the bath, according to the custom
of the Orientals. I now had the same pleasure in

Bokhara; but it was only admissible in some few buildings, since the priests had asserted, that the water of certain baths would change into blood if polluted by a woman or an infidel. A bath is too well known to require description, but the operation is most singular. You are laid out at full length, rubbed with a hair brush, scrubbed, buffeted, and kicked; but it is all very refreshing. The baths of Bokhara are most spacious. Many small vaulted chambers surround a great circular hall with a cupola, and are heated to different temperatures. In the daytime the light is admitted from coloured glasses over the large dome; in the night, a single lamp beneath suffices for all the cells. That portion of the circle towards Mecca is appropriated as a mosque, where the luxurious Mahommedan may offer up his orisons while he is enjoying one of the promised blessings of his prophet's paradise. There are eighteen baths in Bokhara; a few are of very large dimensions, but the generality of them bring in an annual income of 150 tillas (1000 rupees). Each individual pays to the keeper of the bath ten pieces of brass money, of which there are 135 in a rupee. About a hundred people may, therefore, bathe for a tilla; and 150 tillas will give 15,000 people to each bath. Eighteen baths will give a total of 270,000 who enjoy the luxury yearly. But the baths are only used for half the year, during the cold months; and the poorer people are never able to afford them.

I did not omit to pay my respects to the minister

while I rambled about the city, and Dr. Gerard, in
the course of ten days, was sufficiently recovered
to accompany me. The Vizier was equally inqui-
sitive with the Nuwab at Cabool regarding the
preparation of medicines and plasters, of which he
wished the doctor to inform him. We had, however, got into a more civilised region on our approach to Europe, since the Vizier had received
quinine and other medicines from Constantinople.
We sat with the minister while he was transacting
business, and saw him levying duties on the merchants,
who are most liberally treated in this country. The
webs of cloth are produced, and every fortieth piece
is taken in place of duties; which gives the merchant his profit, without distressing him for ready
money. A Mahommedan, indeed, has only to take
the name of the prophet, stroke down his beard,
and declare himself poor, to be relieved from all
duties. One man said, " that he had got witnesses
to prove his being in debt, and would produce
them. The minister replied, " Give us your oath,
we want no witnesses." He gave it; every one
called out " God is great!" and said the " fatha;"
on which the goods were returned without an iota
of charge. With every disposition to judge favourably of the Asiatics, — and my opinions regarding
them improved as I knew them better, — I have
not found them free from falsehood. I fear, therefore, that many a false oath is taken among them.
No people could be more liberal encouragers of
commerce than the rulers of Bokhara. During the
reign of the last monarch, the duties on goods were

never paid till they were sold, as in the bonding
system of a British custom-house. The Vizier, on
this occasion, conversed at great length on subjects
of commerce relating to Bokhara and Britain, and
expressed much anxiety to increase the communication between the countries, requesting that I
myself would return, as a trading ambassador, to
Bokhara, and not forget to bring a good pair of
spectacles, that he might read his Koran with
greater ease. I did not forget his request; and
ere this I hope that that book has been *magnified*,
through the medium of a good pair of glasses, to
his heart's content. Our intercourse was now established on a footing which promised well: I took
occasion, therefore, to express a wish to the Vizier
of paying our duty to the king. I had touched on
a delicate point; for it appeared that the minister
had feared our being charged with some proposals
to his majesty, which we concealed from himself.
" I am as good as the Ameer," said he (so the king
is called); " and if you have no matters of business to transact with the king, what have travellers
to do with courts ? " I told him of our curiosity
on these points, but he did not choose that we
should have the honour, and that was sufficient for
abandoning the suit.

I was, nevertheless, resolved to have a sight of
royalty ; and, at mid-day on the following Friday,
repaired to the great mosque, a building of Timourlane, and saw his majesty and his court passing
from prayers. The king appeared to be under
thirty years of age, and had not a prepossessing coun-

tenance : his eyes are small, his visage gaunt and
pale. He was plainly dressed in a silken robe of
" udrus," with a white turban. He sometimes
wears an aigrette of feathers ornamented with dia-
monds. The Koran was carried in front of him;
and he was preceded and followed by two golden
mace bearers, who exclaimed in Turkish, " Pray to
God that the Commander of the Faithful may act
justly !" His suite did not exceed a hundred
people; most of them were dressed in robes of
Russian brocade, and wore gold ornamented swords
— I should call them knives — the mark of distinction in this country. The present king has
more state than any of his predecessors; but he
may consider it necessary to affect humility in a
temple, and in returning from a religious ceremony.
The people drew up by the wayside as he passed,
and with a stroke of their beards wished his
majesty peace; I did the same. The character of
this king, Buhadoor Khan, stands high among his
countrymen: at his elevation to the throne he gave
away all his own wealth. He is strict in his religious observances, but less bigoted than his father
Meer Hyder. He acts according to the Koran
in all cases; and it is pretended that he even lives
on the capitation tax which is levied from the Jews
and Hindoos. The revenues of the country are said
to be spent in maintaining moollahs and mosques;
but this young king is ambitious and warlike; and I
believe it to be more probable that he uses his
treasures to maintain his troops and increase his
power.

The life of the king of Bokhara is less enviable than that of most private men. The water which he drinks is brought in skins from the river, under the charge and seal of two officers. It is opened by the Vizier, first tasted by his people and then by himself, when it is once more sealed and despatched to the king. The daily meals of his majesty undergo a like scrutiny : the minister eats, he gives to those around him, they wait the lapse of an hour to judge of their effect, when they are locked up in a box and despatched. His majesty has one key and his minister another. Fruit, sweetmeats, and every eatable undergo the same examination; and we shall hardly suppose the good king of the Uzbeks ever enjoys a hot meal or a fresh cooked dinner. Poison is common ; and the rise of his majesty to the throne on which he now sits is not without strong suspicions of a free distribution of such draughts. A native on one occasion presented me with some figs, one of which I took and ate, to show him that I appreciated the gift. The individual cautioned me against such indiscretion in future ; " since," said he, " you should always present some of the gift in the first instance to the giver ; and, if he eats, you may with safety follow his example."

I expressed a wish soon after reaching Bokhara to see some of the unfortunate Russians who have been sold into this country. One evening a stout and manly-looking person fell at my feet and kissed them. He was a Russian of the name of Gregory Pulakoff, who had been kidnapped when asleep at a Russian outpost, about twenty-five years ago. He

was the son of a soldier, and now followed the trade
of a carpenter. I made him sit down with us, and
give an account of his woes and condition: it was
our dinner-time, and the poor carpenter helped us
to eat our pilao. Though but ten years of age when
captured, he yet retained his native language, and
the most ardent wish to return to his country. He
paid seven tillas a year to his master, who allowed
him to practise his trade and keep all he might earn
beyond that sum. He had a wife and child, also
slaves. " I am well treated by master," said he;
" I go where I choose; I associate with the people,
and play the part of a Mahommedan; I appear
happy, but my heart burns for my native land,
where I would serve in the most despotic army
with gladness. Could I but see it again, I would
willingly die. I tell you my feelings, but I smother
them from the Uzbeks. I am yet a Christian (here
the poor fellow crossed himself after the manner of
the Greek church), and I live among a people who
detest, with the utmost cordiality, every individual
of that creed. It is only for my own peace that I
call myself a Mahommedan." The poor fellow had
acquired all the habits and manners of an Uzbek,
nor should I have been able to distinguish him, but
for his blue eyes, red beard, and fair skin. He enquired with much earnestness if there were any
hopes of him and his comrades being released; but
I could give him no further solace than the floating
rumours which I had heard of the Emperor's intention to suppress the traffic by an army. He told
me that the last embassy to Bokhara under M.

Negri had failed to effect that desired end, but that the sale of Russians had ceased in Bokhara for the last ten years, and there were not now 130 natives of Russia in the kingdom; but in Khiva their number increased as before. The whole of those in Bokhara would have been released by the ambassador, had not some religious discussion arisen on the propriety of allowing Christians, who had become Mahommedans, to relapse into idolatry! The moollahs had seen the figures in the Greek church; and no argument will reverse, what they state to be the evidence of their senses, that the Russians worship idols. There is generally some difference of opinion on all points, and that of the Russians and Bokharees on the subject of slavery was much at variance. The Mahommedans are not sensible of any offence in enslaving the Russians, since they state that Russia herself exhibits the example of a whole country of slaves, particularly in the despotic government of her soldiery. " If we purchase Russians," say they, " the Russians buy the Kuzzaks on our frontier, who are Mahommedans, and they tamper with these people by threats, bribery, and hopes, to make them forsake their creed, and become idolaters. Look, on the other hand, at the Russians in Bokhara, at their life, liberty, and comfort, and compare it with the black bread and unrelenting tyranny which they experience in their native country." Last, not least, they referred to their cruel banishment to Siberia (as they called it Sibere), which they spoke of with shuddering horror, and stated that it had on some occasions driven

Russians voluntarily to betake themselves to Bok-hara.   We shall not attempt to decide between the parties; but it is a melancholy reflection on the liberties of Russia, that they admit of a comparison with the institutions of a Tartar kingdom, whose pity, it is proverbially said, is only upon a par with the tyranny of the Afghan.

With Russians, Hindoos, and Uzbeks, our circle of acquaintance at Bokhara soon increased, and most of the Afghan and Cabool merchants sought our society, and we could not but feel gratified at the favourable opinion entertained by them of the British in India.   One of them, Sirwur Khan, a Lohanee merchant of great opulence, to whom we were never introduced, offered us any money which we might require, and did it in a manner that left no doubt of his sincerity.   Another individual, Shere Mahommed, a native of Cabool, afforded me useful assistance in my inquiries regarding the commerce of Central Asia.   We were constantly assailed by Afghans, and even Uzbeks, to give notes of hand, certifying our acquaintance with them; for they believe the hand-writing to be a bond of union with Englishmen; and that the possession of it would secure them an honourable reception in India. We complied with the wishes of those who deserved our confidence.   Among our other friends was a Cashmeer merchant, Ahmedjooee, a clever and talk-ative fellow, who wished me much to assist him in the preparation of a kind of cochineal, which is found, but, I believe, cannot be prepared, in Bok-hara.   There was also an old man, named Hajee

Meeruk, who had seen the world from Canton to Constantinople ; and secretly brought some old and valuable Bactrian coins and rarities, which are acceptable to Europeans.   The most intimate, perhaps, of all our acquaintance was our landlord, an Uzbek merchant, named Mukhsoom, who traded to Yarkund.   He paid us a daily visit, and generally brought some of his friends along with him.   I shall mention an incident regarding this person which is creditable to him.   He was most communicative, and gave us much useful information : as our intimacy increased, I interrogated him closely on the revenues and resources of Bokhara, on its extent and power, and once opened a small map of the country in his presence.   He replied to all my inquiries ; and then, begging I would shut up the map, beseeched me never again to produce such a paper in Bokhara, since there were innumerable spies about the king, and it might be productive of very serious consequences.   He still continued his visits and his information with the same freedom as before.   On our first arrival in the city, the keeper of the caravansary refused us quarters, because we had no character, that is, we were neither merchants nor ambassadors ; but this man kindly let his house to us.   He had been attacked by his neighbours, terrified by his friends, and he himself at first trembled at the risk which he had incurred. The keeper of the caravansary now hid his head in shame ; the landlord shared our intimacy ; his neighbours sought his favour to be brought to us, and our society was more courted than was agreeable.

CHAP. X.

BOKHARA.

TRADITION assigns the foundation of the city of Bokhara to the age of Sikunder Zoolkurnuen, or Alexander the Great, and the geography of the country favours the belief of its having been a city in the earliest ages. A fertile soil, watered by a rivulet, and surrounded by a desert, was like a haven to the mariner. Bokhara lies embosomed among gardens and trees, and cannot be seen from a distance: it is a delightful place, and has a salubrious climate; but I cannot concur with the Arabian geographers, who describe it as the paradise of the world. Ferdoosy, the great Persian poet, says, " that when the king saw Mawuroolnuhr, he saw a world of cities." Compared with Arabia and the arid plains of Persia, this may be true, but some of the banks of the Indian rivers have a like richness, beauty, and fertility. The circumference of Bokhara exceeds eight English miles; its shape is triangular, and it is surrounded by a wall of earth, about twenty feet high, which is pierced by twelve gates. According to the custom of the East, these are named from the cities and places to which they lead. Few great buildings are to be seen from the exterior; but when the traveller enters, he winds

his way among lofty and arched bazars of brick, and
sees each trade in its separate quarter of the city;
here the chintz sellers, there the shoemakers; one
arcade filled with silks, another with cloth. Every
where he meets with ponderous and massy buildings,
colleges, mosques, and lofty minarets. Twenty
caravansarais contain the merchants of different
nations, and about one hundred ponds and fountains,
constructed of squared stone, furnish its numerous
population with water. The city is intersected by
canals, shaded by mulberry trees, which bring water
from the river of Samarcand. There is a belief
among the people, which deserves to be mentioned,
that the loftiest minaret, which is about 150 feet
high, rises to the level of that famous capital of
Timour. Bokhara is very indifferently supplied with
water, the river is about six miles distant, and the
canal is only once opened in fifteen days. In summer the inhabitants are sometimes deprived of good
water for months, and when we were in Bokhara
the canals had been dry for sixty days; the snow
had not melted in the highlands of Samarcand, and
the scanty supply of the river had been wasted before
reaching Bokhara. The distribution of this necessary
of life becomes, therefore, an object of no mean
importance. After all, the water is bad, and said
to be the cause of Guinea worm, a disease fright-
fully prevalent in Bokhara, which the natives will
tell you originates from the water; and they add,
that these worms are the same that infested the
body of the prophet Job! Bokhara has a population of 150,000 souls: there is scarcely a garden or

burying ground within the city walls. With the
exception of its public buildings, most of its houses
are small, and of a single story; yet there are
many superior dwellings in this city. We saw some
of them neatly painted with stuccoed walls; others
had Gothic arches, set off with gilding and lapis
lazuli, and the apartments were both elegant and
comfortable. The common houses are built of sun-
dried bricks on a framework of wood, and are all
flat roofed. A house in an eastern city commands
no prospect, for it is surrounded with high walls on
every side. The greatest of the public buildings is
a mosque, which occupies a square of 300 feet, and
has a dome that rises to about a third of that height.
It is covered with enamelled tiles of an azure blue
colour, and has a costly appearance. It is a place
of some antiquity, since its cupola, which once was
shaken by an earthquake, was repaired by the renowned Timour. Attached to this mosque is a
lofty minaret, raised in the 542d year of the Hejira.
It is built of bricks, which have been distributed in
most ingenious patterns.* Criminals are thrown
from this tower; and no one but the chief priest
may ever ascend it, (and that only on Friday, to
summon the people to prayers,) lest he might over-
look the women's apartments of the houses in the
city. The handsomest building of Bokhara is a
college of the King Abdoolla. The sentences of the
Koran, written over a lofty arch, under which is the

* There is a sketch of this minaret given in " Meyendorff's
Voyage à Boukhara." 8vo. Paris, 1826.

entrance, exceed the size of two feet, and are delineated on the same beautiful enamel. Most of the
domes of the city are thus adorned, and their tops
are covered by nests of the "luglug," a kind of
stork, and a bird of passage that frequents this
country, and is considered lucky by the people.

Bokhara would not appear to have been a large
city in ancient times. Its remoteness from other
parts of the Mahommedan world has given it celebrity, and besides it was one of the earliest conquests of the caliphs. It may be readily imagined,
that the numerous offspring of the first Commanders
of the Faithful would seek for distinction in its
distant and luxuriant groves. Its name was widely
spread by the number of learned and religious men
which it produced; and the affix of "Shureef," or
holy, was soon added to it by the Mahommedan
conquerors. It is considered the sure mark of an
infidel to say, that the walls of Bokhara are crooked;
but, strange to add, the architecture is so defective,
that I doubt if there be a perpendicular wall in the
city. The priests of the present day assert that, in
all other parts of the globe, light *descends* upon
earth; but, on the other hand, that it *ascends* from
the holy Bokhara! Mahommed, on his journey to
the lower heaven, is said to have observed this fact,
which was explained to him by the angel Gabriel,
as the reason for its designation. Besides the pal-
pable absurdity of the tale, I shall only mention that
the affix of "holy" is much more modern than the
days of the prophet, since I have seen coins which
did not bear it, and were less than 850 years old.

Bokhara existed as a city in the days of Kizzil (Alp?) Arslan. It was destroyed by Jengis Khan, and threatened by Hulakoo, his grandson; and we have an anecdote of the negotiations with that destroyer, which, I think, I remember as being told of some other place. The people sent forth a sapient boy, accompanied by a camel and goat. When he appeared before the conqueror, he demanded a reason for selecting such a stripling as an envoy. " If you want a larger being," said the youth, " here is a camel; if you seek for a beard, here is a goat; but if you desire reason, hear me." Hulakoo listened to the wisdom of the boy — the city was spared and protected; and he granted permission for their enlarging its fortifications. The present walls were built by Ruheem Khan, in the age of Nadir; and, since the equity of the rulers keeps pace with its increasing extent, Bokhara bids fair to be a greater city in modern, than in ancient, times.

I now availed myself of the acquaintance which I had made with the Moollah on my road from Kurshee, to visit his college, which was one of the principal buildings of that description in Bokhara, the " Madrussa i Cazee Kulan." I received the fullest information regarding these institutions from my host and his acquaintance, who produced his tea-pot, and gossiped for a length of time. There are about 366 colleges at Bokhara, great and small, a third of which are large buildings that contain upwards of seventy or eighty students. Many have but twenty, some only ten. The colleges are built in the style of caravansarais; a square building is

surrounded by a number of small cells, called
" *hoojrus*," which are sold, and bear a value of sixteen tillas, though in some it is so high as thirty.
A fixed allowance is given to the professor, and
each of the resident students; the colleges are well
endowed; the whole of the bazars and baths of the
city, as well as most of the surrounding fields, have
been purchased by different pious individuals for
that purpose. It is understood by the law, that
the revenues of the country are appropriated to the
support of the church; a fourth of the sum is distributed on that account in Bokhara; and the
custom-house duties are even shared by the priests.
In the colleges, people may be found from all the
neighbouring countries except Persia; and the students are both young and aged. After seven or
eight years of study, they return to their country
with an addition to their knowledge and reputation;
but some continue for life in Bokhara. The possession of a cell gives the student a claim to a
certain yearly maintenance from the foundation, as
well as the revenues of the country. The colleges
are shut for half the year by order of the King, to
enable their inmates to work in the fields, and gain
something additional to their livelihood. What
would the fellows of Oxford and Cambridge think
of mowing down wheat with the sickle? The
season of vacation is called " tateel" (repose), that
of **study** " tuhseel" (acquirement). The students
may marry, but cannot bring their wives to the
college. In the season of study, the classes are
open from sunrise to sunset: the professor attends

constantly; and the scholars dispute in his presence
on points of theology, while he guides their debates.
One person says, " Prove there is a God !" and
about five hundred set arguments are adduced : so
is it with other matters.   The students are entirely
occupied with theology, which has superseded all
other points : they are quite ignorant even of the
historical annals of their country.   A more perfect
set of drones were never assembled together; and
they are a body of men regardless of their religion
in most respects beyond the performance of its
prayers; but they have great pretensions, and
greater show.

I have already mentioned the rigour of Mahommedan law, which is enforced in Bokhara. A few
additional instances will further illustrate it. About
twelve years since, a person who had violated the
law proceeded to the palace, and, in the presence
of the King, stated his crime, and demanded justice
according to the Koran.   The singularity of an
individual appearing as his own accuser, induced
the King to direct him to be driven away.   The
man appeared the following day with the same tale,
and was again turned out.   He repaired a third
time to the palace, repeated his sins, and upbraided
the King for his remissness in declining to dispense
justice, which, as a believer of Mahommed, he en-
treated, might lead to his punishment in this world
instead of the next. The Ulema, or congress of
divines, was assembled : death was the punishment;
and the man himself, who was a Moollah, was prepared for this decision.   He was condemned to be

stoned to death. He turned his face to Mecca,
and, drawing his garment over his head, repeated
the kuluma, ("There is but one God, and Mahommed is his prophet!") and met his fate. The
King was present, and threw the first stone : but
he had instructed his officers to permit the deluded
man to escape if he made the attempt. When dead
the King wept over his corpse, ordered it to be
washed and buried, and proceeded in person to the
grave, over which he read the funeral service. It
is said that he was much affected ; and to this day
verses commemorate the death of this unfortunate
man, whom we must either pronounce a bigot or a
madman. An incident similar to the above happened within this very year. A son who had cursed
his mother appeared as a suppliant for justice, and
his own accuser. The mother solicited his pardon
and forgiveness ; the son demanded punishment:
the Ulema directed his death, and he was executed
as a criminal in the streets of Bokhara. A merchant lately imported some pictures from China,
which were immediately broken, and their value
paid by the government ; since it is contrary to
Mahommedan law to make the likeness of any thing
on the earth beneath. On some subjects their
notions of justice are singular. An Afghan plundered a caravansarai, and was sentenced to die ;
but permitted to purchase his blood according to
the Koran if he exiled himself from Bokhara, because he was a foreigner. Before this arrangement
had been completed, a second robbery occurred by
a party of the same nation : the clergy decreed

their death; and since they thought that the punishment of the first offender, together with the others, would present a more salutary and impressive example, they returned the blood-money, cancelled the pardon, and executed all the offenders.

Our European notions will revolt at such arbitrary changes; but it cannot be said that the punishment was unjust; and, if it had an influence on evil doers, it was assuredly not very injudicious. Whatever we may think of these customs and laws, they have raised the condition and promoted the welfare of this country; and there is no place in the whole of Asia where such universal protection is extended to all classes. Those who are not Mahommedans have only to conform to a few established customs to be placed on a level with " believers." The code of laws is sanguinary, but it is not unjust. When we place the vices of Bokhara in juxta-position with its laws and justice, we have still much to condemn; but the people are happy, the country is flourishing, trade prospers, and property is protected. This is no small praise under the government of a despot.

There is a prevalent opinion in Europe, that this portion of Asia was at one time the seat of civilisation and literature. We cannot doubt but the Greek monarchs of Bactria preserved, in their newly acquired kingdom the arts and sciences of their native land. An eminent author * " harbours " a suspicion of most of the learning of Scythia and

* Gibbon.

" India being derived from these Greek monarchs."
With India we have, at present, no concern; but,
in central and western Asia, I fail to confirm the
opinion of the great historian.   In the sixth century, when Alaric and Attila invaded the Roman
empire, we find them possessed of no arts or literature.   In the eighth century, when overwhelmed
by the caliphs, we hear of none.   In the tenth
century, when the same countries sent forth the
Seljukian line of kings, we still find them shepherds,
and embracing the religion of Islam, which the
caliphs had now firmly planted.   The irruptions of
Jengis, in the thirteenth century, present to us a
horde of barbarians; nor have we any steps towards improvement in the following age, under the
all-destroying Timour.   The whole of these inroads
were undertaken by barbarians; and it is not till
Timour's death that we find a literature in central
Asia.   The astronomy of Ulug Beg has immortal-
ised Samarcand; but he might have drawn his
science from Bactria: for the Arabs were, in early
ages, no mean astronomers; and we may then, with
more probability, trace this department of science
to that people, who over-ran the country a thousand
years after the Macedonians.   In an age later than
the house of Timour, we have had an inundation
of another tribe, the Uzbeks, from the same region
which produced Attila and Jengis; and they, too,
have been as barbarous as their predecessors of a
thousand summers.   It is certain that literature
received great encouragement during Timour's age.
In Baber's days we have also a constellation of

poets of no mean excellence; for he himself gives
us an insight into the spirit of the age by his quot-
ations and rhymes, and it would appear that these
native graces continued till a very late period; for
the people are poetically inclined. They have now,
I fear, taken an eternal farewell of Transoxiana:
the reign of the late king, Meer Hyder or Saeed
(the pure), introduced an era of bigotry and religious enthusiasm. He took the name of " Ameer-
ool Momeneen," or Commander of the Faithful;
and performed the duties of a priest, not of a king:
he read prayers over the dead, disputed in the
mosques, conducted the service, and taught in the
colleges. In the street, he dismounted from his
horse to return the salutation of a Syud or Khwaju;
and he passed the whole of his spare time in religious contemplation. His neighbour of Kokan
pursued a like conduct: he assumed the title of
" Ameer-ool Mooslimeen," or Commander of the
Mussulmans; and, between them, they introduced
a new order of things into Toorkistan. The moollahs of the colleges have since despised all learning
but theology, and all studies but the Koran and its
commentaries. Bokhara and Kokan may be said
to include all Toorkistan, since they are the two
most influential of its states. One cannot but
regret that the colleges of Bokhara should be now
involved in the unprofitable maze of polemical discussion.

After we had been about fifteen days in Bokhara,
the Vizier sent for us about mid-day, and kept us
till evening: he happened to have some leisure

time, and took this means to employ it. We found him in the company of a great many Uzbeks; and it came out that the subjects on which he was to interrogate us were not terrestrial. He wished to know if we believed in God, and our general notions upon religion. I told him that we believed the Deity to be without equal; that he was every where; that he had sent prophets on earth; and that there was a day of judgment, a hell and a heaven. He then entered upon the more tender point of the Son of God, and the prophetic character of Mahommed; but, though he could approve of Christian opinions on neither of these subjects, he took no offence, as I named their prophet with every respect. "Do you worship idols?" continued the Vizier; to which I gave a strong and negative reply, that seemed to excite his wonder. He looked to some of the party, and one of them said that we were practising deceit; for it would be found that we had both idols and crosses hung round our necks. I immediately laid open my breast, and convinced the party of their error; and the Vizier observed, with a smile, "They are not bad people." The servants were preparing the afternoon tea, when the Vizier took a cup, and said, "You must drink with us; for you are 'people of the book,' better than the Russians, and seem to have pretty correct notions of truth!" We bowed at the distinction; and were ever after honoured with tea on our visits to the minister. Since he had begun with our professions of faith, he was resolved to go through them. He wished to know

if we regarded the Armenians as the saints * of the
Christians ; but I assured him that we conceded no
such supremacy to that primitive sect.   He expressed his wonder at our associating with Jews,
since they were so wicked a people.   The determined opposition of the Israelites in Arabia to
Mahommed seems to have disgraced them in the
eyes of his followers.   The minister now wished to
hear of our treatment of the Hindoo and Mahommedan population of India.   I told him that we
respected the prejudices of both — that we alike
repaired their pagodas and mosques, and spared
peacocks, cows, and monkeys, because it was
pleasing to them.   " Is it a truth," said the Koosh
Begee, " that these people worship such beasts?"
I said that they either did so, or respected them.
Ustugh-firrolah!—" God have mercy upon us !"—
was his reply.   The cunning catechist now asked
me if we ate pork; but here it was absolutely necessary to give a qualified answer; so I said we
did, but that the poor people mostly used it.
" What is its taste?" said he.   I saw the cross
question.   " *I have heard* it is like beef."   He enquired if I had tried horse-flesh since my arrival in
Bokhara : I said that I had, and had found it good
and palatable.   He then asked if we had visited
the famous shrine of Bhawa Deen near Bokhara;
and, on expressing a wish to see it, he desired a
man to accompany us, and requested that we would
go quietly.   The Koosh Begee now asked what we

* Peers.

were taking back to our relatives in Europe after
so long an absence, a question worthy of the good
man's heart: but I referred to our distant journey,
and the inconvenience of carrying baggage; adding,
also, that soldiers were never rich. The old gentleman on this rose abruptly from his carpet, and
called for a musket, which he put into my hands,
and requested me to perform the platoon exercise,
which I did. He observed that it differed from the
drill of the Russians, of which he knew a little;
and began, at the same time, to march with much
grimace, across the room. As we stood and enjoyed the scene, the Koosh Begee, who was a tall,
broad-shouldered Uzbek, looked at us and exclaimed, " All you Firingees are under-sized people:
" you could not fight an Uzbek, and you move like
" sticks." Here followed a conversation on the advantages of discipline, which these people may be
excused for disbelieving, since they have had no
good opportunity to judge. The Vizier then com-
municated to us that a caravan was preparing for
the Caspian Sea, as also for Russia, and that he
would take steps to secure our protection if we
proceeded; all of which, as well as the kindness
and great toleration of the man (for an Uzbek)
were most gratifying. He expressed some desire
to know the state of our finances, and the amount
of our daily expenditure; but, little as that was, it
was unnecessary to tell the whole sum. Our funds
were plentiful, but our agents, who were Hindoos,
shuddered at being found out in supplying us. We
did not leave the minister till it was dark; and he

requested the doctor to visit one of his children, whose disease had baffled physic. He found it rickety, and in a very precarious state; the Vizier heard afterwards of its probable end without emotion, saying that he had thirteen sons, and many more daughters.

We took an early opportunity of visiting the shrine near Bokhara, which lies some few miles on the road to Samarcand. I thought little of any tomb while journeying in such a direction; but I did not deem it prudent to sue for permission to visit that celebrated city with our doubtful character. It is only 120 miles from Bokhara; and at Kurshee we had been within two marches of it. We were now obliged to rest satisfied with an account of a capital, the existence of which may be traced to the time of Alexander. It was the metropolis of Timour, and the princes of his house passed their winters at it. " In the whole habitable world," says Baber, " there are few cities so pleasantly situated as Samarcand." The city has now declined from its grandeur to a provincial town of 8000, or at most 10,000, inhabitants, and gardens and fields occupy the place of its streets and mosques; but it is still regarded with high veneration by the people. Till a king of Bokhara has annexed Samarcand to his rule, he is not viewed as a legitimate sovereign. Its possession becomes the first object on the demise of one ruler and the accession of another. Some of its buildings remain, to proclaim its former glory. Three of its colleges are perfect, and one of these, which formed the observatory of the cele-

brated Ulug Beg, is most handsome. It is ornamented with bronze, and its bricks are enamelled
or painted. I could hear nothing of the famous
obelisk which he built, excepting some crude tradition regarding its erection, brick by brick, as the
clock struck. There is another college, called
Sheredar, of beautiful architecture. The tomb of
Timour and his family still remains; and the ashes
of the emperor rest beneath a lofty dome, the walls
of which are beautifully ornamented with agate
(yushm). The situation of Samarcand has been
deservedly praised by Asiatics; since it stands near
low hills, in a country which is every where else
plain and level. We are told, that paper was first
manufactured in Samarcand: but how great is
the change since that article is now supplied from
Russia.

The prohibition to mount a horse did not extend
beyond the limits of Bokhara; and our servants had
the satisfaction of riding our ponies to the gate, as
we walked by their side. When outside the city,
we soon reached the tomb of Bhawa Deen Nukhs-
bund, one of the greatest saints of Asia, who flourished in the time of Timour. A second pilgrimage
to his tomb is said to be equal to visiting Mecca
itself. A fair is held near it once a week, and the
Bokharees gallop out on donkeys to pay their devotions. The reigning king, before he succeeded to
his crown, made a solemn vow to this saint, that if
he would vouchsafe assistance, he would visit the
shrine every week, and walk to it from the city on
foot so many times annually. His majesty, I be-

lieve, keeps his word; since we met his baggage, and were told that he would pray and rest there for the night. There are no buildings at the shrine that require any description, which is a square elevated platform, with a fine mosque and a large college near it. It is circumambulated by every pilgrim, who kisses the inscriptions that set forth its age and date. It is very richly endowed, and the descendants of Bhawa Deen are its protectors. We entered the sacred spot with no other ceremonies than leaving our slippers outside. We were also taken to visit the holy man who had charge of it, and who gave us cinnamon tea, and wished to kill a sheep for our entertainment. He, however, had so many diseases, real or imaginary, that, after a detention of two hours, we were glad to get away. He was most particular in his inquiries regarding the name of the saint, and if it had travelled into India and Europe. It was but Asiatic politeness to bear testimony to his reputation; for Bhawa Deen is really celebrated throughout the Mahommedan world, and the pilgrims of Bokhara are known at Mecca by his name of Nukhsbundee. I observed that this great shrine, and, indeed, most buildings of a similar nature which I saw in my travels, was marked with the horns of the rams that had been sacrificed at the spot. It is said, that these denote power; and it is, perhaps, to this custom that we owe the title given by Asiatics to Alexander the Great, of Zulkurnuen, or two-horned; though we know that he used horns as a son of Jupiter Ammon.

About twenty-five miles north-west of Bokhara, and on the verge of the desert, there lie the ruins of an ancient city, called Khojuoban, and which is assigned by tradition to the age of the caliph Omar. Mahommedans seldom go beyond the era of their Prophet, and this proves nothing.   Many coins are found in this neighbourhood; and I am fortunate in possessing several beautiful specimens, which turn out to be genuine relics of the monarchs of Bactria.*   They are of silver, and nearly as large as a half-crown piece. A head is stamped on one side, and a figure is seated on the reverse. The execution is very superior, and the expression of features and spirit of the whole do credit even to the age of Greece, to which it may be said they belong. They brought numerous antiques from the same place, representing the figures of men and animals cut out on cornelians and other stones. Some of these bore a writing that differs from any which I have before seen, and resembled Hindee. In my search after such curiosities, I heard of some petrified stones shaped like birds, and about the size of a swallow, found in the hills of Budukhshan.   I did not see a specimen, as the owner was absent from Bokhara. I am the more disposed to give credence to the existence of such things, since I have seen innumerable stones of the shape of small turtles or tortoises, which were brought from the higher ranges of the Himilaya.   I could not, how-

---

* A full account of these coins will be found in the next volume.

VOL. II.   T

ever, place the same reliance on their tales of an enchanted and petrified city which was described as lying on the south-western corner of the Sea of Aral, and between Orgunje and Orenburg. They call it " Barsa-gil-mis ;" which, in Toorkee, means, to go and never return ; since such is said to be the fate of the curious. In a country which has furnished Oriental writers with so many tales and metaphors for paradise, as Transoxiana, we may expect to hear stories which are suited to the Arabian Nights. The natives of Bokhara are firm believers in magic ; but they refer to India as the seat of that science. No one, however, doubts its existence ; and I found, according to them, that the art was daily practised in Surat, where the magicians are women, while those of Bengal are men. I passed two years in the city of Surat, and two happy years they were : I had a large native acquaintance, and made many inquiries regarding their customs and popular opinions ; but I heard, for the first time, in Bokhara, that its ladies were magicians. I can at least assert that, if they do possess witchery, it consists in their own native graces. Distance, I believe, gives countenance to most of the fables which gain ground in the world. Aboolfuzzul asserted, some 300 years ago, that there were men who could eat out one's liver in India ; and the opinion has since passed current, and is still believed in all the countries of Asia.

In Bokhara I became acquainted with an Uzbek family of high respectability, and visited them on a Friday. This family had originally come from the

" Dusht-i-Kipchak," and been settled in the country for 150 years : a member of their body had been twice deputed as an ambassador to Constantinople, for which they enjoyed the high title of Bee. They now traded to Russia, and had been considerable losers by the conflagration of Moscow, which had not, with all its horrors, I believe, been supposed to have carried distress into the centre of Tartary. I was received by these people à la Uzbek, and forced to swallow various cups of tea in the middle of a hot day. The Uzbeks have a most unsocial custom at a party, for the landlord becomes a servant, and hands up every dish in person; nor will he himself touch any thing till every member of the party has finished. They are a kind people, and if bigotry be their predominant failing, it is the fault of education ; I never observed them show it by an attack on the feelings of others, though one may discover it in every act of life, and the whole tenour of their 'conversation. We happened to speak of the discoveries of the Russians, who have recently hit upon some veins of gold between their country and Bokhara. One of the party remarked, that the ways of God were unsearchable, which had concealed these treasures from the " true believers," and now revealed them, near the very surface of the earth, to the infidels, or kaffirs. I smiled ; but it was not said in a way that could possibly give offence, and is the manner of speaking about Europeans among themselves. When I left the party to return home, I was much struck with the solemnity with which Friday is observed in the

streets: it is as rigidly kept as a Sunday in Europe,
and, perhaps, more so, for the virtuous Diocesan of
London found of late much to reprehend in his
flock of the metropolis. Not a shop is permitted
to be open till after prayers at one o'clock, and all
the inhabitants are to be seen crowding to the
mosque, arrayed in their best attire. There is a
gravity about the Mahommedans, and something in
their dress which gives an imposing cast to a body
of them proceeding to the temple of God.

A month had nearly elapsed since our arrival in
Bokhara, and it was necessary to think of moving
onwards; but the route that we should follow became a subject of serious consideration, from the
troubled state of the country. The object which
we had in view was to reach the Caspian, and the
higher up we should land on its shores, the better;
but there were difficulties on every side. No caravan had passed from Khiva to the Caspian for a
year, owing to a blood feud with the Kirghizzes of
the steppe. A Bokhara caravan lay at Khiva, and
one from Astracan at Mangusluk on the Caspian:
neither party could advance till some adjustment
was made; which was more hoped for than expected. How much our good fortune predominated,
in not accompanying the Khiva caravan, will hereafter appear. The direct road, by the territories of
Khiva to Astrabad in Persia, was also closed to us;
for the Khan of Khiva had taken the field to oppose
the Persians, and lay encamped in the desert south
of his capital, whither he ordered all the caravans to
be conducted. The route by Merve and Meshid

was open and more safe ; but it appeared advisable
for us to pursue the second of these routes, since
we should see a portion of the territories of Khiva,
then effect our passage to the frontiers of Persia,
and ultimately reach the Caspian Sea by the desert
of the Toorkmuns. All our friends, Hindoo, Armenian and Afghan, dissuaded us from encountering
the Khan of Khiva, who was described as inimical
to Europeans ; but, since we resolved to run every
risk, and follow the route which would lead us upon
him, I waited on our patron, the Vizier, and made
him acquainted with these intentions. He urged
our proceeding by a caravan of two hundred camels
that was just starting for Russia, and which would
lead us to Troitskai in that country ; but this did
not suit our plans, as the route had been travelled
by the Russian mission, and we had no wish to
enter Asiatic Russia, but to reach the Caspian.
The Vizier said that he would make inquiries regarding the departure of the caravan ; and as we
desired to follow the route that would lead us to
the frontiers of Persia, he would afford us his assistance as far as lay in his power. The caravan only
awaited his commands to set out on its journey.

On the 21st of July, we made our farewell visit
to the Vizier of Bokhara ; and our audience of
leave places the character of this good man even in
a more favourable light than all his previous kindness. The Koosh Begee is a man of sixty, his
eyes sparkle, though his beard is silvered by age ; his
countenance beams with intelligence, but it is marked
with cunning, which is said to be the most striking

feature in his character. He showed much curiosity regarding our language; and made me write
the English numbers from one to a thousand in the
Persian character, as well as a few words which
expressed the common necessaries of life. He
spent about an hour in this lesson, and regretted
that he had no better opportunity of acquiring our
language: he then made me write his name in
English, and, handing it over to Doctor Gerard, requested him to read it. He recurred to the subject
of medicine, and was greatly pleased with the lever
of an instrument for drawing teeth, which was explained to him. He fixed it on the wood of the
door, and wrenched out some pieces of it. He then
begged that we would return to Bokhara as " trading
ambassadors," to establish a better understanding
and a more extended commerce with the country.
He now summoned the Cafila-bashee of the caravan,
and a chief of the Toorkmuns, who was to accompany it as a safeguard against his tribe. He wrote
down their names, families, habitations, and, looking
to them, said, " I consign these Europeans to you.
" If any accident befall them, your wives and fami-
" lies are in my power, and I will root them from the
" face of the earth. Never return to Bokhara, but
" with a letter containing an assurance, under their
" seal, that you have served them well." Turning
to us, he continued, " You must not produce the
" ' firman' of the king, which I now give you, till
" you find it necessary. Travel without show, and
" make no acquaintances; for you are to pass
" through a dangerous country. When you finish

" your journey, pray for me, as I am an old man,
" and your well-wisher." He then gave each of us
a dress, which, though far from valuable, was en-
hanced by the remark, " Do not go away empty-
" handed: take this, but conceal it." I thanked the
minister, with every sincerity, in the name of my
companion and myself. He rose, and, holding up
his hands, gave us the " fatha;" and we left the
house of the Koosh Begee. I had not reached home
till I was again sent for, and found the Vizier sitting
with five or six well-dressed people, who had been
evidently talking about us. " Sikunder " (as I was
always addressed), said the Koosh Begee, " I have
" sent for you to ask if any one has molested you in
" this city, or taken money from you in my name,
" and if you leave us contented." I replied, that
we had been treated as honoured guests; that our
baggage had not even been opened, nor our property taxed, and that I should ever remember, with
the deepest sense of gratitude, the many kindnesses
that had been shown to us in the holy Bokhara.
The reply closed all our communications with the
Vizier; and the detail will speak for itself. I
quitted the worthy man with a full heart and with
sincere wishes, which I still feel, for the prosperity
of this country. I now examined the firman which
the Vizier gave us; it was laconic, but most valuable, and set forth our introduction to his Majesty,
which we had not the good fortune to enjoy. It was
in Persian, and may be thus translated: —

" At this time, by the will of God, two persons,

" Firingees, take their departure for their own
" country. It is proper that the people at the ferries,
" as well as the governors of towns and districts
" throughout the kingdom, should offer no hinderance
" to them, as they set out for their country after
" having seen the king, and with his permission."
Then follows the seal of Nussier Oollah, Ameer of
Bokhara.

In the afternoon the camels were laden, and
ready to take their departure. The last person we
saw in our house was the landlord, who came running in the bustle of preparation to bid us farewell.
He brought me a handsome and highly wrought
scull-cap as a present : nor did I consider it necessary to tell him that a few months more would change
my costume, and render his present useless. I
gave him a pair of scissors in return ; and we parted
with the greatest demonstrations of friendship. The
camels preceded us ; and we ourselves, accompanied by an Uzbek acquaintance, took our last walk
through the streets of Bokhara. We were not to
be distinguished from the natives of the country,
for we had adopted their dress and habits, and
trimmed our visages according to their prejudices.
I pushed smartly along, and at all times evinced as
little curiosity as the command I had over my
countenance would admit of. We had excited but
little notice ; though a Jew, to whom our costume
most assimilated, would now and then ask us a
question. I cannot say that I felt much regret at
clearing the gates of the city, since we should now

be more free from suspicion, and able both to ride and write. We had, indeed, managed to use the pen at night with leaden eyes; but, even then, we did it with fear. We joined the caravan about half a mile beyond the city gate, where we bivouacked for the night in a field.

CHAP. XI.

DETENTION IN THE KINGDOM OF BOKHARA.

THREE short marches brought us to the home of
the Cafila-bashee of our caravan; a small village of
twenty houses, called Meerabad, forty miles from
Bokhara, in the district of Karakool. What was our
disappointment to discover, on the eve of prosecuting our journey, that the whole of the merchants
declined to advance, and had taken alarm at the pro-
ceedings of the Khan of Khiva. That personage,
in examining the bales of a caravan from Persia,
discovered some earth from the holy Kerbela, which
had been packed up with the goods, according to
custom, as a spell on their safe transit. But the
precaution, so much at variance with orthodox Mahommedanism, had a very contrary effect. The
greater portion of the goods was plundered; and,
since many of our merchants were Persians, at
least Shiahs, they resolved to run no risks, and
wait either for the withdrawal of the army, or an
assurance of protection to their property, under the
seal of the Khan. The last alternative seemed the
most judicious mode of terminating all anxiety, and
it was discussed in full assemblage.

The merchants formed a congress at the hut in
which we were living; for the Vizier had kindly

made mention of us to all of them. It was a highly amusing sight to witness these gentlemen, with whip in hand and booted, discussing the important topic. After some pressing and refusing, one individual was singled out as the scribe of a letter to the officer of the Khan of Khiva, and he took his seat in the middle of the assembly. He mended his pen, promised to write in a large hand, and begged that but one of the many would dictate. It took about half an hour to decide the style of address, which was even referred to me; but I told the party that I had no such knowledge, since, in our language, we addressed the highest authorities by a brief title and a name. It was at last decided that the document should be headed as a petition; and, with many disputes, the following was produced : —

" The petition of the merchants to the Yooz " Bashee of Merve. We salute you with peace ! " It has been made known to us that the caravan, " which lately passed on its route to Bokhara, has " not only been taxed, as heretofore, but a duty of " 4½ tillas has been levied on each camel, and the " loads of the merchants have been opened in the " highway, and some of them destroyed. On hear- " ing this, two caravans, *en route* to Meshid, have " halted from fear, and we now despatch this paper " by a Toorkmun to inform you. You will render " us a service by giving him a note telling what " duties you will levy on us; and if his Highness " the Khan of Orgunje (Khan Huzrut) ordered " such things, and will offer hinderance to our

" passing, after paying such duties as he has been
" pleased heretofore to accept. When your answer
" reaches us, we shall advance and act accordingly.
" We, a body of merchants, salute you!"

It will be seen that, in matters of importance,
the Asiatics can come to the point, and divest
themselves of their usual rhodomontade. When the
production was read aloud, there was a general
shout of " Barikilla!" (bravo!) and five or six
Toorkmuns, who had taken their seats near the
door, were then consulted regarding its conveyance.
One of them agreed to bring an answer on the
eighth day; the distance of the place being 60
fursukhs (240 miles). He was to have three tillas
for his trouble. When this second matter was
settled, the whole party, holding up their hands,
pronounced the blessing, and stroked down their
beards. The affairs of nations could not have engaged an assembly more earnestly than this occupied the present party. Such grave faces, such
surmises, such whiffing of tobacco, such disputes
about the words, such varied opinions about the
matter: one advocating a measured tone; another
a supplicatory one; and a third a detail of the *outs
and ins* of the whole matter. An intelligent man,
a Moollah, rather far advanced in life, had more
knowledge than the whole body, and the party at last
had the good sense to adopt most of his views.
Will it be believed, after all this serio-comic scene,
these Rothschilds and Barings would not consent
to reward the Toorkmun for conveying the letter:
they would rather wait for a month than diminish

their profits ; and it ended in our paying the money.
It appeared to me a matter of surprise that any
answer should draw them to encounter people whom
they unanimously considered tyrannical and barbarous. After the messenger had been despatched,
the whole of the principal merchants of the caravan
returned to Bokhara, and we were left in an obscure village of Tartary, to consider whether we
should continue in our present abode, or return to
the capital. We resolved to pursue the first course,
and made up our minds to our unlucky detention.

In our journey from Bokhara, we had had some
opportunities of adding to our knowledge of the
country. Four or five miles from the city, we entered on a tract which was at once the extreme of
richness and desolation. To the right, the land
was irrigated by the aqueducts of the Kohik ; and
to our left, the dust and sand blew over a region of
dreary solitude. After travelling for a distance of
twenty miles, in a W.S.W. direction, we found
ourselves on the banks of the river of Samarcand,
which the poets have styled " Zarufshan," or gold-
scattering ; but we must attribute its name to the
incomparable blessings bestowed upon its banks,
rather than the precious ores which it deposits.
This river did not exceed the breadth of fifty yards,
and was not fordable. It had much the appearance
of a canal ; for, a little lower down, its waters are
hemmed in by a dam, and distributed with care
among the neighbouring fields. The stripe of cultivated land on either bank did not exceed a mile
in breadth, and was often less ; for the desert

pressed closely in upon the river. The number of inhabited places was yet great, and each different settlement was surrounded by a wall of sun-dried brick, as in Cabool; but the houses were neither so neat nor so strong as in that country. At this season (July), every cultivated spot groaned under the gigantic melons of Bokhara; many of which were also being transported in caravans of camels to the city. The soil of the country was varied, but, in the neighbourhood of the river, hard and gravelly. I observed that all the pebbles were sharp and angular, and differed much from those which have been subjected to the influence of water. The direct course which we were pursuing to the Oxus led us away from the Kohik; but, after crossing a belt of sand-hills, about three miles wide, we again descended upon it. Its bed was entirely dry; since the dam of Karakool, which we had passed, prevents the egress of its scanty waters at this season. We found that this river, instead of flowing into the Oxus, forms a rather extensive lake, called " Dengiz" * by the Uzbeks, and close to which we were now encamped. The lower parts of the river are badly supplied with water, and it is only in certain seasons that it flows in the district of Karakool. We were now living among the Toorkmuns, who occupy the country between the Oxus and Bokhara. They only differ from the great family to which they belong in residing in permanent houses, and being peaceable subjects of

* The Turkish word for sea.

the King of Bokhara. About forty different " *ro-bats*," or clusters of their habitations, lay in sight of ours; and we passed nearly a month in their neighbourhood and society without receiving insult or injury, or aught, I believe, but their good wishes. In our unprotected state, this was highly creditable to the natives of Toorkistan.

In Bokhara, ample scope had been afforded to observe the manners and customs of the citizen; in the country, we had now like opportunities of remarking the habits of the peasantry. To these we were made known through the means of the Toorkmun chief, to whom we had been introduced at Bokhara. He and the Cafila-bashee used to appear twice or thrice during the day, bringing with them any new acquaintance they might have fallen in with at the neighbouring markets; and we sat down and enjoyed our tea together at all hours. We thus became acquainted with many of the peculiarities of the Toorkmun tribes; and, latterly, I really began to feel an interest in the affairs and prospects of many of the individuals with whom I had been thus associated. The names of tribes and places, which had at one time appeared as far beyond my means of inquiry, were now within its compass. The Toorkmun chief, who was our master of ceremonies on these occasions, was himself a character: he was accompanying the caravan, to instruct his brethren by the way, and prevent our being plundered; but we soon found that he himself had no definite ideas of *meum* and *tuum*; since he had already appropriated to himself three gold

tillas, which he had asked of me as part of the hire
due to the Cafila-bashee, who was also a Toorkmun.
Ernuzzer (for that was the name of our friend) was,
however, both an useful and amusing companion.
He was a tall bony man, about fifty, with a manly
countenance, improved by a handsome beard, that
was whitening by years. In early life, he had followed the customs of his tribe, and proceeded on
"allaman" (plundering) excursions to the countries
of the Huzara and Kuzzil-bash; and some fearful
wounds on his head showed the dangerous nature
of that service. Ernuzzer had now relinquished
the occupations of his youth and the propensities
of his race, but though he had transferred his family
to Merve, as civilised and reformed Toorkmuns,
his aspect and his speech were still those of a
warrior. He himself had for years escorted caravans to Persia and the Caspian; and, under such
a conductor, we had many opportunities of observing the interesting people of which he was a member. The Cafila-bashee was a less sociable person,
and had, besides, much business; but we could not
help contrasting his indifference towards us with
the kind interest of our old friend Hyat. Not-
withstanding the injunctions of the Vizier of Bokhara, the Cafila-bashee left us in our secluded
residence, and proceeded with his camels for a
supply of salt to the banks of the Oxus; nor had
we a single individual except the idle Toorkmun
chief who cared about us.

One of the most remarkable of our Toorkmun
visiters was a man of mature age and blunt address.

His name was Soobhan Verdi Ghilich; which, being interpreted, means *" the sword given by God;"* and his complexion was as ruddy as that of a Bacchanal, though he declared that he had never indulged in the forbidden juice of the grape. He only spoke Toorkee; and my limited knowledge of that language required an interpreter: but, after a few visits, we *almost* understood each other, and no visitor was more welcome than Verdi, who described, in animated strains, his attacks on the Kuzzil-bash. " We have a proverb," said he, " that a Toorkmun on horseback knows neither father nor mother;" and, from a Toorkee couplet, which he quoted with energy, we gather the feelings of his race : —

" The Kuzzil-bashes have ten towers; in each tower there is *only* a Georgian slave ;
    What power have the Kuzzil-bashes?   Let us attack them ! "

Verdi was of the tribe of Salore, the noblest of the Toorkmuns; and he used to declare that his race had founded the empire of the Osmanlis in Constantinople. There is nothing improbable in the assertion; and the traditions and belief of a people are always worthy of record. The Toorkmun shook with delight as I made him detail the mode of capturing the Kuzzil-bash, and sighed that his age now prevented him from making war on such infidels. His advancing years had, in some degree, tempered his prejudices; for he added that, if such things were contrary to the laws of God and the Koran, he did not doubt but the prescribed mo-

dicum of fasting and prayer would expiate his sins.
Verdi now possessed flocks of sheep and camels;
and, since his years did not permit of his continuing
forays, he despatched his sons on that service. He
would tell me that his camels and his sheep were
worth so many slaves, and that he had purchased
this horse for three men and a boy, and that one
for two girls: for such is the mode of valuing their
property. I laughed as the robber detailed the
price of his animals, and requested that he would
tell me my own worth, if I should become a Toorkmun captive: but we were too good people for
slaves, he said; and I did not learn his appreciation
of us. " But," said I to him, " you do not surely
" sell a Syud, one of the sacred descendants of
" your holy Prophet (on whom be peace!), if he
" falls among the list of captives?" — " What,"
replied he, " is the holy Koran itself not sold?
" and why should not I dispose of an infidel Syud,
" who brings its truth into contempt by his he-
" resy?" These are desperate men; and it is a
fortunate circumstance that they are divided among
one another, or greater might be the evils which
they inflict on their fellow-men. This great family
of the human race roams from the shores of the
Caspian to Balkh; changing their place of abode
as inclination prompts them.

The tribe we were now living with is known by
the name of Ersaree; and for the first time, in a
Mahommedan country, we saw the ladies unveiled:
but this is a prevalent custom throughout the
Toorkmun tribes. In no part of the world have I

seen a more rude and healthy race of damsels in form or feature, though they are the countrywomen of the delicate Roxana, the bewitching queen of Alexander, whom he married in Transoxiana. Our Toorkmun chief, Ernuzzer, to dissipate his *ennui*, fell in love with one of these beauties, and applied to me for a magical spell, which he did not doubt I could give him, to secure the girl's affections. I laughed at the old man's love and simplicity. These ladies wore turbans; a becoming dress, the magnitude of which is so increased by their neighbours south of the Oxus, that I must reserve my remarks till I enter on their country. The Ersarees have most of the customs of the Toorkmuns, though their vicinity to Bokhara contributes to their partial civilisation. In our caravan we had five or six Toorkmuns from the south of the Oxus; and if these children of the desert practise the virtues of hospitality at home, they do not forget that it is their due abroad; and the Ersarees had, indeed, reason to complain of the detention of our caravan. Every morning, some one of the party took his sword to the house of a Toorkmun; which passes among these people for the well-known signal that the master must kill a sheep, and that the strangers will assist him to eat it. It is impossible to refuse or evade the notice, and the feast takes place at night. We were not invited to these parties, which were purely Toorkmun; but they would frequently send to us some of the cakes of the entertainment. We had many opportunities to mark the fair treatment which was given to us by

these people.   They knew that we were Europeans
and Christians, and, in speaking of us, they would
yet use the term " eshan;" which is the respectful
address given to Khwajus and holy characters.   A
Persian, who visits Toorkistan, must join his hands
when he prays, and give in to a few other customs,
some of which are not very cleanly; for these practices he has toleration and the protection of the
state.   A Christian has only to speak of Mahommedanism with respect, and avoid discussions, to
secure similar treatment.   The Persian, by his
creed, is enjoined to follow up such conduct.   " If
" there be seventy Shiahs and one Soonee," says
their law, " the whole party are to veil themselves
" on account of that individual."   We found ourselves constrained by no such ordinances, but gladly
conformed to the customs of the people; since the
prejudices of a nation are always entitled to respect.

Though the village in which we were now residing could not boast of more than twenty houses,
there were yet eight Persian slaves; and these
unfortunate men appear to be distributed in like
proportion throughout the country.   They are employed as cultivators, and were at this time engaged
all day in gathering the crop, though the thermometer was 96° within doors.   Three or four of
them were in the habit of visiting us, and I took
letters from some of them to their friends in Persia,
which were afterwards delivered.   Many slaves
save a sufficiency to redeem themselves: for a
Persian is a sharper being than an Uzbek, and does

not fail to profit by his opportunities. At Meerabad, two or three slaves had gathered sums that
would liberate them; but though they fully intended to avail themselves of an opportunity to
return to Persia, I never heard these people, in my
different communications with them, complain of
the treatment which they experienced in Toorkistan. It is true, that some of their masters object
to their saying their prayers and observing the
holidays prescribed by the Koran, since such sanctity would deprive them of a portion of their
labour; but they are never beaten, and clothed and
fed as if they belonged to the family, and often
treated with great kindness. The practice of enslaving the Persians is said to have been unknown
before the invasion of the Uzbeks; and some even
say that it has not continued for an hundred years.
A few Bokhara priests visited Persia, and heard
the three first caliphs publicly reviled in that
country; on their return, the synod gave their
" futwa," or command for licensing the sale of all
such infidels. Sir John Chardin even tells us that,
when a Persian shoots an arrow, he frequently
exclaims, " May this go to Omar's heart." I myself have heard many similar expressions; and,
since the report of the Bokhara priests is true, the
Persians have brought their present calamities upon
themselves. It is said that one of the Persian
princes, in a late communication with the Khan of
Orgunje, sent him the four books which Mahommedans hold sacred, the Old and New Testament,
the Psalms of David, and the Koran, begging him

to point out in which of these sacred writings the
laws of slavery, as practised against the Persians,
were to be found.   The Khan solved the difficulty
by replying, that it was a custom from which he
had no intention of departing; and, as the Persians
do not possess power to suppress it, it is likely to
continue to the detriment and disgrace of their
country.   It has been observed, that Mahommedan
slavery differs widely from that of the negroes, nor
is the remark untrue; but the capture of the inhabitants of Persia, and their forcible exile among
strangers, where neither their creed or prejudices
are respected, is as odious a violation of human
rights and liberties as the African slave-trade.

If the customs and manners of the people among
whom we were residing afforded an interesting subject of observation, there were also a few individuals
belonging to the caravan who deserve mention, and
who, like ourselves, had remained in preference to
returning to Bokhara.   These people were natives
of Merve in the desert, or, rather, descended from
the colony of that people, who were forcibly marched
to Bokhara by Shah Moorad about forty years ago,
and now form the most industrious portion of the
population.   They were not men of condition, and
amused themselves in a manner purely Oriental,
passing most of their leisure hours in telling stories,
and imitating the state and circumstance of the
King of Bokhara.   One enacted the part of royalty;
another petitioned; a third punished; and they
passed one whole day in this manner with an uninterrupted flow of mirth.   Boys would have quar-

relled before evening; but when that time arrived, these people assembled outside to hear a guitar and some Toorkee songs. The style of performance differed from what I have seen in any country; the singer places himself close in front of the musician, so that their knees touch, and the sound is, as it were, conveyed to him by a living conductor, when he sends forth his notes. The Toorkee is a warlike language, and harmoniously sonorous. The bard, I was told, was singing of love, the theme of every clime.

The condition of our own little party, perhaps, afforded as much ground for curiosity and reflection as the strange people among whom we were living. At dusk in the evening we would draw forth our mats and spread them out, and huddle together, master and servant, to cook, and eat within the limited circle. In a remote country, and in an obscure village of Tartary, we slept in the open air, lived without an escort, and passed weeks without molestation. Before one has encountered such scenes, the vague and indefinite ideas formed of them give rise to many strange thoughts; but when among them they appeared as nothing. In every place we visited we had been in the power of the people, and one cross-brained fool, of which every country has many, might have destroyed at once all our best laid plans and schemes. We mixed with the people, and our continued collision placed us in constant danger: but yet we had happily escaped it all. A chain of circumstances, fortuitous indeed, and for which we could not but

feel sensibly grateful, with the tranquil state of the
countries through which we passed, had been the
great cause of our good fortune; for confidence and
prudence, though they be the foremost requisites
of a traveller, avail not in a country that is torn by
factions and rebellion. Experience, also, proved,
that some of the plans which had been adopted for
the journey were to be regretted, since it was
much less difficult to personate the character of an
Asiatic than I had ever believed. The people we
had seen were not of an inquiring turn; but, if
satisfied that such a plan were feasible, I was also
convinced that it would have afforded a far less
share of enjoyment. We had run few risks from
the limited nature of our baggage, though our
cooking pots, few as they were, made me sometimes deplore the propensities of our country. We
were, indeed, living as Asiatics, and had many a
hearty dinner from the "kabobs" of the bazar; but
my faithful Hindoostanee, once my head servant,
but now my cook and factotum, used, I suppose, to
remember the more palatable dinners which he had
seen me eat, and get things from the bazar which
might betray us. We repeatedly prohibited these
luxuries: but even in Bokhara we have had a
breakfast of fish, eggs, coffee, preserves, and fruit,
though it must not be believed that we always
fared so sumptuously. Our party had considerably
diminished since I last described it on the Indus:
one of the Indians had retraced his steps from
Cabool, and the chilling blasts of Hindoo Koosh
had frightened the doctor's servant, who was a

native of Cashmere.   Otherwise we had to bear
the most ample testimony to the patience and perseverance of those we had chosen.   Of these the
most remarkable was Mohun Lal, the Hindoo lad
from Delhi, who exhibited a buoyancy of spirit and
interest in the undertaking most rare in an Indian.
At my request he kept a minute journal of events;
and I venture to believe, if hereafter published, that
it will arrest and deserve attention.   On his route
to Bokhara his tale had run, that he was proceeding
to his friends in that country, and, as we had
passed that city, he was now joining his relatives
at Herat!   The native surveyor, poor Mahommed
Ali, whose loss I have since had to deplore, generally travelled as a pilgrim proceeding to Mecca,
holding little or no open communications with us.
In our retired stay at Meerabad, and under the
azure and serene sky of night, it was impossible to
suppress many a reflection, heightened, I believe,
by the pleasing nature of the climate, and the
success which was attending our endeavours.

In this neighbourhood we did not fail to extend
our inquiries for antiquities, and were fortunate
enough to fall upon the ruins of Bykund; which I
find to be one of the most ancient cities of Toorkistan.   It lies about twenty miles from Bokhara,
and appears to have been once watered by an extensive aqueduct, of which the remains may now be
traced.   In a manuscript history of the country,
called Nursukhee *, which I purchased at Bokhara,

* I have given this work to the Oriental Translation Committee of London.

it is described as a city which is older than that
capital, and to have been formed of a thousand
" *robats*," or clusters of villages. It is also said
to have had many merchants, who traded to China
and on the ocean; though the word which is used
" *durya*," may also mean the Oxus. In after-times,
or about the 240th year of the Hejira, it is said that,
when a native of Bokhara went to Bagdad, he explained himself by saying that he was an inhabitant
of Bykund. The history goes on to describe it as
a most substantial city, which suffered much from
the infidels of the northern countries, who invaded
it in the cold season. At length, Arslan Khan
built a palace, and improved its aqueducts; during
which a circumstance occurred that bears a resemblance to Hannibal's passage of the Alps. Bykund,
it appears, was built on a hillock, which was so hard
as to resist the implements of the artificers. They,
therefore, moistened it with vinegar and butter, and
in the end it yielded to *their* perseverance, since
they dug a whole fursukh through it; which is a distance of about three and a half English miles. The
modern town of Bykund is deserted, and the walls
of some of its buildings are the only remnants of its
former greatness. Since every thing before the
Hejira is fable with the Mahommedans, we must
look to other works and languages for a history of
Bykund, the seat of Afrasiab and the ancient kings
of Toorkistan. I failed in procuring any of its
relics; nor could I search with safety.

We, perhaps, have not come to any satisfactory conclusion regarding the ruins of Bykund, and may not

be more successful in elucidating some of the pas-
sages of the historians of Alexander; but there
are a few facts regarding the river of Bokhara, or
the Kohik, which deserve notice. It is always
mentioned by the Greeks under the name of
Polytimetus, and is thus described by Arrian:—
" Though it carries a full stream, it sinks from the
" sight, and hides its stream in the sand." Curtius
tells us, on the other hand, that, " it was received
" into a cavern, the subterraneous torrent rushing
" on with a noise indicating its course." The termination of this river, as given in our maps, is not
in accordance with fact, since it is represented as
falling into the Oxus; while it really deposits its
waters in a lake, as has been before observed.*
In a great portion of the year the supply is too
scanty to force the passage, and it loses itself in
sands. I venture, therefore, to observe, that we
here verify the text of Arrian, who states it to be
lost in the sands; while, on the other hand, we have
no contradiction to Curtius, who leads its waters
into a cavern or lake,—the modern " Dengiz,"
which is about twenty-five miles long. The village
in which we were residing stood therefore on classical ground, since we are informed that Alexander,
after his detachment had been cut up by Spita-
manes, followed him to where the Polytimetus loses
itself in the sands of the desert, the scene of that
disaster. It required every classical association to
dispel the weariness of our protracted stay in this

* I now find that it is correctly given in the Russian maps.

small hamlet.   Another passage in Curtius, and of
a striking nature, also deserves mention, since I
have met with one of similar import in a Persian
manuscript, descriptive of Bokhara, which I procured in the country.   When Alexander had
marched into the district of Bazaria, which is supposed to be the modern Bokhara, or to lie in
that direction, the following sentence occurs: —
" Of the barbarous splendour prevailing in these
" parts, there is no stronger mark than the ex-
" tensive forests, in which are shut up untamed
" beasts of the grandest kind.   A spacious wood,
" in which numerous unfailing springs give cheer-
" fulness to the scenery, is selected, encompassed
" with a wall, and interspersed with towers for the
" reception of the hunters.   In one park, it was
" said, that the game had remained undisturbed
" during four generations.   Alexander, entering it
" with his whole army, commanded that the beasts
" throughout it should be roused from their lairs."
— B. 8. c. i.   This is the excursion in which Alexander encountered the lion: but the king of the
forest does not now inhabit Transoxiana.   The Persian paragraph, to which I have alluded, runs
thus: —

    " This is the account of Shumsabad, which was
" here built by King Shumsoodeen.   He purchased
" a tract of country half a fursung in extent, and
" laid it out in gardens, orchards, and houses of sur-
" passing splendour; and he dug canals and aque-
" ducts, and expended a great sum of money; and
" he called the place Shumsabad.   In addition to

" this he constructed a preserve for animals, and
" bounded it by walls which were a mile in
" extent: he brought pigeons and birds of every
" description, as well as all the domestic animals,
" and placed them in this preserve; and he like-
" wise introduced the wild beasts of the field, —
" the wolf, the fox, the hog, the deer, the neelghaee,
" &c. &c.: and those which were tame he separated
" from those that were wild; and the latter he
" enclosed by higher walls, that they might not
" escape. When King Shumsoodeen died, his bro-
" ther, whose name was Khizr Khan, succeeded
" him; and he added to the buildings of Shum-
" sabad, and increased the number of the animals
" in the preserve which his brother had constructed."
The work from which this extract is taken presents
us with some curious information regarding the early
condition of the country about Bokhara: it expressly denominates it the Valley of the Sogd, and
as having been at one time a hunting thicket. In
the amusements of Shumsoodeen, long after the
age of the Greeks, we still discover a relish for the
" barbarous splendour" which called for the notice
of the historians of Alexander.

About midnight, on the 10th of August, when
we had almost despaired of the return of our messenger to the Orgunje camp, we were roused from
sleep by the shout of " Ullaho Acbar" from five or
six Toorkmuns. They accompanied their country-
man with the joyful information, that the chief of
Orgunje would not offer any obstacles to the advance of our caravan. A dirty scrap of paper from the

Yooz-bashee contained the information, the authen-
ticity of which I had no desire to question. The
solemn shout which awoke us in the dead of night
might have at one time excited our alarm; but we
now knew that it was nothing more than the blessing, which all Uzbeks and Toorkmuns invariably
give to any one they approach. In other Mahommedan countries this is confined to the ceremonies
on the death of a relative; but in Toorkistan religion is mingled with every affair of life. If a person
visits you, he begins with the " fatha," or the opening
verse of the Koran, happily abridged to an " Ullaho!"
and a stroke of the beard; if you are to travel,
all your friends come and give you the " fatha;" if you
take an oath, all the party present say the " fatha;"
if you meet an acquaintance, you say the " fatha;"
and such good people never, of course, finish a meal
without it. One would really believe the Uzbeks to
be the most religious people on the face of the
earth, uttering as they do the sacred texts of
their faith on the most trivial occasions. We seated
the Toorkmun and his friends, and heard the news
of the Orgunje army, and the prospect of our safe
passage among them. We refreshed the messenger with tea and a hookah, which I called for with
persevering attention, since no person in Toorkistan must ever exceed a single whiff of the same
pipe, which is immediately handed to his neighbour
and circulated through the assembly. We settled
in our small congress that the Toorkmun had better
proceed to Bokhara, and convey the tidings to the
merchants of the caravan. He gave us a frightful

account of the desert south of the Oxus, and the great difficulties of finding the road, which was now hidden by clouds of sand that were disturbed by the wind. I need not mention his adventures, since we ourselves were about to enter on that inhospitable region. We, however, took his advice, and hired two extra camels, which were to be the bearers of six skins of water, the supply which was deemed necessary to store before we took leave of the Oxus.

Our stay near Karakool had now been prolonged to the middle of August, and were I not more anxious to enter on other matters, I might give some account of this region of lamb-skins, supplying, as it does, the whole of Tartary, China, Persia, and Turkey. The caravan soon collected once more at our quarters: and on the morning of the 16th of August, there appeared about eighty camels to prosecute the journey to the Oxus, all of them laden with the precious skins of the little district of Karakool, where we had passed nearly a month, among Toorkmuns and shepherds who talked of nothing but fleeces and markets. Among the arrivals from Bokhara, we were agreeably surprised and delighted to find a small packet to my address, the contents of which consisted of three newspapers and a most kind letter from my friend, M. Allard, at Lahore. The packet had been three months in coming, and afforded us indescribable pleasure, after our long ignorance of what was passing in the world. We had not seen a newspaper since crossing the Indus in the middle of March, and were now indebted to

a foreigner for those which we had received. In
one of the papers it was curious enough to observe
a long paragraph regarding the unfortunate Mr.
Moorcroft, who preceded us in these countries.
We learned from it, that the world were deeply
interested in the lands where we now sojourned,
and that the Geographical Society of London had
resolved on rescuing the papers of the traveller
from oblivion, a portion of which they had already
published under the superintendence of a high
name.* With these circumstances before us, and
even in the absence of any communications from
our own countrymen, we had a pleasing reflection
that we should not be forgotten in our wanderings.
It was impossible, however, to rid ourselves of all
remembrance of the fate of the unfortunate traveller
on whose footsteps we had so long trod, placed as it
was again in more vivid colours before us, and from
a quarter that we least of all expected.

* The Hon. Mr. Elphinstone.

END OF THE SECOND VOLUME.

LONDON:
Printed by A. Spottiswoode,
New-Street-Square.

www.ingramcontent.com/pod-product-compliance
Lightning Source LLC
Chambersburg PA
CBHW062036090426
42740CB00016B/2923